CELEBRITY IN CHIEF

ALSO BY KENNETH T. WALSH

Feeding the Beast: The White House versus the Press

Ronald Reagan: Biography

Air Force One: A History of the Presidents and Their Planes

From Mount Vernon to Crawford: A History of the Presidents and Their Retreats

Family of Freedom: Presidents and African Americans in the White House

Prisoners of the White House: The Isolation of America's Presidents and the Crisis of Leadership

CELEBRITY IN CHIEF

A History of the Presidents and the Culture of Stardom

By

Kenneth T. Walsh

Paradigm Publishers
Boulder • London

Copyright © 2015 by Paradigm Publishers

Published in the United States by Paradigm Publishers, 5589 Arapahoe Avenue, Boulder, CO 80303 USA.

Paradigm Publishers is the trade name of Birkenkamp & Company, LLC, Dean Birkenkamp, President and Publisher.

Library of Congress Cataloging-in-Publication data for this title is available from the Library of Congress

ISBN 978-1-61205-706-4 (hc. : alk. paper) — ISBN 978-1-61205-904-4 (lib. ebook)—ISBN 978-1-61205-905-1 (consumer ebook)

Printed and bound in the United States of America on acid-free paper that meets the standards of the American National Standard for Permanence of Paper for Printed Library Materials.

19 18 17 16 15   1 2 3 4 5

For Barclay

CONTENTS

ACKNOWLEDGMENTS

First of all, I would like to thank my wife, Barclay Walsh. She not only helped to shape this book from the start but also provided essential research along the way. She is one of the best writers I have known during my long career and I have benefited from her talents for decades. Barclay is not only my life partner; she is also my professional colleague. This book is in many ways just as much her project as mine.

Among those who were of great help were David Axelrod, Ross Baker, Doug Brinkley, Marian Burros, Bill Bushong, Jay Carney, Bob Clark, Gregory Cummings, Bob Dallek, Frank Donatelli, Ken Duberstein, Josh Earnest, Marlin Fitzwater, Don Foley, Al From, Bill Galston, Geoff Garin, Ed Gillespie, Ed Goeas, Peter Hart, Rene Henry, Frank Luntz, Mike McCurry, Bill McInturff, Roman Popadiuk, Larry Sabato, Randy Sowell, Sean Spicer, Mark Updegrove, and Brad Woodhouse. Thanks also to the archivists and other employees at the presidential libraries, and to the staff at the White House Historical Association.

Several books provided considerable insight, including Alan Schroeder's *Celebrity-in-Chief: How Show Business Took over the White House*; Tevi Troy's *What Jefferson Read, Ike Watched, and Obama Tweeted: 200 Years of Popular Culture in the White House*; and John Sayle Watterson's *The Games Presidents Play: Sports and the Presidency*.

And I want to thank the wonderful staff at Paradigm Publishers, especially Jennifer Knerr, for believing in this project from the beginning.

Kenneth T. Walsh
Bethesda, Maryland, and Shady Side, Maryland

Introduction
The Rise of the Concept of Stardom
and the Culture of Celebrity

It didn't take long for Barack Obama to make his mark as the biggest superstar ever to occupy the White House. Within nine months of taking office in January 2009, Obama was awarded the Nobel Peace Prize, one of the most coveted honors in the world. The decision was not based on anything the new commander in chief had done up to that point. He hadn't been in office long enough to have had any major achievements. Instead, the Nobel judges were influenced by Obama's charisma, rhetoric, and historic status as the first African American president, and his pledge to be a peacemaker who would bring humility and restraint to America's international role. In other words, his celebrity made the difference.

Since those heady days, Obama has taken the concept of celebrity in chief to even greater heights, exploiting his fame to enhance his image and propel his agenda in both conventional and unconventional ways. He has deftly used both traditional media and social media to carry his message. He has exploited technology and modern forms of networking to make himself seem hip and in touch. He has extended the president's reach to venues and audiences long neglected by the White House. He has associated with other cultural stars, such as entertainers and athletes, more than any of his predecessors, adding to his luster. First Lady Michelle Obama has also developed a vivid presence in American life as an advocate of improved nutrition and exercise, especially for young people, and has appeared frequently and impressively on television. In a highly publicized moment, she even gave out an Oscar for best picture in 2013.

The Obama presidency has been a case study in the potential, and the limits, of celebrity in modern America. It shows how celebrity can wax and wane, depending on the public's mood and the successes and missteps of the president. Obama's cultural superstardom hit new heights during his first term and helped him win reelection in 2012. It faded as his policies grew more unpopular during 2013 and 2014, but his celebrity also propped up his standing by preventing his approval ratings from going into free fall.

Obama's experience showed that celebrity can be evanescent. Americans' attention span is short, and their patience with a president can erode when a chief executive fails to deliver on promises, such as Obama's pledge to bring hope and change to Washington. But, like a pendulum, public opinion can swing back and forth, from positive to negative and back again. A president can recover celebrity under the right conditions, which is also true of other famous people such as singers, musicians, and movie and TV stars.

As this book will show, Obama is the latest illustration of how celebrity culture is changing the presidency and the nation for better and for worse.

*   *   *

AMERICAN PRESIDENTS have always been famous. But it was only after the advent of the mass media and the vast increase in the power and reach of the presidency under Franklin D. Roosevelt that the leader of the United States became a true superstar.

"Celebrity is an ineffable quality," says historian Mark K. Updegrove, director of the Lyndon B. Johnson Presidential Library.[1] But it's clear that for a modern president, being celebrity in chief—the most famous and powerful individual in our culture—rests on several well-defined building blocks. The presidents who adhere the most closely to these criteria tend to be the most successful.

First, presidents need to represent what's best in America. They should stand for the country's fundamental values and aspirations, convey meaning about complex and confusing events, and update the American narrative for their times.

Second, they must define themselves in positive and distinctive ways, depending on each president's personality, character, and background, and adjusting for what the public wants from its leader during a given period. Among the attributes that Americans prize in their presidents are optimism, likability, and courage.

Finally, to reach the height of celebrity, presidents need to master the media to become larger than life in some way—iconic figures. Franklin D. Roosevelt used radio to catapult himself to the status of an unrivaled leader. John F. Kennedy and Ronald Reagan enhanced themselves through television.

Overall, Roosevelt best embodied the concept of celebrity in chief. He stood for optimism and perseverance both in combating the Depression and in winning World War II. He defined himself as a rare leader who was the tribune of the American people. He mastered the dominant media of his time—newspapers and radio.

Roosevelt was very much at home with entertainment-industry stars, which helped him build up his own celebrity. He won over many Hollywood figures and mingled with them during his presidential campaigns, starting in 1932 when he appeared at the Los Angeles Olympic Stadium with Charlie Chaplin, Stan Laurel, Oliver Hardy, Clark Gable, and Boris Karloff. In 1940 he won the support of more than 200 Hollywood stars, including Humphrey Bogart, James Cagney, Henry Fonda, and Katharine Hepburn.

Other presidents who have been celebrities in chief during their time in office include Theodore Roosevelt, Kennedy, Reagan, and Bill Clinton. Barack Obama started out as a superstar but has faded somewhat from that status.

Some presidents never get to the level of celebrity in chief at all, or they fall from the perch once they get there. Lyndon Johnson suffered historic setbacks. After an initial honeymoon with Americans, his image turned harshly negative. As people learned more about him, they found that his personal attributes weren't appealing. And he didn't master the media of his time, especially television. Richard Nixon also failed on all the same counts. And it's significant that these two particular presidents ended up with so little positive luster and came across to the public as unlikable. Both were workaholics who had an obsessive interest in politics and power. Nothing else could compare with those passions for them, and it limited their ability to understand the everyday lives of their constituents.

*   *   *

IN FUNDAMENTAL WAYS, political culture and entertainment culture have melded over the years. As media analyst Robert Lichter has pointed out, "We expect our politicians to be entertaining now." Or at least interesting. "We participate in their lives vicariously, the way we participate in the lives of soap-opera characters," Lichter adds.[2]

Many Americans have wanted to emulate presidents whom they admired and who captured their imaginations, such as Theodore Roosevelt, Franklin D. Roosevelt, Kennedy, Reagan, and Obama. For other presidents it was the reverse. Few Americans wanted to be like the ham-handed and overbearing Johnson or the maladroit and conniving Nixon. These negative perceptions badly damaged their governing abilities.

* * *

THE VAST GROWTH in the power of and expectations for the American president have added to the celebrity of the office. The president has become so central to our national identity that nearly everyone wants to know what presidents say and think, how they act, their strengths and weaknesses, and their intentions. We tend to think of them as superhuman or extranormal, with the power to change our lives and alter the course of the world. No wonder we are deeply interested in what they do and who they are.

"Both Left and Right agree on the boundless nature of presidential responsibility," writes author Gene Healy. "Neither Left nor Right sees the president as the Framers saw him: [as] a constitutionally constrained chief executive with an important, but limited job: to defend the country when attacked, check Congress when it violates the Constitution, enforce the law—and little else. Today, for conservatives as well as liberals, it is the president's job to protect us from harm, to 'grow the economy,' to spread democracy and American ideals abroad, and even to heal spiritual malaise—whether it takes the form of a 'sleeping sickness of the soul,' as Hillary Clinton would have it, or an 'if it feels good, do it,' ethic, as diagnosed by George W. Bush."[3]

Healy argues that all this amounts to a shift to an imperial presidency that is unhealthy for the country even if most Americans don't realize the dangers. "Few Americans find anything amiss in the notion that it is the president's duty to solve all large national problems and to unite us all in the service of a higher calling," he says. "The vision of the president as national guardian and redeemer is so ubiquitous that it goes unnoticed."[4]

But it's also true that Americans are more critical of presidential behavior, hypocrisy, and failure than they used to be. This skepticism derives in part from credibility gaps that various presidents widened over the years, including Johnson and Nixon in waging the Vietnam War, Nixon in presiding over deceptions and law-breaking in the Watergate scandal, and Clinton in lying about his affair with former White House intern Monica Lewinsky.

A half century ago, three-quarters of Americans trusted the federal government to do what was right most of the time, and more than 60 percent said the president should take the lead in deciding what the country needs.[5] Most Americans today don't trust the federal government or the president to do the right thing. As of Obama's sixth year in office in 2014, only 29 percent of Americans said they had confidence in the presidency. Still, it was much worse for Congress; only 7 percent had confidence in federal legislators, according to a Gallup poll.[6]

But even though Americans are more skeptical about their presidents and less confident in them, the public remains intensely fascinated by those who occupy the nation's highest office.

Underlying the fascination, presidents are bathed in an intriguing aura of privilege and frequently treated with awe. This adds to their glitter and celebrity. The life of the modern president is filled with the kind of coddling and adulation that are familiar mostly to super-rich business executives, those with vast inherited wealth, movie stars, rock singers, and big-name athletes. It can lead to massive egotism and a sense that the president has an entitlement to ultimate celebrity status. Dr. Robert B. Millman, professor of psychiatry at Cornell Medical School, calls the resulting self-importance "acquired situational narcissism."[7]

Mike McCurry, Clinton's former White House press secretary, says, "The president is the closest thing we have to a royal entity and the presidential family is the closest thing we have to a royal family. We are interested in everything they do, like sports figures and movie stars. Celebrity says something about values and character. And celebrity, when it comes to presidents, is really about how much we trust the person who governs. It's a measure of the character of the president and what we think of him as a person."[8]

The star power of the American presidency has been so strong in recent years that political eras are often delineated by presidencies, such as the Roosevelt era, the Kennedy era, and the Reagan era.

The best of the presidents have learned that they need to constantly use and expand on their natural celebrity as a way of calling attention to and marshaling support for themselves, their ideas, and their policies.

The presidents who do this effectively, such as Roosevelt, Kennedy, Reagan, and Clinton, tend to succeed. (Obama is still a work in progress.) The presidents who fail at maintaining a positive aura of celebrity, such as Johnson, Nixon, Jimmy Carter, George H. W. Bush, and George W. Bush, often find their approval ratings tumbling and their policy agendas stymied.

* * *

IN SOME WAYS, the presidents have begun operating under the rules that apply to all famous people, not just those in politics. "We make stars into something exquisite, and we want to know what they're doing and thinking because our lives are desperately boring," says gossip columnist Liz Smith.[9] Adds gossip columnist Jess Cagle, "It's just human nature. It goes back to the Greeks who gossiped about the gods on Mount Olympus. . . . We identify with stars. We project our own lives and feelings onto them, and what makes a great star is having this tremendous ability to be projected onto."[10]

It's true that being a celebrity in pop culture means being constantly part of the national conversation, which risks overexposure. Few would doubt that Bill Clinton crossed that line and went too far when he answered a young person's question about the kind of underwear he wore. Americans expect more decorum.

But being a celebrity, when properly balanced with restraint, has become an essential ingredient of modern presidential leadership. Writes political scientist Thomas E. Cronin, "Presidents are the nation's number one celebrity; almost everything they do is news. Merely by going to a sports event, a funeral, a celebration of a national holiday, or by visiting another country, presidents not only command attention, they convey meaning. By their actions presidents can arouse a sense of honor or dishonor, hope or despair. . . . Man does not live by reason alone. Myth and dreams are age-old forms of escape. And people turn to national leaders just as tribesmen turn to shamans—yearning for meaning, healing, empowerment, legitimacy, assurance, patriotism, and a sense of purpose."[11]

The common goals and the overall links between politics and show business have become ever stronger, ranging from the need to stay in the public eye to the desire to use celebrity to get things done. Julia Louis-Dreyfus, formerly a lead player on *Seinfeld* and more recently the star of *Veep*, in which she plays a fictional vice president of the United States, said,

"I think of it as spending celebrity, as Norman Lear once said. Celebrity is a kind of capital. You have to use it wisely, and you can overspend it easily. So I use it carefully, when I can, for just the right thing."[12] One of her top political concerns is the need to limit climate change.

In a joint interview with Louis-Dreyfus, House Democratic Leader Nancy Pelosi (D-CA), former speaker of the House, said, "We're both in the attraction business. Politicians are trying to attract people to issues. But there's nothing like the celebrity that Julia brings to an issue because people pay attention to her. She gives people hope that things can change."[13]

*   *   *

EVEN BEFORE the modern era, which started with the emergence of Franklin D. Roosevelt as a national savior during the Depression and World War II, some presidents were able to harness their star power better than others. They used their celebrity to highlight character traits they thought the country would admire and be drawn to. The best of them realized that this would make them more popular and more persuasive.

"In fact, the job of the presidency demanded symbolic leadership from the beginning," says Cronin. "Washington and his advisers would readily recognize that in leadership at its finest, the leader symbolizes the best in the community, the best in its traditions, values, and purposes. Effective leadership infuses vision and a sense of significance into the enterprise of a nation."[14]

Author Alan Schroeder says, "The relationship between presidents and voters finds a direct analogue in the relationship between performers and fans. In both cases the connection is fraught with mystery and contradiction. Citizens come to 'know' their presidents just as fans come to 'know' movie stars, though in reality the relationship never advances beyond the realm of abstraction."[15]

But unlike celebrities from the worlds of film, television, sports, music, and business, presidential celebrity came to mean more than simply being famous. The most successful presidents embodied American attitudes and values—such as the work ethic, empathy, and grace under pressure—and the talent for personalizing the American ethos became an essential skill for every effective president to master.

Some presidents managed it; some didn't. Many historians have admired Woodrow Wilson because of his idealistic views about promoting world peace. But Wilson's star power while he was president was limited in part because many Americans became disenchanted with American participation in World War I, and because Wilson stubbornly tried to push a League of Nations on a country that wasn't ready for it.

His celebrity also was diminished because of his frail appearance and chronic bad health, which included several strokes both before and after he took office. The charismatic and macho Theodore Roosevelt came up with a sharp-edged but savvy dismissal of his successor. He said Wilson looked and acted "like an apothecary's clerk."[16] It was a superficial standard based on Wilson's looks but it captured the way many Americans saw their president.

"Americans, by and large, decide who to vote for based on the candidates' attributes—personality, image, authenticity, vibe," says GOP pollster and public opinion analyst Frank Luntz. "The media is still in denial about this, and every time I have advanced the notion at press events that issues don't matter that much, the print reporters who cover politics rush to defend a more intellectual perception of what elections are all about. To them, accepting the fact that image matters more than policy would be accepting the fact that what people see through their televisions matters more than what they read in the newspaper."[17]

Luntz adds, "[Commentator] George Will may bemoan the dumbing down of America but our frame of reference and common bond as Americans has become pop culture, not the classics. We are much more likely to bond over an episode of *The Sopranos* than we are over a public reading of the *Federalist Papers*. Sadly, even the core democratic institutions and the people who gave birth to this country are less familiar to the next generation of American adults than the latest *American Idol/Survivor* phenomenon."[18]

During the past three decades, the perceptions of what is legitimate self-promotion and what is out of bounds have changed greatly for presidents seeking to expand their celebrity. While he was president from 1981 to 1989, Reagan was never interested in appearing in nontraditional venues such as talk shows or situation comedies on TV. (His wife, Nancy, made an exception by appearing in 1982 on the popular sitcom *Diff'rent Strokes* to promote her just-say-no-to-drugs campaign.) George H. W. Bush, Reagan's vice president and successor, also wasn't interested in nontraditional media. Both were concerned about diminishing the stature of the presidency.

Democratic challenger Bill Clinton achieved a new level of coolness in the 1992 campaign when he appeared on Arsenio Hall's TV show and played the saxophone while wearing sunglasses. Bush was aghast. It wasn't "presidential," he told aides, and he said he wouldn't do such a thing. Perhaps he should have, because it might have softened his image as an out-of-touch Brahmin who didn't understand everyday people's lives. He lost the 1992 election to Clinton.

President Obama has taken outreach to nontraditional media to an entirely new level, a theme that is discussed at length later in this book. He has used to his advantage every possible venue and media outlet, from the three broadcast TV networks of ABC, CBS, and NBC to cable outlets such as CNN and MSNBC; daytime programs such as *The Ellen DeGeneres Show* and *The View*; the comedy TV shows of Jon Stewart, Jimmy Fallon, and David Letterman; social media such as Facebook and Twitter; and the White House website. Through it all, he has projected an image of an unflappable leader, a nice guy and family man, reinforced by nearly everything he has done. Obama's job-approval ratings have dropped from their initial highs for a number of reasons, but they would surely be worse if not for his constant and unusual outreach.

Presidents are forever walking a tightrope between maintaining convention and breaking with tradition both in policy terms and in public-relations techniques. Taking the conventional approach may be the safer course, but it also could prevent a president from exerting real leadership. Obama illustrated this dynamic when he broke with tradition and his past position and endorsed gay marriage in 2013. He apparently helped persuade many Americans who admired him that their past objections to gay marriage were wrong and out of date. And it didn't appear to hurt Obama politically because American attitudes were already changing on this issue, and Obama and his aides sensed it.

"In its insatiable thirst for information, whether important or trivial, about its leaders or its celebrities, the public demands an account of the president's consumption of popular culture," historian Tevi Troy says. "A meaningful evaluation of the president is hardly possible without that information. It is hard to overstate, for example, the extent to which Ronald Reagan was shaped by the movies. Without them, he would have been a friendly ex-lifeguard from Illinois, perhaps a traveling salesman like his father. With them he achieved fame and fortune, worked a lifetime in a world of images and ideas, and ultimately, ascended to the nation's highest office. The movies provided Reagan with the skills he used to excel in politics and to inspire the nation."[19]

* * *

IT MAY SEEM quaint and hopelessly outdated, but a battle between "high culture" and "low culture" has swirled around the White House for many years. "The highbrows in the 1950s had a rather rough time of it," writes social critic Russell Lynes. "It was the decade of the McCarthy investigations,[20] of Adlai Stevenson's two defeats as a candidate for President, and, perhaps, worst of all, the arrival of television—a symbol of mass middlebrowism. It was, moreover, the era of Sputnik I, the first object put into orbit by the Russians, and the shocked American clamor for more scientific training in order to 'catch up.' While that incident ultimately gave a good many intellectuals an improved bargaining position, it was not the humanists, the preceptors of taste, who benefited. The Eisenhower years did not supply the highbrows with the opportunities that the election of Kennedy, who flirted ostentatiously with the arts, seemed to offer, if only briefly. And despite Lady Bird Johnson's conscientious efforts to continue to hold high the torch of culture, her husband was barely tolerant of what highbrows considered her well-intentioned gestures to the Muses."[21]

As of today, what would have once been called "low culture" dominates the White House as it does our entire society. It's an era when President Obama not only appears on late-night comedy shows and daytime TV chat shows but also, remarkably, on Zach Galifianakis's insult-filled parody interview program on the Web, *Between Two Ferns*.

* * *

IN ADDITION, the lifestyles of America's presidents and first ladies have reflected and shaped popular culture in many ways. These are important parts of the presidency, and always have been, even if this aspect of the office has scarcely been examined.

"A lot of them rise to the level of cultural figures," says Democratic pollster Geoff Garin, who was a senior adviser to Hillary Clinton's presidential campaign in 2008.[22] He puts Obama and Kennedy in this category, but not Nixon or Johnson. People aspire to have the same lifestyles or outlooks of Obama and Kennedy. Garin says, "Role model is the category where at the end of the day, you're trying to be like them in your own life.[23]

*   *   *

PRESIDENTS ARE the repository for America's dreams. Each is both the head of government and the ceremonial leader of the United States.

"As a baseline requirement of the position, the modern chief executive must now be able to present a version of himself that is as audience-friendly as the persona of an entertainment star," writes Alan Schroeder. "In addition to his more solemn duties, the president of the United States is expected to perform the functions of a professional showman. . . . No longer does a president stand apart on a remote civic pedestal, isolated from the hurly-burly; instead the powerful forces of the American celebrity circus have dragged him into the tent and asked him to put on a show. The position has always been demanding, but now there is an added demand: a president must know how to 'fill the frame.' "[24]

Presidents also are using some of the same techniques as entertainers, such as in-house TV producers and directors, stagecraft experts, makeup artists, advance teams, and writers. The goal is to create favorable images of the president and generate positive impressions, just as press agents and "personal managers" do for Hollywood stars. And the White House has become a prime source of material for the entertainment industry, especially movies and TV, blurring the lines between show business and government.[25]

Bruce Reed, former senior adviser to Clinton and former chief of staff to Vice President Joe Biden, says celebrity now can determine whether a presidency succeeds or fails. "The connection a political leader forges with the electorate is the lifeline that will make or break his or her success," Reed says. "That bond is stronger when it's not just fame and celebrity and charisma but it has a higher purpose. It's more important for a leader to unite people behind a course" than just behind the leader as an individual.[26]

"The real magic," Reed says, "is when charisma and celebrity are put to a higher purpose. Celebrity can fade, sort of by default, but purpose endures. That was a great asset for Clinton. There were a few occasions when the chips were down and it wasn't fashionable to be with him but ordinary people stuck with him because they knew he was fighting for them. Politics is a fickle business. You never know who is going to be at your back. If it's only about you, that's an unsustainable foundation for lasting change. But if you can't strike the chord with the people you're trying to lead, then you're not going to get them behind your ideas."[27]

Most presidents who were deeply embedded in popular culture benefited through enhanced influence and the ability to command attention and rally support when they needed to. It's striking how often our most effective, historic, and popular presidents were the biggest celebrities, and how the failures or lesser lights were not cultural stars.

Chapter One
Forerunners of the Modern Celebrity Presidents
Washington to Cleveland

George Washington: The Archetype

George Washington was, of course, America's first president. He was also America's first celebrity in chief, the leader who won the Revolutionary War, whose integrity was considered beyond reproach, and who was almost universally believed to be the only person capable of uniting the new nation and establishing the roots of a stable democracy.

His renown was such that in February 1789 he was chosen unanimously by the Electoral College to be the first president of the United States. On April 16 he began making his way from his estate in Mount Vernon, Virginia, to the president's temporary residence and the nation's first capital in New York City, where he was to be inaugurated.

He was reluctant to leave home and take on the responsibilities and public duties of his new job. He wrote in his journal on April 16: "About 10 o'clock I bade adieu to Mount Vernon, to private life, and to domestic felicity, and with a mind oppressed with more anxious and painful sensations than I have words to express, set out for New York in company with Mr. Thompson, and Colonel Humphries, with the best dispositions to render service to my country in obedience to its call, but with less hope of answering its expectations."[1]

It was a remarkable seven-day journey marked by an outpouring of public affection and jubilation for the savior of the nation. In today's terms, he was treated like a rock star. Local officials and everyday people gathered by the thousands to meet him or at least get a glimpse of him; they cheered when they saw him, amid frequent artillery salutes. There were celebrations in many towns, including Alexandria, Virginia; Baltimore, Maryland; Wilmington, Delaware; Philadelphia, Pennsylvania; and Trenton, New Jersey. When Washington arrived at Elizabeth Town, New Jersey, on April 23, a special ceremonial barge was ready to take him across the river to New York. The barge was rowed by thirteen pilots dressed in white, and various sloops and many small boats bearing local citizens accompanied his vessel across the river. His passage was marked by repeated cannon salutes from still other boats and from a fort in the harbor.[2] When he landed, Washington was greeted by New York Governor George Clinton and other dignitaries, and a large procession accompanied him on foot to a house Congress had prepared as his residence.

He took the oath of office in New York's former city hall, renamed Federal Hall, on April 30, "dressed in deep brown, with metal buttons, with an eagle on them, white stockings, a bag, and sword," according to Pennsylvania senator William Maclay, who attended. Maclay said Washington seemed nervous, "agitated and embarrassed more than ever he was by the leveled cannon or pointed musket." He trembled as he gave a short speech accepting the presidency.[3]

And from the start of his administration, Americans honored him with statues, street names, paintings, and memorabilia. The first permanent capital of the nation, Washington, the District of Columbia, was, of course, named after him.

"The American Constitution, as drafted and ratified in the late 1780s, was a splendid document," writes political scientist Thomas E. Cronin. "Yet it did not guarantee that the American presidency would work and that Americans would enjoy both representative and effective government. Much depended on how George Washington interpreted the Constitution and how his countrymen would respond to his leadership. He carefully would have to lessen the distrust of Americans to a centralized leadership institution and earn respect and legitimacy for the fledgling Republic. . . . His integrity, judgment, and lengthy service (both in and out of uniform) to his country and his devotion to his troops and his countrymen set him apart from his fellow founders."[4]

*   *   *

AS PRESIDENT, Washington set many precedents. He knew that his successors would model their behavior on his as much as possible, and that the new nation would expect this to happen, so he was very prudent in what he did. He was concerned about maintaining his reputation for being above reproach, and he didn't want the presidency to become an imperial office such as the royal courts of Europe. There was debate initially on what to call the new president. Some suggested "Your Highness," and others preferred "Your High Mightiness." But Washington said "Mr. President" would be more appropriate, and this designation has been used ever since.

He felt an obligation to meet as many of his fellow citizens as he could during those early days of the Republic in the late 1700s, and he did so to the extent that he sometimes couldn't relax at his home because of all the visitors. There are accounts of him trying to be polite but struggling to show an interest in the conversations of the people who dropped in on him, both at his estate in Mount Vernon, Virginia, and at his official residence. Sometimes he was bored; at other times he was tired and eager to go to bed after dinner.

He gave up dancing even though he enjoyed it and was good at it. But he considered it frivolous and below the stature of the president.

He limited himself to two terms, and that was the precedent until Franklin D. Roosevelt broke with tradition by seeking and winning election to four terms in 1932, 1936, 1940, and 1944 as he led the nation through the Depression and World War II.

Over the years, all sorts of lore grew up around Washington as the father of his country—tales of how he had chopped down a cherry tree and couldn't tell a lie about it; that he threw a coin across the Potomac River, demonstrating extraordinary strength; that he was a brilliant leader during the Revolutionary War even though he lost several key battles. His celebrity status persists to this day.

*   *   *

WASHINGTON ABSORBED his understanding of the dominant culture of his time in various ways. He was a reader, as were all of the most influential founders, including Thomas Jefferson and John Adams. He had a library consisting of nine hundred books, including classics from ancient Greece and Rome, some fiction, and practical volumes on agriculture. Part of the gentleman's culture of Washington and his associates was not only to read but to discuss books, along with history, philosophy, and current events, at dinner parties. As president, he hosted Thursday dinners, formal affairs in which men and women would gather to eat sumptuously, and then separate into two groups. The women talked among themselves and the men retired to a drawing room to drink and discuss what they considered important matters.

Washington, with his imposing height and bearing, embodied the look and behavior that Americans idealized and sought in their leader. He cultivated this image assiduously. "He knew he was a symbol to his countrymen, and he understood the importance of theatricality in leadership," writes historian Tevi Troy. "He tried to convey a certain image in his dress when on horseback. Jefferson called him 'the best horseman of his age and the most graceful figure that could ever be seen on horseback.' Equestrian skills were held in especially high regard in those days because of the practical value and the symbolic importance of the cavalry from the time of Rome until the end of the Middle Ages. Washington's flair for the theatrical may have come, logically enough, from his own love of the theater. According to [historian] Myron Magnet, Washington exercised 'adroit stagecraft' in his management of the Revolutionary War. He took on the role of stage actor who could skillfully manipulate his audience. He carefully selected his own clothes, recognizing that his impressive military uniform paralleled a costume for an actor playing a character."[5]

He was adept at what we today call "branding," and the country went along, purchasing all manner of Washington memorabilia, from artists' renderings to engravings. "The image of a candidate or a president, whether a portrait or an emblem or what we would now call a brand, was important from the beginning," writes historian Vicki Goldberg. "Engraved portraits of George Washington, which had been popular during his lifetime, remained popular long after his death and still show up daily on dollar bills. There are many ways of impressing an image or perception on a large number of minds, but almost all of them involve repetition and wide distribution—and visual images are particularly likely to stick in the mind."[6]

Washington loved the theater, including Shakespeare, even though it was looked down upon as vulgar and lowbrow in the colonies and early

United States. But he had Joseph Addison's play *Cato*, which celebrated republican values and patriotism in a fight against tyranny, staged for his troops at Valley Forge during the harsh winter of 1777–1778, when morale was low.

Washington combined many roles in his successful quest to manage and enhance his celebrity. Cronin concludes, "In certain ways Washington became the nation's first secular priest or societal shaman. In helping his fellow countrymen to transcend their parochial loyalties he helped instill a new nationalism and a new sense of collective purpose. His combination of *warrior* and *priest*, *liberator*, and *definer* of a national vision presaged additional extraconstitutional responsibilities for future American presidents."[7]

Abraham Lincoln: Uncommon Common Man

Abraham Lincoln was born poor but he was a striver who worked hard to better himself. It was the ultimate American story. This is what his celebrity was based on.

He was a reader of books all his life, and kept up the habit during his presidency in the manner of founders such as Thomas Jefferson, John Adams, and John Quincy Adams. But he also understood everyday American life and, emulating Andrew Jackson, never came across as an elitist, as some previous presidents had. "While every president needs a little John Quincy Adams to govern wisely, he needs a little Andrew Jackson to get elected," Troy writes. "The common touch was never difficult for Lincoln. His origins—the poverty, the rail-splitting, the one-room schoolhouse— were as humble as they come. But long after he left the log cabin, Lincoln retained an ability to connect with ordinary people despite his impressive intellect and knowledge. . . . Lincoln honed this skill as a circuit-riding lawyer whose success depended in part on being a good entertainer. . . . A good actor, Lincoln knew how to play to his audience."[8] This is the same talent that Ronald Reagan would have in the 1980s. Lincoln embodied the concept that someone could rise from nothing to achieve great things, and could even be president, although Lincoln eventually proved that he was hardly an average fellow. Americans, at least in the Northern states, felt he understood them.

*   *   *

A KEY POINT for Lincoln came when he deftly built up and then exploited his personal celebrity in the months prior to his election. The pivotal event was a speech he gave at New York's Cooper Union, an academy in Manhattan, on February 27, 1860. Lincoln scholar Harold Holzer writes that it transformed Lincoln "from a relatively obscure Illinois favorite son into a viable national contender for his party's presidential nomination."[9] He won that nomination three months later and took the presidency six months after that.

Lincoln realized that his speech to an important crowd in the key Eastern state of New York could make or break his chances to win the presidency, so he prepared it meticulously and delivered it brilliantly. It was a principled and reasoned stand against slavery and in defense of the Union, without the zealotry or anger that was inflaming the nation at the time.[10] He would use this address as the basis for many other speeches all across the country.[11] Once nominated, he mostly refrained from making speeches and referred voters to the Cooper Union address and summaries of his seven debates with Stephen A. Douglas in the 1858 US Senate campaign in Illinois. Lincoln said those debates distilled his views very well, even though he lost that Senate race.[12]

"As if to illustrate his metamorphosis," writes Holzer, "the Cooper Union appearance also inspired the most important single visual record of Lincoln's, or perhaps any, American presidential campaign: an image-transforming Mathew Brady photograph. Its later proliferation and reproduction in prints, medallions, broadsides, and banners perhaps did as much to create a 'new' Abraham Lincoln as did the Cooper Union address itself."[13]

Lincoln had sat for photographs before, but he wanted this one to be special because it would be what amounted to his official presidential-campaign image. So he went to Brady, the most celebrated photographer of his day, and sat for a picture at Brady's New York gallery at Bleecker Street on February 27, 1860, a few hours before his Cooper Union speech. He hoped both the speech and the photograph would add to his celebrity. They did, but getting the right photograph was a challenge.

Lincoln, fifty-one, looked weary, haggard, and awkward, and at six-feet-four, his clothes were too small. A friend conceded that his appearance was less than appealing because he had "a large mole on his right cheek and an uncommonly prominent Adam's apple on his throat."[14]

Assessing his subject, Brady hit upon a brilliant idea. He would photograph this unattractive man standing up, at a distance, to emphasize his impressive height, rather than taking the customary head shot. Brady posed Lincoln with a false pillar in the background and a table piled with books and Lincoln lightly touching the top volume with his left hand, to suggest erudition. This technique diverted attention from Lincoln's unappealing facial features and his ill-fitting clothes. Afterward Brady did some retouching, erasing the dark circles around Lincoln's eyes and minimizing the deep lines in his face.[15] He came up with an image of someone who appeared to be dignified and determined.

In May, after Lincoln won the Republican presidential nomination, Brady decided to distribute the photograph as widely as he could. He was hoping to add to his own notoriety as well as Lincoln's.

The photo was sent all over the country, and it introduced the rail-splitter to the electorate not as the country bumpkin portrayed by his critics but as a sophisticated and serious leader. At one point, Brady produced and sold a large number of three-by-four-inch card copies of his original photograph to meet public demand for images of the Republican candidate.

For historians, there was a problem. The photo showed Lincoln clean-shaven but he had grown a beard shortly before his election in November. He posed in Brady's Washington studio for another portrait (taken by Brady associate Alexander Gardner, who would later take other pictures of the president), this time featuring his whiskers.[16] He had learned the value of keeping his image before the public and how important this was to his celebrity and his success as president.

Many enterprising printmakers simply doctored Brady's original photograph by giving Lincoln whiskers, so the first image lived on for years beyond the president's death.[17]

*   *   *

IN MARKED CONTRAST to his image since his assassination, Lincoln was derided by many Americans during his time in office. It's likely that anyone would have endured the same fate as president since the nation was so bitterly divided over slavery and preserving the Union. In addition, the horrific casualty rates of the Civil War caused enormous grief and undermined the credibility of those in power.

The epithets directed at Lincoln were cruel and cutting. He was called an ape, a baboon, a traitor, a tyrant, a monster, a gorilla, an idiot, a demagogue, an imbecile, a lunatic, a charlatan, and "a joke incarnate."[18]

But Lincoln enjoyed popularity among his core supporters because of his appealing personality, storytelling ability, and humorous touch. When political adversary Stephen A. Douglas called him a "two-faced man," Lincoln had a self-deprecating reply. "I leave it to my audience," he said. "If I had another face, do you think I would wear this one?"[19]

Several books claiming to contain examples of Lincoln's humor, such as *Abe's Jokes—Fresh from Abraham's Bosom* and *Old Abe's Jokes, or, Wit at the White House*, were published during his presidency and sold throughout the North, increasing his celebrity.[20]

And of course Lincoln's brilliant use of language, such as his Gettysburg Address and his inaugural addresses, enhanced his stature. His popularity, at least in the North, grew markedly after it became clear that the Union forces would win the Civil War.

But it was after his death by assassination on April 15, 1865, that he entered the realm of truly iconic figures in American history as he took on the mantle of a martyr for a great cause and one of the nation's greatest presidents.

The Military Heroes

Americans have a long tradition of electing military heroes as their presidents. George Washington, winner of the Revolutionary War, was, of course, the first.

Andrew Jackson was the second. Known as Old Hickory, he rode his military celebrity into the White House in 1828 and to reelection in 1832. (He had lost to John Quincy Adams in 1824 after the election was decided by the House of Representatives.) Jackson, a self-made man, won acclaim as an "Indian fighter" and as a general in the War of 1812 when he defeated the British at New Orleans in January 1815 and smashed the forces of many Native American tribes.

"The fact that Andrew Jackson—a rough-hewn, poorly educated, self-made frontiersman—could ascend to the presidency mattered more than the policies he embraced," observed a history of Jackson published by the Miller Center at the University of Virginia. "His rhetorical championship of the plain people against the aristocrats, whatever its substance or sincerity, was itself the sign and harbinger of a massive social shift toward democracy, equality, and the primacy of the common man. Jackson stands in this light not as the leader of a party but as the symbol for a democratic age."[21]

He appealed directly to voters in strong and blunt language, not the words of diplomacy or erudition, and billed himself as the public's prime defender against special interests, greedy businessmen, and craven members of Congress, demonizing his opponents such as John C. Calhoun and Henry Clay.[22]

He thrived partly because of his carefully cultivated image as a man of the people. As president, he expanded executive power and defended everyday Americans from what he considered "money power," and his celebrity as a self-styled public tribune helped him carry the day by capturing the public's imagination.

Jackson was one of America's most popular presidents during his eight years in the White House, and one of the nation's premier celebrities. As a war hero and a populist whose views gained widespread support, Jackson knew how to capitalize on his fame.

On February 22, 1837, as he was preparing to leave office the following month, he invited his fellow citizens to the White House for an unusual event—to devour a huge block of cheddar cheese (measuring four feet in diameter and two feet thick and weighing 1,400 pounds) that had been given to him by an admirer from New York in 1835. Jackson kept it so it could ripen, and he decided to share it with the public as his presidency was ending. It was also the birthday of George Washington. From 1 to 3 p.m. that day, a horde of folks descended on the White House, bearing knives, forks, and spoons, and they set about slicing up the cheese and consuming it on the spot or taking chunks of it home. The rowdy crowd dropped cheese on the floor, smashed it into the carpets, smeared it on the furniture and the walls, and generally made a huge mess.[23]

Following in Jackson's footsteps, Zachary Taylor was regarded as the most popular man in America at the time of his election in 1848, largely because of his record of military success.[24] During the early and mid-1800s, he had been a hero of the Mexican-American War, notably by winning the battle of Buena Vista against a vastly larger force, by decimating Mexican troops at Monterrey, and in fights with Native Americans during his years in the military. He won the nickname Old Rough and Ready.

Taylor's presidency ran into trouble over the hugely polarizing issue of slavery and over his own disengagement from the great debates of his time. He died on July 9, 1850, after only sixteen months in office, due to an illness now believed to have been cholera.

Other military heroes used their celebrity as courageous and successful fighting men to win the presidency and maintain the respect of the public. They included U. S. Grant, commander of Union forces at the end of the Civil War; Theodore Roosevelt, leader of the Rough Riders cavalry unit during the Spanish-American War; Dwight Eisenhower, commander of allied forces in the D-Day invasion of Normandy; and John F. Kennedy, the heroic captain of a US PT boat in the Pacific during World War II.

Grover and Frances Folsom Cleveland: Celebrity Couple

Grover Cleveland was a bachelor when he became president in 1885. In 1886, the forty-eight-year-old commander in chief married twenty-one-year-old Frances "Frankie" Folsom, the daughter of his former law partner. They were wed in the White House's Blue Room and tried to get away for their honeymoon at a secluded resort in the western Maryland mountains. But they were trailed by a trainload of reporters who were as unruly and aggressive as today's paparazzi. President Cleveland was furious and he condemned the journalists as "animals and nuisances."[25]

After the honeymoon, Cleveland's desire for privacy became acute. Even though he continued to work at the White House, he lived for much of the time with Frankie at a house he owned on twenty-three acres in northern Washington, DC, two miles from the White House. Reporters were banned from the property. Frankie called the estate Oak View, but the reporters came up with the name that stuck: Red Top, from the color of the roof on the main house. The Clevelands used it as a year-round retreat, and the first lady made it into a farm with a cow named Grace, and a variety of dogs, cats, chickens, ducks, quail, foxes, and white rats.[26]

The newspapers turned Frankie Folsom Cleveland into a huge celebrity. She received thousands of fan letters and hired a social secretary to deal with all the attention and the many requests for her to make appearances. When she did show up in public, thousands of fans would gather to see her.

President Cleveland wanted his spouse to be a "sensible, domestic wife," and said he should be "pleased not to hear her spoken of as 'the

First Lady of the Land' or 'mistress of the White House.' I want her to be happy . . . but I should feel very much affected if she lets many notions into her head." He told his wife after their marriage, "You will find that you get along better in this job if you don't try anything new."[27]

But the president's preference for a low-key spouse was not to be satisfied. Frankie had irresistible appeal to the country, and the newspapers found her to be a terrific story. She was young, beautiful, and cultured. She was a college graduate, spoke French and German, read Latin, played the piano, and liked photography. She used her celebrity to call attention to the Washington Home for Friendless Colored Girls and encourage white women to support the institution. She also urged donations to the Colored Christmas Club, a charity for African American children.

She held many social events at the White House and this intensified public interest in her and her husband. Businesses used her name and likeness to sell their goods and services, especially fashions, in what were called "Frankie ads"—generally without permission from the first lady or her husband.

Many Americans think of Jackie Kennedy, President John F. Kennedy's wife, as the first glamorous first lady who was a huge celebrity in her own right. Actually, Frances Folsom Cleveland was the first.

President Cleveland was defeated for reelection after one term, but he and his wife returned to the White House after he won the election of 1892. By that time, Grover and Frankie had a daughter, Ruth, and public interest in the Cleveland family was just as intense as it had been during his first term.

CHAPTER TWO
THEODORE ROOSEVELT
THE STRENUOUS LIFE

Six presidents stand out as the biggest stars ever to occupy the White House in modern times: Theodore Roosevelt, Franklin D. Roosevelt, John F. Kennedy, Ronald Reagan, Bill Clinton, and Barack Obama. Each of them learned to dominate the mass media of his day, and each came to represent key parts of the American ethos. This propelled them to iconic status, enabling them to capture and hold the nation's attention, sell their agendas, and, through deft use of stagecraft and propaganda, enhance their popularity.

* * *

BRAWNY, BESPECTACLED, mustachioed Theodore Roosevelt (TR), with his bold progressive agenda, his commitment to action, and his belief in what he called "the strenuous life," was a natural celebrity. His craving for attention was so strong that his daughter Alice Roosevelt Longworth once said, "My father always wanted to be the corpse at every funeral, the bride at every wedding, and the baby at every christening."[1]

He had a flair for the dramatic and an instinct for publicity. All this increased his fame and brought public focus to his agenda.

Roosevelt, who served from 1901 to 1909, was one of the most famous people in the world while he was president, and some of his ideas and catchphrases are still familiar today. He said the presidency offered him a wonderful "bully pulpit" to preach his ideas, generate news coverage, and keep him at the center of national life.

He summarized his muscular foreign policy as to "speak softly but carry a big stick." He confronted and imposed federal regulations on the robber barons of his day and condemned them as "malefactors of great wealth."

In May 1904, when an Arab bandit named Ahmed ibn-Muhammed Raisuli kidnapped Ion Perdicaris, a Greek-American businessman, in Morocco, TR sent a brilliantly succinct message through the State Department to the Moroccan sultan, whom he held responsible: "Perdicaris alive or Raisuli dead." Perdicaris was released unharmed after the sultan paid a ransom.[2]

TR assumed the nation's highest office upon the assassination of President William McKinley in September 1901, after serving as vice president for less than a year. His political, personal, and physical exploits as president quickly became legendary. He and his aides eagerly shared these tales with the newspapers to gain him as much attention as possible. Newspaper cartoonists and reporters portrayed his summers at Oyster Bay on Long Island as a series of physical and mental challenges that Roosevelt set for himself and his family and guests.

In August 1905, Roosevelt took a break from talks designed to end a war between Japan and Russia—negotiations which he was supervising from his estate at Sagamore Hill on Long Island, New York—to ride a new US submarine, *The Plunger*, and refresh his mind. Despite gale-velocity winds, the president boarded a launch that took him across Long Island harbor to the sub, which he rode for three hours. He inspected the vessel, asked the captain and crew many questions, and took the controls for a while. At one point he peered through a porthole and watched fish at the bottom of Long Island Sound. He was the first president to ride a sub.[3]

Reporters would wait for him in the town of Oyster Bay, where he kept an official office, and they would plead with him for information about his activities and what his family was up to. Occasionally he would oblige them. On one occasion he said, with considerable hyperbole, "I want you to know all the facts, so I shall give them to you at first hand. Teddy [Jr.] is now fishing for tadpoles, but really expects to land a whale. Archie shot three elephants this morning. Ethel at this moment is setting fire to the rear of the house; Kermit and the calico pony are having a wrestling match in the garret, and Quentin, four years old, is pulling down the windmill."[4]

During a hunting trip in Mississippi in November 1902, a legend was born when he refused to shoot a small bear that had been brought in for him to kill. A cartoon depicted the incident, and toy makers began producing "Teddy's Bears," which became popular and were the origin of today's teddy bears.[5]

Roosevelt developed traits in himself—and projected the image—of a strong, tough man of action rather than a shy, retiring academic type devoted to the life of the mind even though he was in some ways an intellectual. He loved the outdoors; he had traveled through the West in the 1880s, roughing it and even getting into a fight with a bully in a bar, a tale he told with relish in his autobiography.[6] And of course, in his most famous macho exploit of all, he resigned as assistant secretary of the Navy to join a volunteer cavalry unit in May 1898 in order to participate in the Spanish-American War. He led a daring charge of these Rough Riders at San Juan Hill later in 1898. This heroic incident, which received extensive coverage in the press, helped to push TR into national prominence, and helped him win election as governor of New York in November 1898 and get on the successful Republican ticket as the vice presidential candidate with President McKinley in 1900.[7] When McKinley was murdered in September 1901, Roosevelt, at age forty-two, became the youngest person ever to serve as president. He won a full term in 1904.

Roosevelt made more headlines by attacking the "idle rich," financial trusts, and monopolies. "Theodore Roosevelt's presidency is distinguished by his dedication to prosecuting monopolies under the Sherman Antitrust Act," writes an admirer. "Out of this commitment grew a benchmark of his first term, the 'Square Deal'—a domestic program that embraced reform of the American workplace, government regulation of industry and consumer protection, with the overall aim of helping the middle class. Roosevelt's charismatic personality and impassioned combination of . . . facts and emphatic rhetoric undoubtedly helped him push his agenda."[8]

He became known as a conservationist who preserved nearly 200 million acres of public lands from development. In 1906 he signed the National Monuments Act, which protected the Grand Canyon and other natural sites, such as national forests and wildlife sanctuaries.

He regarded his success in building the Panama Canal, which greatly expedited travel between the Atlantic and Pacific Oceans, as his greatest achievement. In 1906 he won the Nobel Peace Prize for his role in negotiating the end of the Russo-Japanese War in 1905.

As author Peter Collier writes, manufacturers of "everything from baby powder to cigars freely appropriated the president's image to hawk their wares."[9]

"Ever since [Andrew] Jackson, the ability to demonstrate the common touch had been essential for winning the presidency," Tevi Troy says. "In an increasingly democratic nation in which college attendance remained rare, book learning was not necessarily a political advantage. At the turn of the century, only 6.4 per cent of seventeen-year-olds graduated from high school. Roosevelt was not only a college graduate but a Harvard man to boot. Roosevelt addressed this vulnerability in a number of ways. He worked hard to seem like not only a man of the people but also one of the people. . . . First, although he loved books, he never forgot that there were things in life more important than literature."[10]

Roosevelt wrote in his memoirs, "Books are all very well in their way, and we love them at Sagamore Hill [his home]; but children are better than books."[11]

He also wrote, "There are men who love out-of-doors yet who never open a book; and other men who love books but to whom the great book of nature is a sealed volume, and the lines written therein blurred and illegible."[12] But he added, "Among those men whom I have known the love of books and the love of outdoors, in their highest expressions, have usually gone hand in hand."[13]

Writes historian John Sayle Watterson, "Roosevelt, one of his era's best-known participants in ultimate sports, had a need to stalk and kill wild game, to push himself to the limit and to exceed his own expectations. Roosevelt was the undersized boy who challenged everyone and everything. He was competitive in all he did, especially outdoor sports. And for his country and its resources, this personal quest broadened into a national crusade [to protect public lands from development]."[14]

Roosevelt became known as a force of nature, always seeking attention and finding many ways to get it. He drew headlines because of his rambunctious family. His six children considered the White House and its surrounds a giant playground. Once, one of his sons brought a pony into the White House as part of his playtime and gave the animal a ride on an elevator. The press loved the story.

A good example of Roosevelt's celebrity came during a trip he made to the West, including the Yellowstone and Yosemite wilderness preserves, in 1903. He hunted and fished and observed wildlife but also met with people in local towns, and his receptions were tremendous. "He usually spoke from eight to ten times every twenty-four hours, sometimes for only a few minutes from the rear platform of his private car, at others for an hour or more in some large hall," wrote naturalist John Burroughs, who accompanied him. "The throng that greeted him in the vast Auditorium in Chicago—that rose and waved and waved again—was one of the grandest human spectacles I ever witnessed."[15]

TR greeted the American team that went to the Olympics in 1908, hosting them at his estate in Oyster Bay. "By George," he said, "I am so glad to see all you boys." After this, greeting of athletic teams became common practice for American presidents.[16]

Watterson writes, "Indeed, political appearances connected with sporting events such as attending the Army-Navy football game or meeting with sport teams and celebrities—even later trips by train and plane to sporting venues such as golfing meccas—all have their origins in Theodore Roosevelt's athletic presidency."

Typical of TR's derring-do was an incident in the 1912 presidential campaign, when he ran for the White House as the nominee of the Progressive Party, also known as the Bull Moose Party. While delivering a speech in Milwaukee, Wisconsin, TR was shot in the chest by a deranged saloon operator but continued speaking for 90 minutes before seeing a doctor. TR was lucky. The bullet was slowed by a metal eyeglasses case and folded-up speech that the president had in his coat pocket.

In politics, TR wasn't so lucky that year. Democrat Woodrow Wilson won the 1912 election, partly because Roosevelt split the GOP vote with Republican nominee William Howard Taft.

Chapter Three
Franklin D. Roosevelt
Public Advocate

Franklin D. Roosevelt became so much a part of the nation that when he died in 1945, not long after being elected to a historic fourth term, many people feared that no one could replace him. As FDR's funeral train made its way across the country, a man was found weeping along the route and he was asked if he had known Roosevelt. "I didn't know him," the man replied. "But he knew me."[1] It was a testament to the extent to which FDR had entered the emotional life of his fellow citizens.

Cultural historian Fred Inglis writes, "Above all, he retained (what all celebrities seek) a vivid sense of his people's moral convictions and allegiances as they then were constituted by their hardworking lives, their inheritance of the pains of mass migration, their faith in the country. He could reach out and touch these things and, feeling them himself, was rewarded by the reciprocity of trust and affection. He had any number of enemies and people who hated him personally; he opposed the oncoming war in public and steered the United States into it, a little at a time, out of sight; knowing nothing about banking and currencies he restored the nation's bank accounts; and he spoke to his people as to their souls."[2]

A key to FDR's remarkable effect on Americans was his understanding of the power of radio and how it could bring the country together. Americans could hear the same songs and the same programs as never before, and could get to know radio personalities as if they were personal friends. Roosevelt realized that the same could hold true for politicians, and he set about becoming the first radio president.

Roosevelt's nationally broadcast speech at the Democratic National Convention in 1932 had introduced him to the American public in the same way that Barack Obama's televised speech to the 2004 Democratic convention launched him toward the White House.

As president, FDR began a series of what became known as "fireside chats"—radio speeches in which a confident FDR explained how his economic policies would work and urged the American people to do their part in repairing the economy. In 1933, his first year in office, he set the tone by declaring, "You people must have faith; you must not be stampeded by rumors or guesses. Let us unite in banishing fear. We have produced the machinery to restore our financial system, and it is up to you to support and make it work. It is your problem, my friends, your problem no less than it is mine. Together we cannot fail."[3]

"Blessed with a strong, clear, and confident voice, Roosevelt used radio to establish an intimate bond between the president and his constituents throughout the country," writes political scientist Robert E. Gilbert. "The medium of radio enabled Roosevelt to enter people's homes not only as president but as a friend. During his famous fireside chats, he spoke in intimate terms to members of his audience, using language and analogies that they could easily understand. The response was almost always positive, with thousands of ordinary citizens writing the White House and/or Congress, indicating their support for the president's programs."[4]

He delivered only twenty-eight radio talks over the course of his twelve years in office. Roosevelt didn't want to wear out his welcome. He understood that, as the former actor Ronald Reagan would say years later, it's always best for a performer to leave an audience wanting more. So his fireside chats, which began a few days after he took office, took place only two or three times a year. FDR wore a false tooth to close a gap between the teeth in his lower jaw that caused a slight whistle when he spoke. And he used special sheets of paper for his text to minimize rustling noises when he moved from one page to another. Nothing was left to chance. He even noted in the text where he was supposed to pause and where he was to raise his voice or emphasize a point.[5]

His fireside chats, combined with other speeches, conveyed his message of hope and optimism; all wrapped together with his soothing, distinctive voice, they enabled FDR to bond with the country. "You felt he was there talking to you, not to 50 million others, but to you personally," said journalist Richard Strout. Secretary of Labor Frances Perkins, a close friend of Franklin and Eleanor Roosevelt, said FDR would think of his audience as he spoke, picturing people "sitting on a suburban porch after supper on a summer evening" or "gathered around a dinner table at a family meal."[6]

Demonstrating a clear understanding of the public he was trying to lead, Roosevelt said, "The public psychology and for that matter individual psychology cannot, because of human weakness, be attuned for long periods of time to a constant repetition of the highest note in the scale." FDR and his advisers mostly scheduled the fireside chats for one of the first three evenings of a week, when they thought listeners would be most interested and most likely to tune in. They usually limited talks to about 30 minutes so as not to overburden listeners with too much information or too much of a dose of the president at one time. "In all, Roosevelt's fireside chats and other radio speeches became important sources of presidential power, enabling him to achieve a strong national identity and to heighten public morale at a time of great economic distress," Gilbert says.[7]

Gilbert adds, "It is not surprising that the image of dynamic determination that Roosevelt projected was in no way undermined by his severe physical afflictions [caused by polio], since the public remained blissfully unaware of those afflictions. Because of the cooperation of the press, the topic of his crippled legs simply did not reach the public domain. Also, the severe arterial deterioration that finally ended his life in 1945 came as a surprise to much of the nation, which almost believed that he would be on the scene forever."[8]

FDR was extremely confident of his abilities as a dramatist. He once told the actor Orson Welles, "There are only two great actors in America—you are the other one."[9]

FDR used radio to achieve a remarkable degree of celebrity in his own right. He realized that being associated with stars of the entertainment industry would increase his own fame and glamour and open up a wellspring of financial support. But he also knew that establishing too close a link to show-business folk could make him appear superficial and more interested in the glitterati than Middle America. He understood that it would be best for him to establish a direct bond of celebrity with the American people.

Troy adds that Franklin Roosevelt established himself as "the most important figure in the transformation of the president into a media star.

Part of it was simply timing; he was president when Hollywood's influence on American culture exploded. But his greatest contribution to bringing together the worlds of culture and politics was in the realm of radio. Broadcast technologies, destined to help shape American politics with or without Roosevelt, accelerated because of his efforts and insight. . . . Every subsequent president would look to FDR as an example of how to be a media actor as well as a consumer. While previous presidents had highlighted their consumption of the available forms of entertainment in an attempt to convey some of the aspects of the ideal leader, new technologies now allowed them to use the media to broadcast those very characteristics. Thanks to Franklin Roosevelt, the characteristics of the ideal leader would include not only partaking of culture but also using the media of culture to communicate and to lead."[10]

* * *

A MEASURE of Roosevelt's exalted status with the public can be seen in the way he was portrayed in movies. The images of presidents on film today tend to be hard-edged and cynical, as in *White House Down* and *Lincoln*. But FDR was so admired during his presidency that the images of him on film were gauzy and benevolent. In *Yankee Doodle Dandy*, an actor impersonating FDR awed showman George M. Cohan, played by James Cagney, when they met at the White House. Another avuncular actor who resembled FDR appeared in *Grapes of Wrath* as the kindly administrator of a well-run migrant labor camp that served as a safe harbor for poor families during the Depression.

The popular singer and movie star Judy Garland paid FDR a huge compliment in the 1941 film *Babes on Broadway* when she sang "How About You?" and included the line, "And Franklin Roos'velt's looks give me a thrill." It may have been a bit of embellishment about FDR's appearance, but it reflected the respect he commanded throughout the country, including in Hollywood.

* * *

ON JANUARY 30, 1940, FDR reached new heights in blending celebrity with politics when eighteen stars attended his birthday party and related events in Washington. Among them were James Cagney, Gene Autry, Olivia de Havilland, Dorothy Lamour, Elsa Lanchester, Pat O'Brien, Tyrone Power, Edward G. Robinson, Mickey Rooney, and Red Skelton.

They attended a luncheon hosted by the president and first lady Eleanor Roosevelt. That evening the stars attended events around Washington to raise money for the National Foundation for Infantile Paralysis, the polio-stricken president's favorite charity. At the end of the evening, the Hollywood troupe returned to the White House to watch FDR address the nation on the radio.[11] The tradition of Hollywood stars celebrating FDR's birthday had started in a low-key way in 1934 and continued through his presidency with increasing fanfare.[12]

Roosevelt didn't mind that people knew he had polio, but he kept the extent of his disability a secret from the public. Even news photographers at the White House were part of the cover-up. They wouldn't take or use photos of the president in a wheelchair showing that his legs were useless. Photographers starting work at the White House were told these ground rules in no uncertain terms.

As his presidency progressed, parties were held on his birthday each year at many venues around the country, and they were attended by everyday people, not just Hollywood types. These events included both lavish settings such the living rooms of the rich and more humble locations such as civic centers and barns. The goal was to raise money for polio research and treatment. These fund-raisers evolved into the March of Dimes, a title invented by entertainer Eddie Cantor. He said it was a March of Dimes and to send dimes to the White House. The White House was flooded with envelopes filled with dimes and dollars. A special card was made with slots for the dimes, which became well known and used widely around the country.

Journalism professor Alan Schroeder writes, "The FDR birthday celebrations represent the first sustained effort by a president to forge a direct alliance with stars of the entertainment world. Previous occupants of the Oval Office had curried favor with Hollywood's studio bosses, as did Roosevelt himself. But this was something different: a deliberate, personal courting of the faces that lit up the nation's movie screens. In large part the birthday balls came about because of Roosevelt's status as a devoted fan of American pop culture, films in particular. Celebrating his birthday with the top stars of the day seemed appropriate for FDR because he understood the ways in which his job intersected with theirs. Without embarrassment, he recognized himself as a member of their firmament."

Schroeder continues, "FDR, like only three other presidents in history—Kennedy, Reagan, and Clinton—spoke fluently the language of show business, and he had the natural temperament to get along with performers on a personal basis."[13]

Bob Clark, archivist at the FDR Library, said Roosevelt was an icon during his time in office. "He kind of permeated the culture," Clark told me.[14]

Not only did FDR master radio; he was also adept at providing an early form of "sound bite" for newsreels. After giving a speech on the radio, which he would often do in the ground-floor Diplomatic Reception Room of the White House, he read excerpts that he particularly liked for the newsreels, which played in theaters before movies were shown.[15]

CHAPTER FOUR
JOHN F. KENNEDY
GLITTER AND COOL

John F. Kennedy mastered TV as Franklin D. Roosevelt had mastered radio, but Kennedy went further, cultivating his image in a more methodical and comprehensive way. As the nation's celebrity in chief, Kennedy emerged as a charming and cool operator and America's leading man. He exhibited enormous grace under pressure while seeming to be a good husband and father with a gorgeous wife and two beautiful children. In some ways this image was a sham, since Kennedy was a womanizer who had deep trouble in his marriage. But he used his celebrity status to keep the nation's attention and to capture America's imagination, a dynamic that exists to this day.

"What Kennedy had was a kind of celebrity, a kind of star power," says historian Robert Dallek. "All the womanizing seems to enhance rather than detract from his star power." And his assassination has deepened his mythic qualities, embedding into the nation's psyche the idea of a talented young president whose promise was cut short by an assassin.[1]

Kennedy stood out for his charisma and his ability to build on his celebrity. "There is an old saying in politics that a candidate is greatly advantaged if he likes and enjoys people and even more if people know that he likes and enjoys them," writes political scientist Thomas E. Cronin. "Kennedy won praise in this regard. He liked himself, he liked politics, he liked and enjoyed people, and people knew it. He had stage presence and star quality."[2]

A large part of Kennedy's success came from his simple recognition of the power of TV. Presidents are in our living rooms with great regularity through television, and Kennedy realized that he needed to be a star to have the most impact and to boost his own popularity.

Despite his strength and charm on TV, as evidenced by his performance in the 1960 presidential debates with Republican nominee Richard Nixon, Kennedy only won the 1960 election very narrowly. But as he settled into power at age forty-three, he used TV more and more to cement his celebrity status and fascinate the public with his youth, vigor and seemingly new ideas, such as the Peace Corps and his goal of sending astronauts to the moon. His staff and supporters reminded people of his heroism in World War II, when he swam for hours pulling one of his men with him in the Pacific after his torpedo boat, *PT-109*, was destroyed by the Japanese. He was charmingly self-deprecatory about his wartime courage and grit. "It was involuntary," he once said. "They sank my boat."[3] Americans loved his style.

Kennedy was the son of a Hollywood film mogul and, like his father, "Jack Kennedy developed an early appreciation of the uses of celebrity," writes Alan Schroeder. "In the late 1940s, visiting a friend who worked for actor Gary Cooper, JFK became fascinated by the connection between movie stars and their audiences. Kennedy and the friend, Chuck Spalding, would talk for hours about the popularity of various celebrities. . . . Kennedy wondered about his own star quality. 'He was always interested in seeing whether he had it—the magnetism—or didn't have it.' Spalding said."[4]

He had it.

Some felt that his affinity for show business enabled him to more easily romance beautiful women in the industry. But he also loved being with show-business folk in general, and this made him more popular in the entertainment community. Actress June Havoc, emerging from a 1961 White House meeting with the president, excitedly told reporters that Kennedy's "vernacular is very theatrical. He talked show folk talk." JFK's exposure to the movie industry through his father, a producer, and his curiosity about the charisma of show-business people caused him to fit in naturally with entertainers.[5] His connection to the entertainment world was deepened in a personal way when one of his sisters married the actor Peter Lawford. This also gave him a link to Lawford's pals, known as the "Rat Pack," the hippest stars on the scene. Other members were Frank Sinatra, Dean Martin, Sammy Davis Jr., and Joey Bishop.

The Democratic National Convention, which nominated Kennedy for the presidency in 1960, showed how strong the bond had grown between JFK and Hollywood luminaries. Parties celebrating Kennedy proliferated throughout Los Angles, the convention's host city and the location of Hollywood itself. Among those on the Kennedy bandwagon were Sinatra, Davis, Steve Allen, Nat King Cole, Tony Curtis, Judy Garland, Janet Leigh, Shirley MacLaine, and Shelley Winters.[6]

Kennedy used his lifestyle in the White House to enhance his celebrity. He and his staff cleverly parlayed photographs of him with his wife and two adorable children into the image of a devoted family man. Americans were delighted at photos of his son John Jr. hiding under Daddy's desk, his daughter Caroline romping in the Oval Office as her doting father looked on, and his wife Jacqueline on his arm at many glittery social events. Privately there were troubles in the Kennedy marriage, in large part because of his philandering, but this was kept from the public.

The high point of Kennedy's social climbing was his hosting of world-famous cellist Pablo Casals at the White House. The president was not a big fan of music and wasn't familiar with Casals's work. But his wife persuaded him to invite the cellist to entertain. Casals's famous performance at the White House on November 13, 1961, cemented JFK's reputation as an arts maven. The legendary cellist had played there in 1904 for Theodore Roosevelt but had not performed in the United States since 1928. The White House invitation to Casals was an enormous PR coup. But Kennedy was at a loss about how to behave—to such an extent that the president received, and followed, instructions from his social secretary, Letitia Baldrige, on what to do during the evening, including a reminder that he should wait for an encore rather than move from his seat abruptly.[7]

It worked. The media had high praise for Kennedy's hosting Casals along with an audience that included many famous people from the music world, such as Leonard Bernstein and Aaron Copland. This sealed the new president's reputation as a patron of the arts and a man who mingled easily with America's high-culture celebrities.

In some ways this was a false image. Theodore Sorensen, one of Kennedy's closest advisers, said JFK's cultural tastes were actually rather simple even though the new president tried to convey an image of sophistication. "He had no interest in opera," Sorensen observed; he "dozed off at a symphony and was bored by ballet." He liked Broadway songs, Irish tunes, country-and-western music, and songs from Hollywood musicals, and was interested in rock and roll.[8]

But Kennedy and his handlers were intent on making him as much of a celebrity as possible to every stratum and cohort in the country, highbrow or lowbrow.

One of the high points of his social calendar was a glitzy party and Democratic fund-raiser thrown for his forty-fifth birthday on May 19, 1962 (his birthday was actually on May 29) at New York's Madison Square Garden. More than 15,000 people attended, including stars such as Harry Belafonte, Jack Benny, Maria Callas, Bobby Darin, Jimmy Durante, Ella Fitzgerald, Henry Fonda, and Greer Garson. The president seemed delighted with all the tributes as he smoked a cigar and beamed.[9]

The three-hour extravaganza ended when Marilyn Monroe, the sex icon of the era, appeared on stage in a skintight gown and sang seductively, "Happy birthday to you. Happy birthday to you. Happy birthday, Mr. President. Happy birthday to you." Kennedy later told the crowd, "I can now retire from politics after having had 'Happy Birthday' sung to me in such a sweet, wholesome way." It was a brilliant moment of political theater, and it bolstered Kennedy's reputation as one of the most glamorous celebrities of the age, dominating the intersection of politics and entertainment.

Throughout his brief 1,000 days in office, Kennedy and the entertainment world continued to cultivate each other with star-filled fund-raisers and dinners.

*   *   *

THE PRIVATE TRUTH was that, despite his reputation as an all-around arts enthusiast, Kennedy loved books above all cultural pursuits, and he estimated that he could read 1,200 words a minute, a very rapid rate.[10] As president he preferred history and biography to fiction, and enjoyed reading about how individuals had shaped history. His favorite book was *Melbourne*, by Lord David Cecil, a 1939 biography of Lord Melbourne, Queen Victoria's prime minister in the early nineteenth century.[11] But he made an exception to his overall preference for nonfiction by relishing Ian Fleming's novels about Secret Agent 007, James Bond.

Kennedy also read several newspapers every morning, paid close attention to the newsweeklies, and perused journals of opinion.

His success at achieving immense celebrity status was reflected in the popularity of Kennedy impersonators as entertainers.[12] This showed how pervasive JFK had become as a celebrity and a major figure in popular culture during fewer than three years in office. One of the leading Kennedy impersonators was Vaughn Meader, whose TV appearances and 1962 album *The First Family* reached a mass audience, capitalizing on JFK's distinctive voice and mannerisms and the public's desire to know more about him.[13]

*   *   *

THE KENNEDY FAMILY'S celebrity had been carefully constructed by the family patriarch Joseph Kennedy, John F. Kennedy's father. "It goes back to the 1920s, when the father was a producer in Hollywood," says Barbara Perry, senior fellow at the University of Virginia's Miller Center. "That was the beginning of the family's celebrity."[14] Joe Kennedy's role producing movies got noticed, and it drew media attention to him and his glowing family in the newsreels and in the glossy magazines of his day. It also taught him "what sells and what doesn't sell," Perry says. "He realized that sex appeal sold. Sex appeal, good looks, being different, standing out, and a certain charm and superstar quality was going to attract attention and draw people in."

When Joe later became US ambassador to the Court of St. James's in London, he encouraged publicity and there was an enormous amount of it, focusing on the attractive, smart and engaging family of the ambassador, his wife Rose, and their nine children. As Irish Catholics, their ethnic background and their faith also helped draw attention to them in a United Kingdom that had a long and troubled history with heavily Catholic Ireland. Perry says, "They were the toast of London. . . . They were the reality show of the era."

For a while, the wealthy Kennedy patriarch thought he could be the first Catholic president of the United States, but after that dream died he groomed and promoted his sons for political careers. He bankrolled JFK's successful White House bid in 1960.

Jack learned much from his father about the importance of image. Jack's marriage to the wealthy, beautiful, and well-connected Jacqueline Bovier in 1953 was staged as a major social event, attended by 3,000 guests and receiving much publicity (with deft encouragement from the bride and groom). They were celebrities even before JFK started campaigning for the White House. When he was running for president, he and his wife and their young daughter would score a PR coup by appearing on the cover of *Life* magazine, building up his positive image in the mass media of his day. The son also had the father's magnetism. A friend once said that Jack and Joe "could charm the birds out of the trees."[15]

Jack served relatively briefly in the US House of Representatives from Massachusetts and then, with financial backing from his father, won an upset victory to the Senate in 1952 against Republican incumbent Henry Cabot Lodge.

"Kennedy became a backbencher in the U.S. Senate," writes Cronin. "He was never a member of what was then called the Senate 'inner club.' Moreover, he often seemed distracted by his social life and, again, he was often sick. Still, he was in great demand as a celebrity for he was a member of the alluring Kennedy clan, and he was its youthful golden boy, a promising young man with a fortune and a future. The longer he stayed in the Senate the more publicity he received, despite his ineffectiveness as a senator."[16]

JFK cultivated his celebrity for the remainder of his life and throughout his time in the White House, using it to increase his personal popularity and call attention to and boost support for his agenda. One image-making breakthrough was the release of *PT 109*, a film starring charismatic leading man Cliff Robertson depicting Kennedy's heroism as an attack-boat commander during World War II in the Pacific. Released in July 1963, the year before he was planning to run for reelection, it was panned by critics as too reverential and, at two-and-a-half hours, too long, but it showed how enamored the entertainment industry remained with the country's young leader.[17]

Frank Donatelli, White House political director for President Ronald Reagan, told me, "Issues do matter, but people want to know about their presidents. Today you have to tell your [personal] story as president."[18] Donatelli traces this development to President Kennedy. "The personality dimension of the presidency blossomed under Kennedy," Donatelli said. "When you are a celebrity, people want to learn more about you. You have an advantage in that way."

Writes cultural historian Fred Inglis, "The celebrity he engendered mingled glad excitement with a delicious fearfulness. This was a new current of feeling, not yet established as a structure, coming through as all that the sixties were later to signify. Kennedy, out of his completeness as politician, his utter absorption in its day-to-day conversation, his needful cynicism, his rhetorical tropes, vacuous but rousing ('Ask not what your country can do for you—ask what you can do for your country'), brought all these qualities together and radiated them to his nation as thrilling novelty, a transformative surge of new feelings and world-changing possibility."

Inglis continues, "It could not last. It had insufficient content. Only his appalling death gave longevity to the myths of Camelot. Celebrity itself, however—the concept and its value to the American people, to *all* people come to that—is still charged up by Kennedy's ghostly force. It reminds us how once upon a time sheer attractiveness, physical presence, calm resolution in manner, grace in conduct, and the signal good fortune of the Cuban Missile Crisis in 1962, combined to colour the old political machine with the brilliance and exhilaration of heroism."[19]

Writes Cronin, "President John F. Kennedy also fits the defender of the faith and the renewer of the dream symbols closely associated with the symbolic presidency. In part, it was his glamour, style, youth, and wit. Yet it was also the Kennedy message of hope and the promise of new possibilities. . . . He liked to stress that this country 'cannot afford to be materially rich and spiritually poor.' We needed, he said, to complete the unredeemed pledges of the Roosevelt-Truman period, and we similarly needed to reclaim our political and military dominance in world affairs. His Peace Corps, man-to-the-moon program, overseas economic development initiatives, belated but significant civil rights action, and similar endeavors were intended to recapture the spirit and idealism of distinctive aspects of the American Dream."

In death, Kennedy's celebrity expanded and perceptions about his accomplishments outran reality, to the extent that today he is remembered as one of America's greatest leaders.

CHAPTER FIVE
RONALD REAGAN
THE ROLE OF THE CENTURY

Ronald Reagan took the TV age to a new level. A former movie and television actor, he was a brilliant political performer, and it helped him sell his policies. Reagan also understood the dangers of overexposure and wearing out his welcome, so he tried to limit his TV presence to when it really counted. He knew how much attention he could get as a political star, having already been a movie star, and he used it to good advantage to dramatize his administration, his policies, and his persona.[1]

When he was running for the White House, Reagan was amused when commentators and critics wondered whether it was a good idea for a former movie actor to be elected president. When a reporter asked him about this during his successful 1980 campaign, Reagan said, "How can a president not be an actor?"[2]

He was making a good point, because today's presidents need to not only be policy makers, world diplomats, and legislative strategists; they also need to be showmen.[3] Reagan handled his TV appearances exceptionally well, which I discuss at length in Chapter 10, on the presidents and television. And he knew how to give a great speech. "He's an actor," a Reagan aide said. "He's used to being directed and produced. He stands where he is supposed to and delivers his lines; he reads beautifully; he knows how to wait for his applause line."[4]

Michael Deaver, Reagan's chief media adviser in the White House, writes, "Politics and Hollywood have a lot in common. Both are full of phony moments—photo ops, self-serving anecdotes, spin doctoring."[5] Reagan was well versed in the entertainment arts that have become so important to a successful presidency.

Some presidents affected and shaped popular culture; some didn't. Some presidents had a natural affinity for everyday Americans and some didn't. Reagan did. He knew that Americans wanted and needed a leader who was sunny and optimistic, and that's what he provided.

Antitax activist Grover Norquist says, "Reagan was a celebrity going in. People wanted to be seen with him. It's like they wanted to be seen with a movie star. . . . He was validating that they were cool."[6]

In public President Reagan acted like a celebrity, gregarious and forever affable. But privately he could be distant from those around him. Larry Speakes, Reagan's White House press secretary, says, "Privately, he tends to be a loner, content to spend most of his time with his wife and no one else."[7] Nancy Reagan has written of her husband that "although he loves people, he often seems remote, and he doesn't let anybody get too close. There's a wall around him."[8]

Reagan and his media advisers understood the power of the visual, something that even TV reporters underestimated at the time. When he was running for reelection in 1984, Lesley Stahl of CBS did a story about Reagan's policies that she thought was hard-hitting and negative. "I was worried that my sources at the White House would be angry enough to freeze me out," she recalled. But she got an unexpected reaction when White House Deputy Chief of Staff Michael Deaver, Reagan's media strategist, called. "Way to go, Kiddo," Deaver told Stahl. "What a great piece. We loved it." Stahl was nonplussed and asked, "Didn't you hear what I said?" Deaver answered, "Nobody heard what you said. . . . You guys in televisionland haven't figured it out yet, have you? When the pictures are powerful and emotional, they override if not completely drown out the sound. I mean it, Lesley. Nobody heard you."[9] It turned out that the images Stahl used of Reagan were positive, making him look strong, amiable, and upbeat. This is what the viewers remembered.

Day in and day out, Reagan's advisers orchestrated his public appearances based on irresistible visuals, depicting the president in a positive way. They often surrounded him with, or prominently included in the TV frames, lots of American flags, uniformed police officers, soldiers, children, diverse audiences, and other images designed to increase Reagan's appeal and stature. This relentless TV strategy, combined with an improving economy and public approval of Reagan's leadership, lifted him to a huge victory for a second term in 1984.

The Reagan presidency was "rich with symbolism and meaning for many Americans," writes political scientist Thomas E. Cronin. "Reagan came to the White House promising a new American Dream—a dream that spoke of more freedom from government, lowered taxes, and less regulation of the entrepreneurial impulses of the nation. Reagan's definition of the American Dream differed in many ways from Roosevelt's, yet like Roosevelt, Reagan's initiatives often polarized the nation. In common with Roosevelt, Reagan received unusual public support and won an impressive reelection, perhaps in part because he was willing to take a stand, willing to defend his version of the American mission. If Reagan's was more of an act of restoration or redirection than an act of rebirth or liberation, some of Reagan's more ardent supporters view his role as very much as significant as the visionary, transcending leadership of a Lincoln or a Roosevelt."[10]

Political analyst Sidney Blumenthal, a former White House adviser to President Bill Clinton, writes of Reagan, "He was, after all, more than a pure-bred politician; he had descended to politics from the ether of popular culture. In his first race, he finessed the 'actor issue' by casting himself as a 'citizen-politician,' asserting his lack of qualification precisely as his salient qualification. He aspired to be the enchanting ruler of society, over which he would spread 'stardust.'"[11]

Adds Blumenthal, "His rhetoric was filled with shards of kitsch, ripped from the context of popular culture. On budget policy, Reagan threatened Congress by quoting Clint Eastwood: 'Make my day.' Here the president played Dirty Harry, the vigilante cop. On terrorism, he said he would act like Rambo. On taxes, when the movie *The Untouchables* was in commercial release, he cited Eliot Ness: 'If any tax hike ever comes across my desk, my handling of the veto pen will make the way Eliot Ness went after Al Capone look like child's play.' Then he referred to Vanna White, the comely *Playboy* featurette and letter-turner on the television game show *Wheel of Fortune*: 'I'll veto it in less time than it takes for Vanna White to turn the letters V-E-T-O.'"[12]

"Reagan's references to popular culture, making him seem familiar and, by extension, his policies more acceptable, were mostly lifted from the entertainment world that had supplanted much of genuine small-town culture," Blumenthal writes. "Reagan himself was part of that irreversible process. . . . The themes promoted by the president were given their greatest elaborations in certain television series and films. On TV, the family, riven by conflict in the 1960s and 1970s, was restored: *Home Front* with a Hollywood ending. The message, however, varied from show to show and was not necessarily simple."

Blumenthal continues, "*Dynasty* and *Family Ties*, about two very different families, were two of the 1980s' most popular and durable television series. . . . *Dynasty*, which began airing in January 1981, carried the spirit of the Reagan inaugural forward through the 1980s. The show centered on a nouveau riche family in Denver—plutocrats from Pluto. Their wealth was equated with an outrageously camp and deadbeat glamour. . . . Greed was depicted at its most snarling and grasping, a view of Reagan-period parvenus as if scripted by Thomas Hobbes. . . . *Family Ties*, by contrast, featured a humorous and sympathetic portrait of an ambitious young Reaganite, Alex Keaton, played by Michael J. Fox, the star of 'Back to the Future.' (The treatment of his values was gently satiric.) Adding to the irony was Reagan's declaration that it was his favorite show. . . . Like most teenagers, Alex frequently made claims of omniscience, but father—and mother—still knew best."[13]

*   *   *

REAGAN HAD carefully thought out the connections between show business and politics. He once said, "Politics is just like show business. You have a hell of an opening; you coast for a while; you have a hell of a closing."[14] He also realized that politicians, like movie stars, have to be entertaining or they will flop.[15]

And Reagan knew that his associations with celebrities would increase his own celebrity and appeal. "Both Ronald Reagan and George Bush took time out from running the country to pose with Michael Jackson, then at the height of his enormous popularity," recalls journalist Alan Schroeder. "The 1984 meeting with Ronald and Nancy Reagan marks a particularly memorable encounter in the presidential celebrity pantheon. Jackson showed up in full regalia: sunglasses; a spangled blue jacket decorated with gold braiding, epaulets, and sash; white-sequined socks, and a single glove. The Reagans stood in elegant contrast, Ronnie in black, Nancy in white. These three professional performers cut a striking visual ensemble for the cameras, which was of course the entire point of the exercise."

Schroeder adds: " 'Well, isn't this a thriller!' Reagan told the hundreds of onlookers, mostly White House staffers and their families, who had assembled for the occasion on the South Lawn. 'We haven't seen this many people since we left China.' The ostensible purpose of Jackson's visit was to pick up a plaque, and the president got quickly to the point. Because Michael Jackson had permitted the use of his song 'Beat It' in a traffic safety campaign, the twenty-five-year-old superstar received from Reagan a Presidential Public Safety Communication Award. The ceremony lasted only a few minutes, and Jackson spoke a mere two sentences: 'I'm very, very honored. Thank you very much, Mr. President and Mrs. Reagan.' The whole thing was over almost before it began, the three stars slipping out of view inside the mansion. But preserved on videotape and film, this brief encounter forever remains a key moment in the Reagan pop cultural iconography."[16]

*   *   *

REAGAN'S AIDES say he was self-effacing about being president. He felt that he was the temporary custodian of the office and didn't get carried away with his own importance. But he was extremely proud of his career as a Hollywood actor. He seemed to attach more of himself personally to that occupation and the celebrity he achieved, and sometimes this would show through.

One incident was particularly telling. On a Friday afternoon, the family of a Reagan associate visited him in the Oval Office and a woman in the group said the wrong thing. "I saw a lot of your movies back in your Hollywood days," she said. "I just want you to know, I think you're the best president I've ever witnessed running this country, but I never liked you as an actor." Reagan was offended. "You could see that he was stunned," recalled James Kuhn, Reagan's personal assistant, who observed the scene and described it later in an oral history. "He was almost frozen in his tracks, standing still. Feelings hurt, taken aback, totally stunned over that comment."[17]

Reagan soldiered on graciously and didn't mention the slight. But when the group left and he was alone with Kuhn, the president told his aide, "I've never had anybody tell me that before, Jim. That was the first time. Nobody's ever told me that they thought I was a bad actor." Reagan must have meant that no one had criticized his acting skills to his face, because he had gotten plenty of ridicule from media commentators and opposition Democrats for being in "B movies."

Kuhn tried to make him feel better. "I understand," the aide replied. "I don't think that she really meant it that way either, she was just making a contrast." But Reagan persisted. "I just had never heard that before," he complained sadly.[18]

On another occasion, Reagan was campaigning for a Republican candidate in New Jersey as his second term was winding down in 1988. An elderly woman in line to shake his hand remarked, "We loved you in 'Death Valley Days' [a TV show he had hosted many years earlier] but we love you even more as president." Reagan was delighted by the double compliment.[19]

Both incidents showed how much Reagan was still wrapped up in the worlds of cinema and TV, where he had achieved stardom on his own and of which he remained proud.

*   *   *

REAGAN WAS KEENLY aware of the power of image, and was always eager to improve his standing with the public and enhance his reputation for being a strong, vigorous leader. This came to the fore as he prepared to meet then–Soviet leader Mikhail Gorbachev for the first time. No one knew what to expect. Reagan had famously called the Soviet Union an "evil empire" years earlier and he was now going to sit down with the leader of that empire at a historic meeting in Geneva in front of the world's media.

Just beforehand, as Reagan was getting ready to greet his counterpart upon his arrival outdoors, he moved to get his coat. Kuhn was troubled. What if Gorbachev wasn't wearing a coat and Reagan was all bundled up? Wouldn't the septuagenarian commander in chief look like a "feeble old man" in contrast? Kuhn made his case, but Reagan's more senior advisers, including Secretary of State George Shultz and White House Chief of Staff Donald Regan, disagreed and said Reagan should wear a coat. It would be no big deal.

But when they left the room, Kuhn made his case again. Reagan bit his lip the way he did when he was getting annoyed, but finally he relented. He wouldn't be wearing the coat.[20]

Kuhn recalled, "Gorbachev got out, fedora on, a scarf, all bundled up in his heavy coat, looking like this old sinister man, and there's Reagan, standing there, looking beautiful, in this tailored blue suit, looking spectacular, no coat on. I mean, we one-upped the Soviets like you could not believe. That was written about and written about and written about. The photos that ran—Reagan looked A-plus, Gorbachev looked like a D-minus."[21]

* * *

DURING THE COURSE of his eight years as president, Reagan had a real impact on popular culture. Marlin Fitzwater, his White House press secretary, said Reagan introduced Eastern America to Western America, especially the political West and the affluent lifestyle of rich California. As former governor of California and a Western conservative, he introduced America's Eastern elites to the concepts of Main Street conservatism rather than Wall Street conservatism, the focus on less government, individual freedom, lower taxes, and the market, and, on an international level, fighting communism.

In terms of lifestyle, he and his wife Nancy enjoyed luxury, although President Reagan was more in tune with middle-class life than his wife. When she was away, he preferred meat loaf, mashed potatoes and gravy, and macaroni and cheese, foods he loved as a young man and that she wouldn't allow the White House chefs or the cooks on *Air Force One* to serve him. Instead she made sure he had seafood, vegetables, and other nutritionally correct dishes.

* * *

IN SUM, Ronald Reagan relished his role as celebrity in chief, and he used it to good effect. He appreciated "the need for the president to reaffirm our basic goals, to celebrate liberty and freedom, and to participate fully in the rituals that both give meaning to American life and help people understand the larger events of which they are a minor part," Cronin observes. "Few presidents have been better than Reagan at helping the nation observe its rituals such as Memorial Day, the Fourth of July, Thanksgiving, Veteran's Day, our participation in the Olympics, summit diplomacy, and similar ceremonies. No one was better at performing national chaplain services—as Reagan did in comforting Americans after the *Challenger* disaster, or as he grieved with and gave meaning to those who mourned the tragic deaths of U.S. Marines in Lebanon or the army troops downed in a transport crash in Canada as they returned from the Sinai. Reagan understood that Americans have a civil religion with semisacred symbols and that these reflect our human need to make sense out of scattered experiences, and to thereby instill meaning, form, order and assurance."[22]

He understood that he could use his personal celebrity to achieve those goals, and he did so brilliantly.

Chapter Six
Bill Clinton
Pop Icon

Americans should have realized what they were getting in the White House when, during the 1992 campaign, Bill Clinton appeared in shades on *The Arsenio Hall Show* and played the saxophone. The appearance was criticized for lacking presidential dignity, but it also succeeded in getting Clinton noticed as someone who had a youthful outlook and would try new things, in keeping with his theme of being the representative of a new generation. He was so eager for public attention that he embarrassed himself by answering a personal question about his underwear at an MTV town-hall meeting early in his presidency. A young woman asked, "Mr. President, the world's dying to know: Is it boxers or briefs?" Clinton laughed and replied, "Usually briefs."[1] It was widely considered too much information, and Clinton was roundly criticized for making the revelation.

Clinton knew pop culture better than any of his predecessors. But as with the boxers-or-briefs incident, sometimes he got carried away and lost some dignity in the process. This was illustrated by his love for junk food. At first it seemed appealing when the president wanted to get a regular helping of burgers and fries from McDonald's. But after a while he seemed to be simply seeking publicity and trying to come across as an average fellow. This reinforced the idea that he was hopelessly self-absorbed and always craving attention. And his love of junk food set a bad example and damaged his health. After he left office, this became clear when he had heart surgery in 2010 and became a vegetarian.

A former adviser to President Bill Clinton told me, "Being a celebrity means people are drawn to know you and people pay attention to you. Clinton always kept things interesting. He would get angry at the press but he loved the attention. Clinton felt he could give as well as he could take. Clinton was the rare blend of charisma and brains."

Adds Mike McCurry, Clinton's ex-White House press secretary, "When you talk about celebrity, you have these pods—sports, movie stars and politicians. . . . Presidents are always gaga when they meet actors and athletes. They are cool to be around and a president thinks, 'Maybe some of that will rub off on me.' "[2]

Celebrity can help presidents publicize themselves and their ideas. On the other hand, McCurry says, "Celebrity, when it comes to presidents, is really about how much we trust the person who governs. It's a measure of the character of the president and what we think of him as a person. Every American saw a piece of themselves in Bill Clinton. Every American made mistakes and screwed up like he did, but people were comfortable with where the country was."

Celebrity can help presidents draw attention to themselves and their ideas. On the other hand, "The more you become a celebrity, the less you become a person of substance," McCurry told me. "The more you become a celebrity, the less serious a person you are." Presidents need to strike a balance. "And the president needs to go beyond glamour," McCurry says. "You don't have to be glamorous to earn the confidence of the people."[3]

*   *   *

CLINTON, BORN IN 1946, always kept in touch with popular culture. He brought a baby boomer's baggage to the White House, including self-indulgence, an intense desire for attention, a minimal but embarrassing history of having used marijuana, and opposition to the Vietnam War that caused him some difficulty among conservatives. He also had the undignified image of a womanizer. But these aspects of his life actually helped him bond with his own generation and younger people because he had so much in common with them.

He was an enthusiastic movie fan from his boyhood in Arkansas. Among the films he loved, he once told movie critic Roger Ebert, were *Love Me Tender* and other Elvis Presley films, including *Loving You, Jailhouse*

Rock, *King Creole*, and *Blue Hawaii*. Clearly, Clinton shared the tastes of many in his generation. He also enjoyed epics, such as *Samson and Delilah*, *The Robe*, *Ben-Hur*, and *The Ten Commandments*. As president he saw as many movies as he could in the White House theater, including *Midnight in the Garden of Good and Evil*, *Shine*, *Casablanca*, *Shakespeare in Love*, *Billy Elliott*, *Boyz n the Hood*, *Schindler's List*, *Shadowlands*, *Mrs. Doubtfire*, *American Beauty*, *Three Kings*, and *Sling Blade*.[4] The list reveals a wide-ranging taste and an interest in virtually all aspects of American life depicted on film, reflecting Clinton's intellectual curiosity.

"Clinton combined the movie habits of other recent presidents," writes Tevi Troy. "Like Carter, he loved to watch; like the Bushes, he used the White House theater as a political tool; and like Reagan, he understood the importance of popular culture in appealing to the American public. Clinton fit in perfectly as one of the baby boomers, but he also served as a leader for that generation. Speaking the language of the movies had become the twentieth-century way of speaking to the common man, and it was a language Clinton had mastered."

All this helped Clinton win two terms as president. He seemed to be much more in touch with Middle Americans than Republican incumbent George H. W. Bush in 1992 and GOP challenger Bob Dole in 1996. "Both of these candidates, who were old enough to have served in World War II, predated the pop culture that Clinton and his fellow baby boomers had absorbed," Troy says. "Clinton devoured movies, invited Hollywood stars to screenings at the White House, and discussed films with anyone and everyone. He even appeared on TV with Roger Ebert to discuss his love of movies."[5]

Clinton also was adept at using his love of music to appeal to young people and baby boomers like himself, who had a huge interest in music. He adopted the popular Fleetwood Mac hit from 1977, "Don't Stop," as his 1992 campaign song. He and his wife Hillary named their daughter after a Judy Collins tune, "Chelsea Morning." His taste in music ran from top-forty hits from his youth to gospel, blues, and jazz, and he truly knew how to play the saxophone. Rock-and-roll singer Joe Cocker said, "For a president to be associated with rock and roll is kind of cool."[6]

Clinton was even able to use a musician entertainer as a foil when he criticized Sister Souljah, a rap artist who reacted outrageously after policemen were acquitted in the beating of Rodney King, an African American motorist, prompting a riot in Los Angeles. Souljah told the *Washington Post*, "I mean, if black people kill black people every day, why not have a week and kill white people?" Clinton condemned her remarks, saying, "Her comments before and after Los Angeles were filled with a kind of hatred that you do not honor." The incident showed that Clinton was willing to stand up to an African American activist even though it might alienate black voters. "The Sister Souljah moment" entered the popular lexicon, defined as confronting a member of a key constituency for the greater good and to demonstrate one's independence.

* * *

THE INTERSECTION of politics and entertainment is clear at the annual White House Correspondents' Association dinner in Washington, when celebrities from the entertainment industry, politics, government, and the business world mix and mingle at a star-studded formal event. During the Clinton years, I invited cast members of *The West Wing*, a hit TV show about a fictional White House, on behalf of *U.S. News & World Report*, my employer. Martin Sheen, the series's star who played President Josiah Bartlet, was one of my guests.

I arranged to meet him in the lobby of the Washington Hilton Hotel, where the dinner was held, and he arrived fashionably late. Bystanders who crowded into the lobby clamored to shake his hand and take pictures, some calling his name or shouting, "Mr. President!" Martin savored the attention.

After a while I pulled him aside and said, "Martin, I have to get you to the reception being given by *U.S. News*, and then to the VIP reception that features the *real* president, and then to the actual dinner, so we need to move along." He said that would be fine but asked if I could give him another five minutes talking to the fans. I agreed. After that we were side-kicks for the rest of the evening and he was a genial, approachable guest.

At the VIP reception, there was another moment of celebritization. After Clinton arrived, he and Sheen saw each other across the room and they began a mock stare-down. Attendees realized what was happening and the crowd parted. The two men walked slowly and theatrically toward each other, like gunfighters ready to draw. Suddenly they shook hands, Sheen said "Mr. President," and Clinton said "Mr. President," and both of them burst into laughter as the crowd cheered.

Clinton thoroughly enjoyed the company and affection of entertainers. And he spent time with them as often as he could. After an evening with the legendary movie couple Paul Newman and Joanne Woodward in 1993, White House Press Secretary Dee Dee Myers said, "He grew up watching movies like *The Hustler*, *Hud*, and *Cat on a Hot Tin Roof* and he still gets genuinely blown away by spending time with some of these people. There's still a lot of the kid from Hope, Arkansas, in him." Among the many other stars Clinton enjoyed palling around with were Tom Hanks, James Taylor, Carly Simon, Jimmy Buffett, Whoopi Goldberg, Billy Baldwin, and Barbra Streisand.[7]

During his first year as president, Clinton was derided for associating too much with entertainment figures. Press coverage of the president's celebrity fixation grew more intense. Among Clinton's newfound "friends," who attended a number of White House events at the president's invitation, were movie icons such as Streisand, Jack Nicholson, Warren Beatty, Lauren Bacall, and Macaulay Culkin; music legends such as Bob Dylan, Michael Jackson, Tony Bennett, Aretha Franklin, and Linda Ronstadt; and comedians Goldberg and Bill Cosby.[8]

Schroeder writes, "Like the new president himself, the 1993 inaugural was a study in excess. But anticelebrity backlash against Clinton did not reach its zenith until several months later, following a series of encounters between the White House and its newfound friends from the world of entertainment. The associations began to draw notice in mid-March. On the fifteenth of the month Paul Newman and Joanne Woodward accompanied Bill and Chelsea Clinton to dinner at a Washington restaurant called Galileo. The next night the president again met Newman and Woodward at an American Ireland Fund dinner at the Capital Hilton. Judy Collins spent the night of March 23 at the White House and went jogging with the president the next morning. Four nights later Barbra Streisand took her turn as an overnight guest of the Clintons, attending the Gridiron show with the presidential party before retiring to the mansion. Although each of these incidents was reported in the press, none generated more than cursory attention."[9]

But Clinton's fascination with Hollywood celebrities got even more intense. At the end of March, White House officials hosted several entertainment-industry executives, including television comedy producer Gary David Goldberg, at the White House to discuss how to explain the administration's proposals to overhaul the health-care system. On April 3, President Clinton hosted a group of entertainment personalities at his Vancouver hotel suite during a visit to Canada that featured a Clinton meeting with Russian president Boris Yeltsin. During breaks in those talks,

Clinton met in his suite with actors Sharon Stone, Richard Gere, Cindy Crawford, and Richard Dreyfuss. This fostered the impression that Clinton was regularly distracted and overly impressed by famous dilettantes.[10]

It didn't stop there. To celebrate the Washington premiere of a new film called *Earth and the American Dream* in April 1993, Clinton hosted actors Christopher Reeve, John Ritter, Lindsay Wagner, and Billy Crystal. They were treated to a tour of the White House, met briefly with the president and vice president, and received environmental briefings from top administration officials, including Interior Secretary Bruce Babbitt. And on May 12 Clinton attended a Democratic fund-raiser in New York City where he sat at a table next to Sharon Stone, who was known for her raunchy persona in *Basic Instinct*.[11]

The former working-class boy from Hope, Arkansas, was at the top of the celebrity pyramid, and he let it go too far. In the spring of 1993, Clinton got a haircut on *Air Force One* while the famous jet was parked on a runway at Los Angeles International Airport, which at least had the potential of delaying other flights waiting for the president to take off. Making matters worse, the "barber" was a Beverly Hills stylist named Christophe, who sometimes charged $200 for a haircut. The media picked up the story and portrayed the new president as starstruck. Ross Perot, the Texas billionaire who had run unsuccessfully for president as an independent the previous fall, said, "When you've got a different movie star in the House every night, and you've got somebody up there from Hollywood pleading the cases for the Dalai Lama, the average hard-working American in work clothes can't relate to that."[12]

Stung by the furor, Clinton told a town-hall meeting, "I mean, look, I wear a forty-dollar watch. I wasn't raised that way. I've never lived that way. That's not the kind of person I am." When a questioner said the administration seemed "a little infatuated with Hollywood and celebrities," Clinton denied that he had "gone Hollywood": "The answer to that is no, heck no, never, no, never, never."[13]

Bill Clinton's admiring circle of celebrities eventually would grow to include Ted Danson, Neil Simon, Steven Spielberg, and Mary Steenburgen. His critics said he was so chummy with the show-business elite in order to boost his ego, and these luminaries represented the kind of self-centeredness that was a growing problem in American society.

"On balance, did Bill Clinton's celebrity associations hurt more than help him?" asks Schroeder. "Certainly the men and women of show business never stopped filling his coffers, starting with the presidential election of 1992 and continuing into the Senate career of Hillary Rodham Clinton. But entertainers demonstrated their enthusiasm in another important way: by accepting him early on as one of their own, the celebrity caste validated Clinton as a member in good standing of the aristocracy of fame. His high-profile supporters welcomed him into their circle at a time when he had not yet ascended to their heights. Well before he became president, Clinton crossed a threshold of visibility that psychologically boosted his qualification for the job."[14]

Chapter Seven
Barack Obama
Making History and Taking New Paths

As the first African American president of the United States, Barack Obama was a huge celebrity and a historic figure from his first day in office. Today he is the most famous person in America, and possibly the world. He is a divisive figure, with millions of Americans supporting him but millions also detesting him. Yet despite his polarizing qualities, Obama tries to stay in touch and show that he understands the lives of everyday Americans. To those ends he holds town-hall meetings with users of Facebook, Twitter, and Zillow, and he is the first president to participate in a sustained way in social media; he uses his smartphone to keep in touch with friends and to surf the Internet. He watches popular TV shows and movies and keeps up with music, partly because his young daughters want him to. He is a big sports fan, making predictions about the NCAA basketball playoffs every year, giving him a bond with millions of other Americans, especially men. He makes the rounds of the TV talk shows, which his predecessors disdained while they were in office (though not as candidates), trading quips over the years with Jimmy Fallon, Jay Leno, David Letterman, and Jon Stewart.

Obama projects an easygoing, approachable persona, even though he is often detached and distant in private and has been widely criticized for failing to develop long-term relationships with members of Congress, civic leaders, media figures, and others with whom he deals regularly. But in terms of his public image, Obama has made himself into more of a celebrity than any president in history. And except, perhaps, for Jackie Kennedy, Michelle Obama is more of a celebrity than any previous first lady.

"The Obamas are hooked on it," says Ken Duberstein, former White House chief of staff for President Ronald Reagan. "President Obama certainly likes being a real star and in certain communities, he is—he is a rock star in Hollywood. But I'm not sure that's done anything for him to get votes in Washington."[1]

Duberstein makes a good point. Obama's celebrity did not prevent him from entering a second-term slump, or help him move his agenda forward in Congress, or save his Democratic party from big losses in the midterm elections of 2014. That's when opposition Republicans took control of the Senate and added to their majority in the House of Representatives. The results were widely considered a rebuff to Obama and his unpopular policies, such as his failure to end wage stagnation for the middle class and his setbacks in foreign policy such as the Russian annexation of Crimea and the territorial gains of Islamic extremists in Iraq and Syria.

The lesson from Obama's experience is that being celebrity in chief can improve a president's effectiveness if he uses his fame properly to call attention to his ideas and cultivate support for them, but it is no panacea. In short, celebrity is perishable.

And Obama has often seemed to be using his celebrity not to get votes in Congress but to win personal approval and affection from the country at large.

Historian Tevi Troy writes, "As president, Obama has put all of his knowledge of and experience with pop culture to work. His great insight has been that by being part of pop culture—being a celebrity himself—a president can influence how pop culture portrays him. . . . Kennedy was glamorous and Reagan was a movie star, but Obama has worked more aggressively than any other president to establish his preferred image through a variety of media—not only books, television, and movies but new media such as Twitter, Reddit, and Google. Embracing the celebrity culture, he became a rock star himself."[2]

In short, he managed to be, at least for that portion of the country that stayed supportive of him, trendy and cool. This made him fascinating enough so he could capture and hold people's interest and get them to take seriously his ideas and policies. Doing this is no small achievement at a time when the public tires quickly of public figures and America's attention span is short. Obama also managed to portray himself as a model of idealism and good intentions, and a genuinely nice man, and this kept him from being savaged by the media and by the TV comedians, which in turn added to his mystique.

"There are a few situations when we've used the president's notoriety to put some weight behind his priorities," a senior administration official told me. "We wanted to reach certain audiences through popular culture." One gambit centered on the Affordable Care Act, which became the focal point of a public information campaign with a special emphasis on encouraging young people to sign up for health insurance under Obama's program.

Obama sees his notoriety as an updated version of what Theodore Roosevelt called the White House "bully pulpit"—a way to capture public attention, educate people about policies and trends, and provide lessons from his own life. He calls his approach the "pen and phone" strategy: using his pen to sign executive orders to bypass a balky Congress, and his phone to persuade legislators and other leaders to go along. Inside the White House, Obama and his aides use shorthand to describe his use of the bully pulpit—"the phone thing."

He has moved from one nontraditional venue to another. Obama appeared on the Zach Galifianakis interview parody show *Between Two Ferns*, did interviews on the late-night talk-show circuit, appeared on *The View* and *Live with Kelly and Michael*, and personally recruited other celebrities to spread the word about his policies.

When Obama decided to appear on Jimmy Fallon's popular TV show, White House officials got together with Fallon's joke- and skit-writers and they all decided to base a skit on Obama's program to make it easier for former students to pay off their student loans. They did it as part of a gambit in which Fallon "slow jams" the news—gives a report using the slang of a musical rap artist. Obama was on a trip to North Carolina, and Fallon joined him there to do the segment.

Obama also decided to promote the merits of his health-care law through these venues, making use of his access to and understanding of popular culture.

Obama sees himself as a role model. He believes that it's helpful for him to talk about his unique background to educate the country about different issues, such as race and staying in school. So from time to time he will "reveal himself" for a higher purpose. He did this in talking about how he and his wife were burdened by a large debt from student loans, which took a long time to pay off. He also used the Trayvon Martin case, in which an unarmed African American man was killed by a neighborhood watchman, as a teachable moment to explain how racial problems can occur and intensify. Obama used as an example his own background as a young African American man who was racially profiled.

"He identified an opportunity when he would offer a point of view to the country which otherwise would not be well understood," a key Obama aide told me. "He drew on his unique experience to communicate with a lot of white folks about how African Americans felt [about crime and being always under suspicion, or worse], and also to educate African Americans why white people had such intense feeling about all this and what other people in the country were going through."

One program he was eager to promote was My Brother's Keeper, designed to motivate and inspire young African American men to turn away from crime and use their talents to better themselves and achieve in mainstream society. He also saw much merit, in the present and in the future, for his initiative to wire a large number of schools for broadband, to give them an edge in understanding and using technology.

"There's no way to quantify the impact he's had but years from now, in retrospect, I have a feeling that we'll see he's had a big impact," a senior White House adviser told me. White House officials say Obama is particularly proud of having been flexible enough to change his mind and express support for gay marriage. They told me his change of heart probably persuaded many other Americans to adopt his view, and he believed there had been a huge change in public attitudes toward supporting same-sex marriage.

His interview with TV reporter Robin Roberts about his evolution on gay marriage was likely instrumental in changing people's minds. "Maybe 20 years from now it will be seen as a seminal moment," a senior White House official told me. And Obama encouraged a more enlightened and tolerant view of new arrivals to the United States because of his repeated comments that Americans should welcome immigrants, the official said.

*   *   *

BARACK OBAMA's winning the Nobel Peace Prize within a few weeks of taking office as president in 2009 showed the extent of his celebrity from the start of his administration. His eagerness to pay attention to social media and to keep his BlackBerry made him seem hip to technology and modern forms of communication. (He stayed with BlackBerry while millions of other Americans moved on to other smartphones because the Secret Service said a BlackBerry could be kept more secure.)

To some extent, Obama has been judged not on what he does but rather on who he is—a vigorous young politician with enormous promise and the first African American president. This, not his accomplishments, is where his celebrity originally came from. Obama was an inspiring symbol of change as a candidate in 2008, but he has had trouble translating that into being president and getting things accomplished in Washington's rancorous atmosphere.

Obama took presidential celebrity to a higher level by exploiting social media and other forms of communication. In the process, he has reached Americans in their own habitats rather than using only the traditional formats that were being ignored by more and more Americans, including news conferences, official speeches, and interviews with mainstream media heavyweights.

Part of the reason that the Obamas resonate with many everyday people is that they choose to show themselves to the media as parents, far more than, say, Bill and Hillary Clinton did. The Clintons were very concerned about protecting their daughter Chelsea's privacy. So they didn't do a lot publicly with her or let it be known what they were doing with her privately. But the Obamas have been more open about being photographed with and attending events with their daughters, Malia and Sasha, such as taking hikes on vacation, attending sports events, and including them in official activities such as pardoning the Thanksgiving turkey, an annual rite at the White House (where in 2014 the girls looked quite bored). "We didn't see President Clinton as a father or Hillary Clinton as a mother as we do Barack and Michelle Obama. For all the talk that he is too elitist, people really relate to them," Democratic pollster Geoff Garin says. "The first lady personally is very accessible," he adds, and she attempts to convey an image of "affordable glamour."[3] And she is all over popular culture. She gave out an Academy Award, danced with Jimmy Fallon on his TV show, and planted and harvested vegetables in the White House garden with local kids.

For his part, President Obama made it known that he tweeted Katy Perry in August 2013 after she expressed support for his health-care law.

Capitalizing on her fame, he used the occasion to urge young people to sign up for the program.

* * *

OBAMA ENTERED a deeper phase of celebrity during his second term as he cultivated his relationships with show-business personalities.

Some conservatives said he was going too far and was demeaning the presidency and making himself into too much of a show-biz figure. This critique was nothing new. During the 2008 presidential campaign, Republican nominee John McCain, a senator from Arizona and former prisoner of war in Vietnam, ran a television ad complaining about Obama's rock-star status. As pictures were shown of entertainment personalities Britney Spears and Paris Hilton, along with the scene of a crowd shouting Obama's name, the ad's narrator said, "He's the biggest celebrity in the world. But is he ready to lead? With gas prices soaring, Barack Obama says no to offshore drilling and says he'll raise taxes on electricity. Higher taxes, more foreign oil—that's the real Obama."[4]

During the 2012 campaign, American Crossroads, a conservative political action committee associated with GOP strategist Karl Rove, ran an ad mocking Obama for being a "celebrity president." The forty-five-second video, entitled "Cool," featured clips portraying Obama as a chief executive who loved being famous and who was preoccupied with trivia, and partly as a consequence was an ineffective leader. It showed Obama "slow-jamming" the news with TV personality Fallon, singing Al Green's song "Let's Stay Together," and swatting a fly during a CNBC interview.[5] Obama was also mocked for dancing with talk-show host Ellen DeGeneres. The ad said, "Four years ago, America elected the biggest celebrity in the world," and called Obama "one cool president." Noting that 85 percent of recent college graduates had moved back with their parents and that student-loan debt had exceeded $1 trillion, the ad asked, "After four years of a celebrity president, is your life any better?"[6]

Rove, the former chief political strategist for President George W. Bush in his successful campaigns of 2000 and 2004 and a deputy White House chief of staff under G. W. Bush, was back on the attack in late 2013. He criticized a video parody of Snoop Dogg's "Drop It Like It's Hot" for sending a strongly pro-Obama message. The video also had a political and substantive message; it urged young people to sign up for health insurance under the Affordable Care Act, Obama's signature domestic legislation.

At the time, the law was undergoing a messy rollout during which millions couldn't enroll because of a faulty website. The video, sponsored by Obama supporters outside government, featured an Obama impersonator rapping about the health-care law, known as Obamacare, and advising, "So don't stand and diddle, my health care's the shizzle. It's chock-full of top-notch health-care provizzles." Rove told Fox News, "I worry about something that seems [to] aim to glorification of the commander in chief, the president of the United States as opposed to simply advocating young people go out and sign up for this entitlement program. . . . This disturbingly gets too close to the line. I think it, in fact, crosses it."[7] Rove added, "Could you imagine if such a thing had been run by George Bush or Bill Clinton or Bush 41 [G. W. Bush] or Reagan? 'I have two terms. I'm really cool. I'm really hip.' How much public outcry there could have been?"

Some conservatives say the presidency has been demeaned because the chief executive has become so familiar. But a president can get more support for his agenda, or at least get the country to pay attention to him in order to make his arguments, by playing celebrity in chief and intersecting with popular culture. And from the start Obama understood popular culture and the need to reach out in different ways far better than his critics did. Peter Roff, a Republican analyst, made this point in a *U.S. News* column in early 2014.[8] Referring to a *New York Times* report in December 2013 about Obama's television preferences, Roff wrote, "The president prefers things that are 'edgy, with hints of reality,' including AMC's 'Breaking Bad,' HBO's 'Game of Thrones' and 'Boardwalk Empire,' and Netflix's 'House of Cards,' an American remake of a British miniseries of the same name about a ruthless politician's unethical climb to the top of what Benjamin Disraeli called 'the greasy pole.'"

Roff wrote some conservatives complained that Obama was "unpresidential" for revealing these preferences because "somehow the president's television preferences are not the business of the American people." But Roff called the White House's disclosure of such preferences "a stroke of brilliance" and added: "What the liberals understand and conservatives fail to grasp is that in the age of information everything is media. By disclosing what the president's favorite television shows are or what his picks for the NCAA brackets may be or what music he likes to listen to, his political team is giving him the opportunity to meet the people where they are, not where they might want them to be. . . . Obama was sold to the American people like new and improved laundry soap, the latest model sports car coming out of Detroit or Hollywood's newest teen idol. The American people met him in places that were essentially on the fringes of the political arena rather than in the middle of it. By talking about what he likes to watch on television, his political team is keeping that conversation going, even stepping it up because—as his approval numbers continue to drop—the ancillary conversations about seemingly extraneous subjects become all the more important. Rather than attack the communications strategy it represents, Republicans would do well to analyze it, understand it and adopt it."[9]

* * *

ON MARCH 11, 2014, Obama appeared on Zach Galifianakis's tart-tongued talk show *Between Two Ferns*, airing on the satirical Funny or Die website, causing another stir. The show's format called for Galifianakis as the host to insult and try to embarrass his guests rather than take the fawning route often favored by TV hosts, especially on entertainment shows such as *The View*. Obama participated happily in these entertainment shows, and excelled.

But *Between Two Ferns* was different. It called for Obama to be combative so he wouldn't seem like a wimp or a foil. And even though Obama was again criticized by traditionalists who felt he was degrading the presidency, he did well in the snarky format, with the help of his speech writers and quip meisters. The president traded jibes and insults in a six-and-a-half-minute interview with Galifianakis. At one point, the host asked the president, "What's it like to be the last black president?" Obama responded, "Seriously? What's it like for this to be the last time you ever talk to a president?"[10]

Obama used the occasion to urge young people to sign up for insurance under his Affordable Care Act. White House officials said more than three million people went to the government's health-care website within several hours of the mock interview. Signups for Obamacare were also attributed to the administration having recruited Miami Heat basketball star LeBron James to do a thirty-second public-service announcement that aired during the college basketball playoffs on television. The TV spot encouraged athletes and stars from other fields to go on Twitter and use additional ways to urge young people to enroll in Obamacare. All in all, it was a successful attempt to use celebrities and celebrity culture to promote a policy initiative.[11]

Obama showed his gratitude on May 1, 2014, by holding a reception at the White House for many pro-Obamacare celebrities and others who had supported the law. Among those attending were TV stars Mayim Bialik, Connie Britton, Kal Penn, Adam Scott, and Aisha Tyler.[12] On May 6, 2014, Obama took another unusual step into the world of celebrity when he granted brief interviews to eight meteorologists from national and local TV, including Al Roker of NBC's *Today Show*, Ginger Zee of ABC's *Good Morning America*, and Megan Glaros of *CBS This Morning*. The topic was climate change; Obama used the interviews to argue that the federal government ought to do more to fight it.[13]

In April 2014, Obama named five famous people to the President's Council on Fitness, Sports & Nutrition, which First Lady Michelle Obama helped to reinvigorate in 2010 as part of her effort to encourage people to eat healthy food and to exercise. The appointees were pro basketball player Jason Collins, the first openly gay player in the National Basketball Association (NBA); former NBA star Alonzo Mourning; celebrity chef Rachael Ray; ballet dancer Misty Copeland; and publicist Rob Shepardson.[14] It was one more move to cement the Obamas into celebrity culture.

On May 3, 2014, Obama appeared at the annual White House Correspondents' Association dinner, held at the Washington Hilton Hotel, and the celebrity cavalcade continued. Among those drawn to the Obama-centered event were Rosario Dawson, Omar Epps, Kevin Hart, Steve McQueen, Sofia Vergara, and Robin Wright.[15]

Obama's efforts to deepen his connections to the world of celebrity included hosting dinner parties with athletes, actors, famous intellectuals, and other stars of various fields. Sometimes these events lasted until after midnight. Often they became akin to seminars in which the president discussed philosophy, ideas, and art. Among those attending have been the singer and philanthropist Bono, actors Samuel L. Jackson and Will Smith, former pro basketball player Alonzo Mourning, investor Warren Buffett, Apple CEO Tim Cook, former secretary of state Colin Powell, and *Vogue* editor in chief Anna Wintour.[16]

The president was growing tired of all the hassles of Washington, where congressional Republicans were blocking most of his agenda and where the news media were scrutinizing and criticizing him more than ever. So he seemed more invested in doing things that interested him personally, such as hanging out with celebrities.

Obama's supporters included many on the entertainment industry's A-list, including George Clooney, Morgan Freeman, Tom Hanks, Scarlett Johansson, Eva Longoria, Natalie Portman, Bruce Springsteen, and Kerry Washington.[17] It was a case of reflected glamour for everyone involved, including the president.

* * *

THERE WERE OTHER efforts to give Obama a strong pop luster. As his second term progressed, he made a habit of breaking out of the White House "bubble" as often as he could, not only to gain publicity as a leader in touch with the people but also because, like other presidents, he felt that the White House was too isolating.

For example, during the spring of 2014 Obama repeatedly escaped from the presidential cage. In May he took a ten-minute walk from the West Wing to a speech at the Interior Department. "The bear is loose—I broke out of the cage," he declared happily, with his suit jacket slung over his shoulder in the muggy Washington afternoon. He didn't use his armor-plated limousine, which the Secret Service prefers because it's easier to protect him that way. But his bodyguards remained nearby.[18]

When he arrived at Interior, accompanied by senior adviser John Podesta, he seemed more than a bit frustrated by his cloistered lifestyle. "I think about the thrill of going on a hike without a security detail behind me," he said. "It's a wistful feeling." On his stroll back to the White House, again without using his motorcade, he greeted surprised and delighted tourists, saying, "We can shake hands. I won't bite."[19]

Obama's "the bear is loose" moment—comparing himself to a circus bear that got out of its cage—was the second time he'd escaped briefly from his bubble in a single week. He also dropped in on a Little League baseball game one night en route to a fund-raiser. He chatted with the people he encountered, posed for photos, and seemed to be having a grand time as the young people and their parents met the celebrity in chief. Some squealed with joy; others cheered him.[20]

In June he broke free again. He walked to a Starbucks near the White House for some hot tea, and he left the West Wing to have lunch at a restaurant in nearby suburban Alexandria, Virginia, with the education secretary, Arne Duncan. They had burgers at FireFlies restaurant after the owner wrote to invite the president to sample her food.[21]

In mid-June Obama spent a couple of days relaxing in Rancho Mirage, California. He also continued his pattern of playing as much golf as possible, both in the Washington, DC, area and when he was traveling. He loved spending hours on the links with friends and other people he found interesting because it gave him a sense of normalcy.

But Obama has had cabin fever for a long time. In January 2014 he enjoyed a burger at The Coupe diner not far from the White House. He also has had sandwiches at Taylor Gourmet in DC and took former French president Nicolas Sarkozy to Ben's Chili Bowl, a locally famous eatery. His food jaunts were welcomed by local restaurant owners and foodies who liked the attention to the District of Columbia restaurant scene. "I think in some way, shape or form, President Obama has made food hip to people who may not think that way or may not look at food that way," said Casey Patten of Taylor Gourmet.[22]

On July 29, 2014, Obama continued his outreach by having a barbecue dinner in Kansas City, Missouri, with four people who had written him about their economic situations. They ate at Arthur Bryant's restaurant, a popular informal eatery. The president had a half slab of ribs, beans, fries, and a beer.[23]

All this reveals a larger reality: presidents sometimes feel so cloistered and coddled that they need to reestablish contact with everyday people to remind themselves what normal life is like. They also like to take soundings on how popular they really are, and how much respect the office of president commands among everyday people.

*   *   *

OBAMA SOLIDIFIED his hold on Hollywood in several ways. "The change occurred thanks to the rise of the [ultraconservative and zealous] tea party, which galvanized West Coast liberals, and the President's sudden conversion to the legalization of gay marriage, which happened to come at a time when local reports indicated that his Hollywood money was in danger of drying up," writes historian Timothy Stanley. "Almost overnight, Hollywood assumed a structural importance in his re-election campaign to rival that of organized labor, liberal PACs or even the DNC [Democratic National Committee]."[24]

Stanley says Obama has been doing what other presidents have done—using Hollywood stars to set his image. "Richard Nixon used John Wayne to define his foreign policy," Stanley writes. "Ronald Reagan's Western swagger was pure Hollywood invention. But this kind of celluloid fantasy-making is far from healthy. Congress isn't a place that can be navigated by idealism; a dangerous world cannot be managed with superhero theatrics (such as drone strikes)."

He explains, "Expectations are raised excessively by promising to solve all these problems with the same ease that they do in the movies. Moreover, talking in clichés encourages partisanship. While the Democrats cling to being Jed Bartlets, the Republicans see themselves as Men With No Name—and there's little common ground that can be reached between people competing to be more stubbornly archetypal than the rest. . . . Hollywood might still imagine him to be a superhero, but Obama has really become the thing that in 2008 he set out to avoid: another Clinton Democrat."[25]

* * *

OBAMA IS ALSO LEARNING that celebrity worship has its limits. Presidents have trouble when their policies don't work or when their behavior doesn't match up with the public's expectations, no matter how much they are connected to popular culture or how much they are surrounded by an aura of celebrity.

Republican pollster Bill McInturff told me in December 2013 that President Obama had suffered a major blow because Americans' trust in him had declined so much: "He has lost his personal connection and is not perceived as being honest."[26] A *Wall Street Journal*/NBC News poll, which McInturff helped conduct that month, found that 54 percent of Americans disapproved of Obama's job performance and 43 percent approved. Only 37 percent said Obama was honest and trustworthy.

One big reason was Obama's broken promise that Americans who liked their health insurance and their doctors could keep them under the Affordable Care Act. These promises turned out to be false, and millions of Americans were learning that winter, as the program was implemented, that their policies had been cancelled and their insurance would no longer include the doctors they liked.

But there was more. Obama no longer opposed widespread government spying on US citizens in order to catch terrorists, reversing his position, or at least changing his civil-libertarian tone, from his 2008 campaign. Beyond this, his willingness to compromise with congressional adversaries, which he also promised to do, seemed to fluctuate from week to week. So the drumbeat of media coverage of the stalemate and dysfunction in

Washington caused many Americans to blame both Obama and Congress. People were increasingly angry and upset that Washington officials were taking care of the privileged but the middle class wasn't being protected by the powers that be.

"It's corrosive," McInturff told me. "He is being perceived through a different filter today. He's become a lot like a typical politician. He seems to be one more politician making promises. [Trust in Obama] is being compromised. That's a terrible thing for a presidency. . . . It's like a breach of trust between two sides in a marriage. It will take a long time to heal."[27]

* * *

IN THE SPRING of 2014, faced with a variety of problems at home and abroad—including setbacks for American diplomacy in Ukraine, in Syria, and in the Middle East peace process and a continued congressional stalemate on his agenda—Obama began to lose even more luster in popular culture.

He was harshly criticized by *New York Times* columnist Maureen Dowd, widely read in elite circles and an influential interpreter of popular culture. "You are the American president," she wrote, "and the American president should not perpetually use the word 'eventually.' And he should not set a tone of resignation with references to this being a relay race and say he's willing to take 'a quarter of a loaf or half a loaf,' and muse that things may not come 'to full fruition on your timetable.' An American president should never say as you did to the New Yorker editor, David Remnick, about presidents through history, 'We're part of a long-running story. We just try to get our paragraph right.' Mr. President, I am just trying to get my paragraph right. You need to think bigger."[28]

At the same time, media critic Howard Kurtz wrote, "The thrill up the leg is gone. There's not even a tingle in the toes. President Obama's media supporters are abandoning him. Even the liberal culture seems to be abandoning him. And as he slips into the low 40s [in job approval] in two recent polls, it's hard to see how he recasts his once-glittering image. This is the kind of sea change that goes beyond polling numbers. The very mass culture that celebrated Barack Obama, that turned him into an international icon, is now migrating toward the darker side of his legacy, perhaps fueled by a sense of frustration and disappointment."[29]

Obama and his aides seemed to understand this slippage and took some steps to correct it. One was an interview the president and his wife gave to *Parade* magazine, a staple of middle-class culture and a very traditional medium. The interview appeared June 22, 2014, and was highlighted by a flattering full-page cover photo of the first couple under the headline "A Conversation About Family." The Obamas talked about their earlier struggles with low-paying jobs and how it took them a long time to pay off their college loans, making them appear to have very modest backgrounds. "We pinched pennies," the president recalled. "But we also got help. My grandmother helped a little bit on the down payment [for a condo]. And we scraped together what savings we had."[30]

* * *

OVERALL, it should have come as no surprise that Obama continually tried to stay in tune with popular culture during his presidency. He had been immersed in it from boyhood while growing up in Hawaii, where he lived with his mother and grandparents. In his memoir *Dreams from My Father* he wrote of his after-school routine, which included checking out the comics at a newsstand, watching cartoons and sitcom reruns at home while his grandfather took a nap, and doing his homework before dinner, which young "Barry" and his grandparents ate in front of the television set: "There I would stay for the rest of the evening, negotiating with Gramps over which programs to watch, sharing the latest snack food he'd discovered at the supermarket." Obama would go to sleep to the sounds of top-forty music on the radio.[31]

His absorption with television continued through college. He loved watching sports on TV, especially basketball, which he started playing seriously in high school. He also sat with friends late at night at his home in Hawaii to watch Johnny Carson's opening monologue on *The Tonight Show*, which was often topical and widely considered a good measure of how much ridicule of politicians Americans would tolerate. Carson was a master of staying close to the edge but not going over it in his mockery.

* * *

TODAY, TRUE TO HIS PAST, President Obama is still trying to stay in tune with popular culture. During times of crisis, he clears his mind by playing sports, especially golf, and watching ESPN. He also watches other types of TV shows to escape the tedium and pressure of his job.

Michael Lewis reported in *Vanity Fair* that from 10 p.m. to 1 a.m. Obama will watch television and use his iPad to keep track of entertainment news, such as reports of what's happening on *Real Housewives* and *Jersey Shore*. He says he doesn't watch these shows in full and doesn't enjoy them, but he has expressed a liking for *Homeland, Mad Men, Boardwalk Empire, Entourage,* and *The Wire*—the latter of which he has called "one of the best shows of all time." Such shows are often edgy fare, and First Lady Michelle Obama has little or no interest in them. She and the Obama daughters, Malia and Sasha, prefer lighter programming such as *Modern Family.* They also like *iCarly*, and Michelle Obama was a guest star on that show. It was the first time a first lady had appeared in a sitcom since Nancy Reagan promoted her "Just Say No" antidrug campaign on *Diff'rent Strokes* in 1983. Given how different the president's taste in TV is from his family's, he usually watches his shows alone.[32]

"Like the TV shows he prefers," Troy notes, "Obama's movie choices tend to the dark side. *The Godfather* and *One Flew Over the Cuckoo's Nest* number among his all-time favorites. Among new films, he likes the gritty and the edgy. Early in his White House tenure, he watched *Slumdog Millionaire* and *The Wrestler*—definitely edgy even if not classic."[33]

Obama's sophisticated tastes in TV and movies display a connection to pop culture and a certain coolness that's appealing to intellectual elites, the Hollywood crowd (including donors), and the young.

CHAPTER EIGHT
SECOND BILLING
FROM TRUMAN TO THE BUSHES

Sometimes presidents just can't connect to popular culture, despite their best efforts. They subsequently lose much of the celebrity status they are accorded immediately after being elected. Those who lose star power tend to be less successful leaders than those who enhance their celebrity.

Harry Truman was a hybrid figure, proud of his middle-class roots and well intentioned but not charismatic. Initially the nation rallied around him as FDR's successor following Roosevelt's death in 1945. (Truman had been FDR's vice president.) But as president, Truman's tough decisions eventually outran public opinion and he left office as a very unpopular leader. Yet his certainty didn't fail him, even on cultural issues where he had little or no expertise. Truman once remarked to reporters that he wasn't impressed with a picture by respected American painter, photographer, and printmaker Yasuo Kuniyoshi. "If that's art," Truman declared, "I'm a Hottentot."[1]

Dwight Eisenhower was an enormously popular figure as the leader of Allied forces in Europe during World War II and emerged as an example of how war heroes are often propelled into the White House. As president, however, Ike lost some of his celebrity luster because he was widely considered competent but boring.

Other presidents lost touch with the country and lacked star power. Their problem was that they didn't have a powerful weapon in their political arsenal—the ability to motivate and inspire people through celebrity.

Lyndon B. Johnson: Star-Crossed

Lyndon B. Johnson was insecure about his appearance on TV—he realized that The Tube deepened the lines in his face and showed him to be a much less attractive man than his predecessor, John F. Kennedy. Johnson wasn't as quick on his feet as Kennedy was in repartee or in showing a sense of humor, and this also weighed on him. He knew he wasn't very adept in handling questions at news conferences or in media interviews, so he was reluctant to do them.

Johnson tried to parlay his Western roots into the image of a compelling larger-than-life Texan at the start of his presidency. But this backfired as he escalated the Vietnam War, as casualties mounted, and as Americans turned against the conflict. By the end of his presidency he was seen as a reckless and belligerent cowboy who had gotten the country into a morass. He was far from being a celebrity, and in fact was so unpopular that he faced massive demonstrations when he gave speeches and his travels were consequently curtailed.[2]

But he was a news junkie and was fascinated by the way the media covered him. He had a Teletype machine installed in the Oval Office, along with a cabinet containing three television sets so he could watch the three major networks (ABC, CBS, and NBC), sometimes all at once, sometimes shifting from one network to another and back again in rapid succession. He also had three TV sets installed in the bedroom and living room of his Texas ranch.

Johnson had no qualms about complaining, often harshly, to network executives when he didn't like their coverage. This reinforced his image as a man with a thin skin, making matters worse for him. He was deeply upset with negative coverage, and became preoccupied with keeping track of what journalists, especially those on TV, were saying about him.

Once he phoned the head of CBS, Frank Stanton, to complain about a report showing a Marine setting fire to a Vietnamese hut with a Zippo lighter. The president said the network had "shat on the American Flag" and added that the Canadian-born correspondent, Morley Safer, was way off base. "How could CBS employ a communist like Safer?" Johnson asked. "How could they be so unpatriotic as to put on enemy film like this?" In 1965, after guests at a White House Festival of the Arts protested the Vietnam War, Johnson was livid. He told his aides that communists had too much influence. "The communists already control the three major networks and the 40 major outlets of communication," he said.[3]

*   *   *

IT WAS NO WONDER that LBJ had trouble staying in touch. He had no interest in popular culture. "Sports, entertainment, movies—he couldn't have cared less," said a friend.[4]

Johnson would frequently fall asleep during movie screenings at the White House. But one movie he liked, and watched twelve times at the White House, was *A President's Country*, a 1966 documentary about the Texas hill country where LBJ was raised and that also described the president's boyhood. Produced by the US Information Agency and narrated by actor Gregory Peck, it was sent to ninety-eight US embassies for promotion but not released in the United States.[5]

Politics was Johnson's obsession, but not the politics of selling his ideas to the country. Instead he focused on personal politics in Washington, the many techniques of cajoling, bullying, pleading, sweet-talking, and deal-making, one on one, that he had learned as a member of Congress and perfected as Senate majority leader. He never understood the importance of image-making or marketing himself and his programs to the voters, as other presidents did, and he suffered for it. "He exuded power, not celebrity," says Mark Updegrove, director of the LBJ Presidential Library.[6]

Even though Johnson's legislative record during his first two years was astounding—his bills passed Congress partly because they were seen as a continuation of the agenda of the martyred Kennedy—Johnson's overreaching on domestic policy with his vast expansion of federal power and especially his escalation of the Vietnam War made him extremely unpopular. He declined to seek reelection in 1968.

At the end of his presidency, he was so widely detested and was so far away from being a popular celebrity that he almost became a prisoner of the White House, reluctant to give speeches on liberal campuses or in major cities because of the likelihood that violent protests would break out upon his arrival.

Some presidents were star-crossed when they tried to cultivate Hollywood stars, and occasionally their events with celebrities completely backfired. LBJ was one of them.

On January 18, 1968, fifty women from around the country attended a luncheon organized by Lady Bird Johnson, LBJ's wife, at the White House to discuss ways that individual citizens could fight crime. One of the guests was Eartha Kitt, an African American singer who played Catwoman on the Batman television show.[7] After a lunch of seafood bisque, chicken, and peppermint ice cream, and following brief remarks from President Johnson and others, the first lady said she would take some questions. That's when Kitt saw her moment.

Puffing on a cigarette, she announced, "I think we have missed the main point at this luncheon. We have forgotten the main reason we have juvenile delinquency. The young people are angry and parents are angry because they are being so highly taxed and there's a war going on, and Americans don't know why. Boys I know across the nation feel it doesn't pay to be a good guy. They figure that with a (criminal) record they don't have to go off to Vietnam." Pointing at the first lady, Kitt went on: "You are a mother, too, although you have had daughters and not sons. I am a mother and I know the feeling of having a baby come out of my gut. I have a baby and then you send him off to war. No wonder the kids rebel and take pot—and Mrs. Johnson, in case you don't understand the lingo, that's marijuana."[8]

Mrs. Johnson politely responded: "Because there is a war on . . . that still doesn't give us a free ticket not to try to work for better things. . . . I cannot identify as much as I should. I have not lived the background you have nor can I speak as passionately and well. But we must keep our eyes and our hearts and our energies fixed on constructive areas and try to do something that will make this a happier, healthier, better-educated land."[9]

Kitt was criticized for staging a publicity stunt to gain attention, but she was unrepentant. She later told reporters, "If Mrs. Johnson was embarrassed, that's her problem. . . . I should put on my claws because I am the Cat Woman of America."[10]

Richard Nixon: Uncool

Richard Nixon was one of the least cool presidents of the modern era, in some ways an anticelebrity. He tried repeatedly to connect with popular culture but failed. His reputation as "Tricky Dick" and memories of his campaign against the sainted John F. Kennedy turned off many cultural celebrities and everyday Americans.

He lost the 1960 presidential election to Kennedy partly because the Democratic candidate was a much better TV performer in their debates. But Nixon reinvented himself in his 1968 campaign with clever TV packaging. He emphasized sixty-second TV ads and staged town-hall meetings that made him seem affable and down to earth. Ray Price, a Nixon speech writer, said, "The response is to the image, not to the man, since ninety-nine percent of the voters have no contact with the man. It's not what's there that counts, it's what's projected—and carrying it one step further, it's not what he projects but what the voter receives."[11]

As president, Nixon did try to stay in touch with popular culture. He had enjoyed movies since he was a young man and during his younger days he liked *The 39 Steps* and *Mutiny on the Bounty*, both released in 1935. As president, he watched films often at the White House, at the presidential retreat at Camp David, and at his homes in San Clemente, California, and Key Biscayne, Florida. It was a way for him to find out what was going on in the wider world and to relax, and he watched films most frequently with Bebe Rebozo, his close friend. The two viewed 153 different movies together during Nixon's five-and-a-half years in office.[12]

Nixon watched twenty-five films of John Wayne, his favorite actor, known for macho roles that glorified the individual in righting wrongs and overcoming adversity, often with a patriotic theme. One of Nixon's favorite movies was the stirring World War II epic *Patton*, starring George C. Scott as General George Patton. Nixon watched it five times and urged members of his staff to see the picture. The president appreciated Patton's hard-charging attitude, as depicted in the film, and the fact that he overcame many obstacles to accomplish his goals and got into trouble with the press, traits that Nixon saw in himself. There was so much speculation that the film had an unhealthy effect on the commander in chief by encouraging his bellicose tendencies that Nixon felt compelled to deny it in an interview with British TV personality David Frost in 1977. Nixon said the movie had "no effect on my decisions."[13]

Journalism professor Alan Schroeder makes a good point when he asks, "How does it make a president feel to take a backseat to an actor? In January 1973 Richard Nixon got miffed when *Time* magazine featured Marlon Brando on the cover in lieu of the second Nixon inaugural. As retribution the president ordered his lieutenants not to talk to *Time* correspondent Hugh Sidey. Given the disparity in star power between popular performers and charisma-deprived politicians, one can almost understand the frustration some presidents face as they seek to maintain their hold on the public imagination."[14]

Making matters worse, overall Nixon had bad relations with Hollywood. They went back to his 1950 Senate campaign against onetime actress Helen Gahagan Douglas in California. He revived a nickname a past opponent had given her—"The Pink Lady"—because of her supposed left-wing views, and she dubbed him "Tricky Dick" because of his supposed untrustworthiness. Nixon won the race but had to deal with the epithet for the rest of his career, and Nixon and Hollywood remained at odds.

*   *   *

AS OPPOSITION TO THE WAR grew even more intense, Nixon endured a Vietnam-related embarrassment similar to the one LBJ's wife experienced with Eartha Kitt years earlier.

It happened at a White House dinner in which Nixon was to present the Medal of Freedom to DeWitt and Lila Wallace, cofounders of *Reader's Digest* magazine. After dinner, the president and his guests moved to the East Room for coffee and entertainment, which featured the Ray Conniff Singers, a group that specialized in light and breezy music that Nixon praised as "square." But just as the eight men and eight women were about to begin their show, a member of the troupe, Carole Feraci of Los Angeles, unfurled a homemade banner she had smuggled into the room, hidden in the bosom of her dress, and that read, "Stop the Killing." She looked at Nixon in the front row and said, "President Nixon, stop bombing human beings, animals, and vegetation. You go to church on Sundays and pray to Jesus Christ. If Jesus Christ were here tonight you would not dare to drop another bomb."[15]

Ray Conniff, who was on stage, quickly apologized and said, "Mr. President, the first part of the program was as much a shock to me as it was to you," and he asked Feraci to leave, which she did.

Later, Feraci told reporters she was acting out of conscience. "I thought that it would make a nationwide impression if an oobie-doobie-doo girl like myself made this protest on a stage inside the White House." The incident was national news, seeming to reflect the increasing intensity of the antiwar movement.[16]

Over time, celebrities in the entertainment industry became increasingly supportive of the Democratic party and its liberal views. But Nixon sought to throw a line to minorities and the music industry shortly after he took office in 1969, when he invited jazz great Duke Ellington to the White House to celebrate Ellington's seventieth birthday and give him the Presidential Medal of Freedom. Nixon revealed his ignorance of music when he ordered his chief of staff H. R. Haldeman to invite "all the jazz greats, like Guy Lombardo." The evening wasn't the smash hit that Nixon had hoped for since Nixon and most of the government officials who attended were not very appreciative of jazz.

On December 21, 1970, Nixon went all out to connect with popular culture, especially young people: he met at the White House with Elvis Presley, "The King" of rock and roll. Presley had suggested the meeting because he hoped Nixon would make him a "federal agent-at-large" in the Bureau of Narcotics and Dangerous Drugs (even though it would later be revealed that Elvis had a problem with overusing prescription drugs). It was one of the most bizarre moments in the history of presidents and entertainers.

Elvis showed up dressed in a purple velvet cape and a white shirt open halfway down his chest, a gold chain, and huge sunglasses. Nixon referred to his guest as "Mr. Presley" and Elvis referred to Nixon as "Mr. President." Elvis showed his host photos of his wife Priscilla and daughter Lisa Marie, and produced several police badges that he had collected. "I really support what our police have to do," the rock-and-roll icon said, and the president replied, "They certainly deserve all the support we can give them. They've got tough jobs."[17]

At one point Nixon awkwardly told The King, "You dress kind of strange, don't you?" And Presley replied, "You have your show and I have mine." A photo of the meeting, in which the president looks more uncomfortable than the iconic rock-and-roller, is one of the most famous of the Nixon era. And Elvis got his federal agent's badge.[18]

In 1973 Nixon invited country singer Merle Haggard to the White House, in part to celebrate what Nixon considered an anthem to the country's long-suffering middle class, "Okie from Muskogee." But it didn't work out. Haldeman wrote in his diary that the "Evening with Merle Haggard" was "pretty much a flop because the audience had no appreciation for country/western music and there wasn't much rapport, except when Haggard did his 'Okie from Muskogee' . . . which everybody responded to very favorably, of course."[19]

But Nixon was increasingly convinced that country-and-western singers were among the few entertainers who might be considered conservative, and in 1974 he visited the Grand Ole Opry in Nashville, a citadel of country music. "Country music is American," Nixon said in Nashville, and not "something that we learned from some other nation. It isn't something that we inherited. . . . It's as native as anything American we could find." He said country music was patriotic and celebrated America and religion, unlike rock and roll.

This attitude only deepened the animosity of rock stars and Hollywood celebrities toward Nixon, whom they felt was trying to undermine them and destroy the liberal movement. They were correct. Undermining the left was part of Nixon's comprehensive Southern strategy of using issues such as crime, race, and the Vietnam War to drive a wedge between Southern conservatives and the Democratic party. This strategy resulted in the South becoming a reliable Republican region in presidential elections for many years.

Nixon's relations with the TV industry were also rocky. He claimed to rarely watch television but some of his associates said that he did, and that he stewed about what he saw. He felt the programming was left-wing and un-American.

There was a remarkable irony in Nixon's hatred of TV, because the medium helped his career more than once. In 1952, after Dwight Eisenhower chose him as his vice presidential running mate, Nixon, then a US senator from California, got into trouble when he was linked to a secret slush fund. Suddenly his spot on the ticket was in jeopardy. He decided to gamble everything and appear on television to explain himself. At one point in that speech, in which Nixon defended himself effectively and credibly, he admitted that supporters had given his family a dog that his daughters named Checkers. "And you know, the kids, like all kids, love the dog," he said, speaking into the camera, "And I just want to say this right now, that regardless of what they say about it, we're gonna keep it." The speech generated a huge favorable response and Nixon stayed on the GOP ticket.

In 1968, eight years after losing the presidential election to John F. Kennedy, Nixon was aiming for a comeback as "the new Nixon," a wiser, more approachable, and more likable man. He appeared on the hit show *Rowan & Martin's Laugh-In*, a fast-paced, irreverent series of skits that often made fun of politicians and others in public life. All that Nixon did was say the show's catchphrase, which Nixon interpreted as a question, "Sock It To Me?" He seemed much more relaxed and self-deprecatory than people expected, not the gloomy and negative Tricky Dick of his past. Again, the reaction was very favorable.

One of the shows he came to hate was *All in the Family*, one of the most popular programs of the Nixon era. It featured Carroll O'Connor playing Archie Bunker, a racist, sexist, hopelessly behind-the-times right-winger who was held up to ridicule week after week. President Nixon told White House aides that the show promoted homosexuality. "Do you know what happened to the Romes, the Romans? The last six Roman emperors were fags. The last six. Nero had a public wedding to a boy."[20]

*   *   *

NIXON WAS a poor athlete. "Not since Calvin Coolidge have we had a more awkward uncoordinated locker-room character in the White House than Richard Nixon," *New York Times* columnist James Reston wrote. A caddie said that when he was on the links, Nixon's golf balls "spent more time in the trees than most squirrels."[21]

But one area where Nixon really could connect with everyday people was as a sports fan. He had an encyclopedic knowledge of baseball and football history. He followed sports in the newspapers and magazines, attended sports events, and watched football and baseball on television. "Like many who never made the team, I am awed by those who made it," he told all-star baseball players. "I'm proud to be in your company."[22] He told a sports reporter, "My favorite vacation, if I had an opportunity to take a week off at the right time, would be to travel with a baseball club. The dugout chatter and, particularly, the conversation on the train or plane between cities would be a welcome relief from some of the heavy discussions in which I participate in my office!"[23]

*   *   *

NIXON'S POLICIES and his personality became so unpopular, and the Watergate scandal was considered so outrageous, that he could never be a true political celebrity. By the end of his presidency in 1974, he was widely detested, an anticelebrity whom people didn't want anything to do with. Historian Rick Perlstein writes that Nixon left behind a nation split more deeply between liberals and conservatives, "two American identities, two groups of Americans, staring at each other from behind a common divide, each equally convinced of his own righteousness, each equally convinced the other group was defined by its evil."[24]

Perhaps the greatest reason Nixon was reviled was what Perlstein described as his "stoking and exploiting anger and resentment, rooted in the anger and resentments at the center of his character. For what was his injunction to join his Silent Majority if not also an invitation to see one's neighbors as aliens, and to believe that what was alien would destroy us?"[25]

Gerald Ford: Image Woes

Gerald Ford had been a member of the House of Representatives from Michigan for many years by the time Richard Nixon elevated him to the vice presidency, after incumbent Spiro Agnew resigned amid a scandal. Ford was well liked on Capitol Hill and was a good legislator. But his reputation suffered after the media and his critics created the impression that as president he was a stumblebum and an intellectual lightweight. Once this image settled in, Ford was unable to use his celebrity to his advantage.

Liberal adversaries were looking for ways to undermine Ford following his pardon of Nixon for any crimes committed as president. The pardon was Ford's way of trying to move the country beyond the bitterness of the Nixon era and the Watergate scandal. It made matters worse for the new president when the media resurrected old quotes attributed to President Lyndon Johnson: that Ford had played too much football in college without a helmet and that, as a congressman, he couldn't walk and chew gum at the same time.

But what really intensified the bumbler image was an unfortunate incident when Ford fell down the stairs of *Air Force One*. On May 3, 1975, Ford exited his presidential jet in Salzburg, Austria, and decided to help his wife Betty down the rain-slick stairs rather than firmly grip the handrail. He had one arm around his wife's waist and held an umbrella in his other hand, and he lost his footing and took a tumble. The photos of his fall got worldwide attention.

From then on, reporters and critics were constantly on the lookout for Ford missteps. And they found quite a few, from falling on the ski slopes to hitting errant shots on the golf course and sometimes striking spectators. Comedian Chevy Chase popularized this image of Ford by impersonating the president on *Saturday Night Live*, hitting his head, dropping things, tripping over furniture, and making stupid comments. President Ford added to his bumbling reputation when, during a debate with Democratic challenger Jimmy Carter, he appeared to be confused as to whether the Soviet Union dominated nations in Eastern Europe.[26]

Ford in reality was an athlete and an industrious and intelligent student of government, but he could never convey those qualities to the country. At his core, he was a decent but bland Midwesterner, and he could never break into pop culture or become a celebrity. Just as important, he could never emerge from the shadow of having been Nixon's vice president.

Some of Ford's efforts to seem cultured and hip flopped miserably. When he held a dinner for Queen Elizabeth II in 1976 to mark the US bicentennial, he brought in pop singers The Captain and Tennille, who sang "Muskrat Love," an odd choice for such a highbrow occasion. The audience of straight-laced dignitaries was not impressed.

He hosted some pop icons at the White House, including former Beatle George Harrison and singer Billy Preston, but never established a bond with them. In the end, the country just couldn't accept the idea of Jerry Ford, the dull former congressman from Grand Rapids, as cool.

Ford failed in his attempt to win a full term on his own, losing to Democratic nominee Jimmy Carter in 1976 in a public repudiation of the Nixon-Ford years.

Jimmy Carter: Losing the Common Touch

Jimmy Carter was elected in 1976 in reaction to the corruption and political abuses of the Watergate scandal. He was a peanut farmer and former governor of Georgia, and portrayed himself as an honest man and a truth-teller who would bring an outsider's perspective to Washington.

At first Carter was popular as he cut down on the trappings of the imperial presidency, such as the public playing of "Hail to the Chief" wherever he went. He regularly carried his own bags aboard *Air Force One* when he traveled. His desire to reduce US reliance on foreign oil was considered admirable. He seemed to make sense when he argued for energy conservation and a measure of austerity, and he tried to live a relatively simple lifestyle free of ostentation at the White House while minimizing the perks of office as much as possible. He wore sweaters and turned down the thermostats of the White House in winter and limited the air conditioning in summer.

Initially people saw this as fresh and different, and possibly the way of the future. Carter as a new president seemed to be an intriguing public figure, fascinating to everyday people and the elites in New York, Hollywood, and Washington, DC. But this changed dramatically. By the end of his administration Carter seemed hapless and ineffective. He couldn't cope with the many problems he had to deal with, including an oil shortage and an overall energy crisis, a bad economy, a bellicose Soviet Union, and the country's desire for more uplifting and effective leadership than the dour Carter was providing.

Gradually, Carter lost whatever celebrity or novelty status he had, and he became very unpopular amid reverses on the economy and international affairs. His image on *Saturday Night Live*—which was a barometer on and shaper of public impressions—turned negative. He started out being portrayed as a brilliant and sensitive leader Americans could be proud of, but he morphed into a smirking know-it-all.

Carter tried repeatedly to connect with popular culture, especially musicians, hoping this would get him more of a hearing with the public. "He entertained Dizzy Gillespie (with whom he sang 'Salt Peanuts' on the White House lawn), Sarah Vaughan, and Earl 'Fatha' Hines, noting in his diary that he had at one point been 'an avid jazz fan,'" Tevi Troy reports. "Carter recalled that when he 'was in trouble in the White House or needed to be alone, just to relax,' he would go into his study and tie flies for fishing while 'Willie Nelson's songs played on the hi-fi,' he joked, 'So all the good things I did or, of course all the mistakes I've made, you could kind of blame half that on Willie.'"[27]

* * *

CARTER ENJOYED movies more than most other presidents. He watched 480 films during his four-year presidency, an average of 120 a year. Among them was *All the President's Men*, about the Watergate scandal, which he saw shortly after his January 1977 inauguration.

Carter also loved the theater. He attended twenty-eight productions at the Kennedy Center, a haven for the arts near the White House—more than any other president up to that time. "Carter, compared to many other presidents, went to the theater more for genuine appreciation and intellectual stimulation," said Thomas A. Bogar, a retired history professor and author of the 2006 book *American Presidents Attend the Theatre*. "He had eclectic taste, and such a wide appreciation for all the different genres of theater."[28]

After only a few weeks in office, Carter attended *Madame Butterfly* at the Kennedy Center following church one afternoon with his wife Rosalynn, their preadolescent daughter Amy, their pastor, and several friends. They stayed for the entire three-hour performance and met the cast backstage afterward. This became his pattern. He enjoyed the theater so much that he often invited cast members to the White House for a tour and a chat.

One of Carter's biggest problems was that he lost whatever common touch he had. *Washington Post* book reviewer Jonathan Yardley, assessing Carter's presidency, expressed a widely held view when he wrote, "He was his own worst enemy: smug, self-righteous, sanctimonious, humorless, vindictive and exhibitionistic about his piety. He was too haughty and aloof to deal effectively with friends and foes in Congress—foreshadowing the presidency almost three decades later of Barack Obama—and he never understood how to talk to the American people, as made all too plain by his well-intentioned but tin-eared address to the nation in July 1970 about the 'crisis of confidence' from which the country ostensibly was suffering."[29]

Carter came across as the nation's scold, and presidents rarely do well or connect with everyday people in that role. He lost his bid for a second term to Ronald Reagan in the 1980 election.

George H. W. Bush: The Preppie Factor

George H. W. Bush, Reagan's vice president who was elected in 1988 as Reagan's heir and the forty-first president, was mocked by his critics for being a rich "preppie" out of touch with the country.

His image was wrong from the start, even on small aspects of his lifestyle. At first, President Bush ate pork rinds and wore multicolored wristwatch bands that were popular among wealthy men of his generation who had attended prep schools, but neither the pork rinds nor the watch bands caught on widely during his time in office. He was ridiculed by pundits and comedians for being highfalutin in the case of the watchbands and inauthentic over the pork rinds (people didn't believe a rich fellow who attended Yale really had a yen for this particular snack). He stopped wearing the watchbands and talking about the pork rinds, at least publicly.

President Bush had a misfortune in his 1988 campaign when his handlers tried to use Bobby McFerrin's upbeat reggae song "Don't Worry, Be Happy" as the unofficial campaign anthem, but it backfired when McFerrin announced his opposition to candidate Bush. The campaign dropped the song.

He had better luck with Arnold Schwarzenegger, the champion bodybuilder-turned-movie star. Schwarzenegger endorsed Bush over Democrat Michael Dukakis in 1988 and, during a campaign appearance in New Hampshire, derided Bush's political rivals as "girlie men." It wasn't a popular reference with feminists but many voters liked Schwarzenegger's bluntness and sense of humor and agreed with his point that the rivals were weak on national defense.

But this association with Schwarzenegger lifted Bush's fortunes only temporarily. After he was elected, Bush's efforts to connect with popular culture flopped. He was unpopular (as modern Republican presidents tend to be) with many in the entertainment industry, which seems increasingly populated by liberals. One exception was country-and-western artists, who tend to be more conservative. In Bush's corner were country entertainers including Loretta Lynn and the Gatlin Brothers. However, Bush's effort to reach out to them wasn't enough to improve his aristocratic image.

He suffered a huge setback, which seemed to reinforce the claim that Bush was an out-of-touch Brahmin, when he visited an exhibit of technological advances in supermarket scanners. He inspected a machine designed for use at a checkout counter, and marveled at it. The subsequent news stories, including one in the *New York Times*, made it seem that Bush was nonplussed by an everyday supermarket checkout scanner. This was unfair to Bush. He was reacting to sophisticated equipment that could read bar codes that had been torn up and thrown on the scanner's screen. But the damage was done, and Bush's image suffered because of it.

Because of incidents such as the one involving the scanner and, more broadly, because of his failure to show that he cared enough about everyday people and was able to effectively address the country's economic problems, George H. W. Bush lost his bid for reelection to Bill Clinton in 1992.

George W. Bush: Willing to Go It Alone

George W. Bush, the former Republican governor of Texas, was the forty-first president's son and namesake. He cultivated ties with his party's right wing, and this helped him win the 2000 GOP presidential nomination and go on to win the general election over Vice President Al Gore. The Supreme Court, in a controversial 5–4 decision, awarded Bush the state of Florida, which was enough to give him an Electoral College majority. But Bush had lost the popular vote to Gore by 500,000 votes nationwide, and a large chunk of the country didn't consider him a legitimate president.

He got off to a lackluster start, and then came the terrorist attacks of September 11, 2001. This gave Bush a mission for his presidency: beginning what he called a global "war on terror." He handled the immediate aftermath of the attacks with steadiness and resolve, and his job-approval rating soared. Part of it was the natural rally-around-the-president effect that almost always occurs in a crisis. But gradually Bush's ratings declined amid unpopular wars he had launched in Iraq and Afghanistan and a souring economy. He didn't have a reservoir of support among everyday people, especially Democrats and independents who had their doubts about him from the start.

Bush stubbornly refused to watch much television news, preferring sports programming. He felt that his staff would tell him anything he needed to know, and he didn't need the "mainstream media" for information. Like Bill Clinton, Bush was a baby boomer who had grown up with television. But he felt it had developed a liberal bias and a yen for sensationalism and stirring up conflict, so he divorced himself from it. Adding to his anti-TV sensibility was his feeling that the masters of the television industry were liberal and didn't respect him for his views or his intellect.

In 2005 it was revealed that Bush had never seen some of the most popular and trend-setting TV programs, including *The Daily Show with Jon Stewart* and *Desperate Housewives*. He felt that, from what he had heard, they didn't share his values and he would only get riled up if he watched. He was probably correct, but it might have helped him stay in touch with the country if he had seen firsthand the kind of culture and criticism he was up against.[30]

His dismissive attitude, which White House officials gleefully conveyed to the media and the country, alienated him further from the nation's opinion leaders.

Bush even had trouble within the country-music world, traditionally pro-Republican, or at least more conservative than other segments of the music industry. In 2003 Natalie Maines, a Texan singer with the Dixie Chicks, told an audience in London she was "ashamed the president of the United States is from Texas." The remark caused criticism of Maines among country-music fans, but the incident showed how far Bush had gone from being really connected to pop culture.

It got worse. After Hurricane Katrina devastated the Gulf Coast and New Orleans in 2005, Grammy Award–winning singer Kanye West, an African American, said Bush "doesn't care about black people" because federal relief to so many African Americans (and others) in Katrina's wake was badly botched. Bush didn't respond at the time but he later said West's remark hurt his feelings and was "one of the most disgusting moments in my presidency." West's career wasn't hurt, however, suggesting the depth of Bush's unpopularity among liberal segments of the population.

Chapter Nine
First Ladies
Partners in Celebrity

First ladies have played a key a role in popular culture over the years and often shaped perceptions of their husbands, sometimes softening harsh impressions or helping people to understand what made their spouses tick.

* * *

DOLLEY MADISON, the wife of James Madison, was a celebrity in the nation's capital during the early years of the Republic, largely because of her skills as the "first hostess" from 1809 to 1817. She had also served as a hostess for ladies' receptions during the presidency of Thomas Jefferson, a family friend who was a widower.

She had married John Todd, a lawyer, in 1790 but he died of yellow fever three years later, leaving her in Philadelphia with a small son, Payne. She was active in political circles when Philadelphia became the new nation's temporary capital, and she met Madison there. He was seventeen years her senior. They were married in September 1794. They had no children together.

She became famous for redecorating the White House in a grand style, as well as for the parties she organized there and for her personal style, which included wearing a trademark turban. A chronicler at the time wrote, "She looked a Queen. . . . It would be absolutely impossible for anyone to behave with more perfect propriety than she did."[1]

She also made history by helping to save a priceless portrait of George Washington by painter Gilbert Stuart. She moved it out of the White House at the last moment when the British were about to take the American capital and burn the president's residence down during the War of 1812.

Other early first ladies who achieved a degree of celebrity included Martha Washington, George Washington's wife, who was a national mother figure; and Mary Todd Lincoln, spouse of Abraham Lincoln, whose overspending ways were an embarrassment to her husband.

*   *   *

BUT THE FIRST LADY who was the first true celebrity was Frances Folsom Cleveland, a twenty-one-year-old who married the forty-nine-year-old President Grover Cleveland in 1886 while he was serving the first of his two nonconsecutive terms. There was tremendous media interest in her from the start.

Little was known publicly about Frances until the president's aides revealed her identity the week before the Clevelands' White House wedding. She was the daughter of Oscar Folsom, the president's longtime law partner, and Cleveland had known her as "Frankie" or "Frank" since she was an infant. He had even bought her a stroller when she was a child and babysat her as "Uncle Cleve." She was a college graduate, poised, sophisticated, and lovely. The newspapers couldn't get enough information about her.[2]

Grover and Frankie were married at the White House in front of family and a few friends on the evening of June 2, 1886. Afterward the couple left Washington on a train heading for a resort at Deer Park, Maryland, for their honeymoon. But they were trailed by a horde of reporters and sketch artists eager to cover what was considered one of the biggest stories of the year. It quickly became a media feeding frenzy. After spending their wedding night in Deer Park, the newly married couple looked out at the grounds the next morning to see reporters everywhere, some in trees with binoculars. President Cleveland was furious at the invasion of their privacy, and he labeled the journalists "animals and nuisances."[3] But this was only the start of the press and the public's fascination with the first lady. Frances Folsom Cleveland quickly became a cultural superstar.

"The media were besotted by [Frankie's] appearance," writes journalist S. J. Ackerman. "Although 'girlish,' her face was intelligent and thoughtful. Although the dimples came readily, the smile was exceedingly sweet, and seemed a fitting accompaniment to her well-modulated voice. When the Women's Christian Temperance Union scolded her 'decollete' gowns, she ignored them. In fact, she was an instant arbiter of fashion. First came her coif, lovely auburn hair swept up from the forehead, then gathered behind above her shaved neck. Her arms were bare above leather opera gloves. She turned to American designers to fill her closets."[4] On more substantive topics, she showed a sensitive side when she played with children at a Christmas party for African American orphans and dedicated a home for young women who worked in factories.[5]

Advertisers used her likeness and name to promote products without her permission, and people came to Washington hoping to catch a glimpse of her on the way to a party or traveling around town.[6] Her fame was so intense that the president moved with his wife to a secluded twenty-three-acre farm he owned not far from the White House so they could escape the glare. The Clevelands made that farm their primary residence in 1886. The estate, which Frankie named Oak View but which reporters called Red Top, for the color of the roof on the main house, offered the couple more privacy and featured a menagerie of foxes, quail, chickens, ducks, horses, rabbits, deer, white rats, dogs, and cats, and a cow named Grace. The president commuted by horse or carriage to the White House, but he also did some of his presidential work at an office on the farm.[7]

The interest in Frankie and Grover continued during his second term, when he made a successful comeback after being defeated in his first bid for reelection. The Clevelands were the first true celebrity couple in the White House.

*   *   *

ELEANOR ROOSEVELT was a celebrity for more than a decade as first lady and in her post–White House years.

Born in New York City on October 11, 1884, she was the daughter of Elliott Roosevelt, who was President Theodore Roosevelt's younger brother. Her mother was Anna Hall, a member of another affluent family from the Northeast. She married Franklin Delano Roosevelt, her fifth cousin, on March 17, 1905, and they became the parents of six children. In 1921 her husband contracted polio, which caused enormous difficulty for her and FDR for the rest of their lives; he never recovered the use of his legs.

Eleanor became vital to her husband's political success, serving as an important sounding board for his ideas and, through her many fact-finding trips, as a way for him to stay connected to the world outside Washington. He called her his "eyes and ears."

After FDR won the presidential election in 1932, Eleanor informed the nation that Americans should not expect the new first lady to be a paragon of elegance but instead "plain, ordinary Mrs. Roosevelt."[8] As the years passed, Mrs. Roosevelt became a celebrity of the first order because of her commitment to good works and helping the American people during the Depression, not because of her glamour or her beauty.

She did things that first ladies had never done before. Eleanor visited a coal mine, relief projects, poor neighborhoods in the cities and rural areas, and many military posts during World War II. She would report back to the president what she had observed. From her husband's inauguration in 1933 until the United States entered World War II in 1941, when wartime activities limited her domestic schedule, Eleanor traveled an average of 40,000 miles per year within the United States.[9]

Mrs. Roosevelt's travels became legendary. She once visited migrant-labor camps in California's San Joaquin Valley and ordered the driver of her car to stop when she saw a few shacks in the distance. She walked across a field toward some migrant workers, and one of them quickly recognized her. "Oh, Mrs. Roosevelt, you've come to see us," he said matter-of-factly. He was already familiar with her many trips to see how everyday people lived and worked.[10]

She was a pioneer in other ways that added to her celebrity and increased people's interest in her. In 1933, her first year as first lady, Mrs. Roosevelt became the first presidential spouse to hold a news conference. She allowed only female reporters to attend in an attempt to boost women in journalism, since women were traditionally barred from presidential news conferences.

She bonded with millions of Americans by writing a six-day-a-week newspaper column, "My Day," which was widely distributed from 1935 until her death in 1962. Through her writing, her travels, and her speeches she became known as an advocate for minorities and the poor. In 1939 she resigned in protest from the Daughters of the American Revolution (DAR) when the organization refused to allow African American opera singer Marian Anderson to perform in a DAR auditorium in Washington. Instead

Mrs. Roosevelt arranged for Anderson to sing before 75,000 people at the Lincoln Memorial.

* * *

JACQUELINE BOUVIER KENNEDY was an icon of her time, known simply as "Jackie" to millions of Americans and others around the world. She was the perfect candidate for celebrity in an age of mass entertainment—beautiful, glamorous, stylish, and educated, with a distinctive kittenish voice and a strong desire to control and promote her image and the image of her husband as youthful, vigorous, forward-thinking people. She was particularly eager to be seen as a good mother and wife. She also was known as a patron of the arts and a lover of fashion.

Her celebrity was embellished when she traveled abroad and beguiled men who led nations from France to Pakistan. Acknowledging the media frenzy that surrounded his wife on their trip to France in May 1961, President Kennedy introduced himself publicly as "the man who accompanied Jacqueline Kennedy to Paris, and I have enjoyed it."[11]

Mrs. Kennedy was only thirty-one (and her husband forty-three) when she became first lady, but by then she already had an impressive resume. Trained in ballet as a girl, she was an expert horseback rider and had a classical education that had given her fluency in languages other than English, including French and Italian. She graduated from Miss Porter's School, a boarding school for girls in Connecticut. She attended Vassar College in New York, spent her junior year studying in Paris, and finished her final year at George Washington University in Washington, DC, from which she graduated with a BA in French literature in 1951. That same year, she worked for $42.50 per week as the "Inquiring Camera Girl" for the *Washington Times Herald* newspaper in the District of Columbia. Her job was to photograph and interview local citizens by asking them a question of the day.[12]

She met John Kennedy when he was a member of the House of Representatives from Massachusetts and soon to be elected senator from that state. On September 12, 1953, they were married at St. Mary's Church in Newport, Rhode Island, in a highlight of the New England social calendar. She had two small children, Caroline and John Jr., when she became first lady in January 1961. She told a reporter, "If you bungle raising your children, I don't think whatever else you do will matter very much." This notion—that she was a devoted mother and wife—was central to her appeal, in addition to her looks and glamour.

Jackie Kennedy set off a fashion craze when she attended her husband's inauguration wearing a beige wool coat rather than the traditional fur coat, and a pillbox hat. Women around the world loved the look, and they were entranced with the beautiful young first lady. They started paying attention to what she wore. Within weeks, women around the world were buying pillbox hats, white gloves, and A-line dresses—Jackie trademarks.[13] She popularized wraparound sunglasses for women when she started wearing them in 1962.[14]

She became one of the most photographed women ever, for magazines, newspapers, and television. Women wanted to copy her outfits, to look like her, to emulate her. Hollywood costume designer Edith Head called Jackie Kennedy "the greatest single influence (on fashion) in history."[15]

On February 14, 1962, she led CBS News on a tour of the White House, which she had redecorated as a showplace for American history and culture. A massive audience of eighty million Americans watched the broadcast, reinforcing Jackie's hold on the popular imagination as a modern, successful, and talented woman. The dinners and social events that she organized at the White House, in which she feted artists, writers, musicians, and scientists, became legendary and she grew extremely popular with the elites.

Cultural historian Fred Inglis says she succeeded in public and in private because of several factors: "In public, her beautiful smile, her gracefulness and poise, her self-effacement and (successful) concealing of rogue emotions; in private, with her . . . husband, careful often nervous, wounded by her husband's infidelities but never openly reproachful, girlish in her uncertainties and political ignorance."[16]

Later she became a beacon of inspiration and admiration when she behaved with bravery, dignity, and stoicism after her husband was assassinated in November 1963.

*   *   *

JACKIE KENNEDY went a long way toward elevating her husband to mythic status after his death. She promoted the idea that his administration was a magical, unique moment for the country symbolized by the popular musical *Camelot* that began a long Broadway run in 1960. For an article in *Life* magazine, Mrs. Kennedy told journalist Theodore White, an admirer of her late husband, "At night, before we'd go to sleep, Jack liked to play some records; and the song he loved most came at the very end of this record. The lines he loved to hear were: 'Don't let it be forgot, that once there was a spot for one brief shining moment that was known as Camelot.' "[17]

*   *   *

NANCY REAGAN was a strong player in her husband's government. She didn't push Ronald Reagan very much on policy, but she was very interested in maintaining an image of him as a vigorous, engaged leader, even if in private he was often laid back and disengaged. "Even though she wasn't a policy person she knew what was going on," said former Reagan aide James Kuhn. "She was his ultimate protector," he recalled.[18]

And that extended especially to personnel. Nancy was always watching to see if the staff was promoting and protecting her husband or if they had their own agendas. When she felt that White House Chief of Staff Donald Regan was too imperious and was alienating too many people in Washington—and after he treated her dismissively—she undermined him with her husband and he was forced to resign.

She kept an eye on her husband's schedule, trying to ensure it made him look as good as possible. Kuhn, the president's longtime personal assistant, said, "She watched everything." And sometimes it was with the help of an astrologer. She never recovered emotionally after her husband was nearly assassinated in 1981. And from then on she consulted an astrologer to determine when it was safest for her husband to travel, and she often made demands on White House schedulers to protect him according to the position of the planets and the stars.

When she called Kuhn, at 4:30 p.m. many days, it was frequently with complaints. "There was something wrong that she saw," Kuhn recalled. "She could have seen it on CNN or the news . . . and she'd say 'What are you guys doing? Why did you do this? Why did you let him say that or do this? Why did he get pinned down here by the press?' Or whatever. . . . [S]he'd do this with everyone, the chief of staff, deputy chief of staff, where she would stop people in their tracks. 'Why is Ronnie giving this speech? Why is he going this way in his policy? Why is he even getting involved in this?' And I couldn't answer. I'd go, 'You're right.' And I would have to modify my course. She was always looking ahead, always watching everything, protecting him and pushing things the way things needed to be pushed."[19]

Her most important contribution in terms of policy was urging her husband to reach out to Soviet leader Mikhail Gorbachev in hopes of reducing superpower tension and, in Nancy's mind, softening her husband's reputation as a bellicose, jingoistic cowboy. Partly under her influence, Reagan formed a partnership with Gorbachev that lowered international tensions and eased the way to the dismantling of the Soviet empire.

While not personally popular, Nancy Reagan entered the wider culture with her signature policy initiative, an antidrug campaign appealing to children under the slogan "Just Say No." She came up with the idea after learning how extensive drug use was among the young, and she promoted the campaign heavily. By her husband's final year in the White House, 1988, there were 12,000 Just Say No clubs around the country.[20]

The public, however, always perceived Nancy as too interested in luxury, wealth, and expensive fashions. But she did cause a brief fad in fashion when her preference for red boosted sales of red women's garments, such as dresses and blouses.

Mrs. Reagan attempted to soften her image in an appearance at Washington's Gridiron Club, where she made fun of herself, wearing what she called secondhand clothes and singing a self-deprecatory song. This at least showed Washington insiders that she had a sense of humor. But she was never as popular as many other first ladies.

* * *

BARBARA BUSH used her position to shape cultural perceptions of AIDS. She visited hospitals and other facilities to comfort patients with AIDS and made a habit of embracing those with the disease and holding AIDS-stricken children in her arms. Her goal was to show Americans that they couldn't catch the disease through casual contact.[21] There are no studies on the impact she had, but the attention she gave to AIDS must have had a positive effect on educating the country about the disease. She was also active in promoting reading and education.

* * *

HILLARY CLINTON stood out as a historic first lady and a first-tier celebrity while her husband was president from 1993 to 2001. Part of the reason was that she was the most influential policymaker of any first lady in history; her husband placed her in charge of a massive overhaul of the health-care system. She failed to win congressional passage for the legislation, but in fighting for the bill she earned fame and a reputation as a tough infighter and a smart policy wonk.

Her fame intensified even more—unfortunately for her—when her husband was accused of and finally admitted to having an affair with a former White House intern named Monica Lewinsky. The House of Representatives impeached Bill Clinton for lying under oath, but the Senate refused to remove him from the presidency. Even though he survived in office, the barrage of often salacious coverage, day after day, month after month, gave Hillary and Bill Clinton starring roles in a sordid soap opera that appalled and fascinated the country.

In the process, Hillary became one of the most famous people in the world. "No one had been featured more often than Hillary Clinton on Barbara Walters' *Ten Most Fascinating People of the Year* program," reports journalist Edward Klein. She made the list in 1993 when she became first lady, again in 2003, and a third time in 2012, which "meant that she continued to pull in solid Nielsen ratings," Klein says. "Barbara was a personal friend of Hillary's," he writes. "But that was not the reason she had Hillary on her annual show. However you felt about Hillary—whether you loved her or hated her, whether or not you thought she deserved all the accolades that came her way—she was the feminist movement's success story par excellence. She had been co-president with her husband for eight years, a U.S. senator for another eight, secretary of state for four, and the 'Most Admired Woman' in Gallup's poll for the past eleven years. And now, as she prepared to leave the State Department [after serving as secretary of state during Barack Obama's first term], she was the odds-on favorite to become the Democratic Party's next presidential nominee" in 2016.[22]

Mrs. Clinton even became a subject for musical theater. "Like Eva Peron in 'Evita' and Imelda Marcos in 'Here Lies Love' (not to mention the Founding Fathers who crowd '1776'), Mrs. Clinton is a larger-than-life political leader whose career cries out for music," wrote journalist Amy Chozick in the *New York Times* in July 2014.[23] Hillary was the key figure in two shows then being developed in New York, *A Woman on Top*, and *Clinton: The Musical*.

Chozick added, "Depending on whom you ask, Mrs. Clinton is either one of the world's most admired women or a political animal who attracts scandal. The more positive view mostly wins out in these stage depictions."[24]

*   *   *

MICHELLE OBAMA, the only African American first lady to date, quickly rose to the status of cultural icon. She shares with her husband a desire to use her position to publicize her causes, and she has followed through vigorously. "We can't waste this spotlight," she said at a public forum in 2014. "It is temporary and life is short, and change is needed."[25]

Michelle Obama is leading a national campaign to fight childhood obesity and to encourage proper nutrition, and has gotten lots of attention for her White House garden, where she and the East Wing household staff grow fruits and vegetables. Michelle Obama may have had some impact on reducing childhood obesity, or at least convincing some mothers and fathers to feed their children more nutritious food and convincing some young people to make better food choices themselves, such as cutting down on snacks and sugary beverages.

She also is an advocate of programs to help military personnel and their families, and emphasizes the need to encourage the education of girls in societies around the world. A more subtle goal is to set an example for young African Americans to emulate Michelle and Barack Obama as strivers and devout advocates of education to get ahead.

Like her husband, she loves the attention. And like Jackie Kennedy, Michelle Obama is a style maven, and she celebrates the "cool" aspects of popular culture. At her fiftieth birthday party at the White House in January 2014—she called herself "fifty and fabulous"—she hosted a red-carpet lineup of stars, including former Beatle Paul McCartney, actor Samuel L. Jackson, former pro basketball greats Magic Johnson and Michael Jordan, and singers Beyoncé and Stevie Wonder, who performed. The dancing went on until the wee hours.

The first lady caused a stir among the adoring fashion elites, as she often did, by wearing a red silk jumpsuit. Tara Luizze, sales and merchandise manager at Hu's Wear in Georgetown, told the *Washington Post*, "If you have great arms and the body that can pull it off, 50 is the new 30, so why not try it?" Added wardrobe consultant Cathy Starnes, "Jumpsuits are transitioning into a realm of a more classic style, and it's not quite as risky. Let's face it. Michelle doesn't often get it wrong when it comes to style." Author and style adviser Lauren Rothman gushed, "The confidence that the first lady has to make that style choice is what's so empowering. That she's not scared to wear a jumpsuit to her 50th birthday party, I think that's awesome."[26] At this same party, President Obama caused his own stir when he danced with singers Janelle Monae and Usher. "I did not drop and split, but I did bust a move," he said later, with considerable pride.[27]

In sum, Michelle's participation in popular culture has been extraordinary. She even announced the Academy Award for best motion picture in February 2013. Beamed from the White House on TV, she gave the Oscar to *Argo*, in the perfect intersection of politics and pop culture.

During her husband's first term in the White House, Michelle Obama was careful to focus on projects that were noncontroversial, and she was seen as a nonconfrontational figure. Nearly everyone could rally around her campaign for good eating habits and exercise. But she has moved into hard-edged politics. In May 2014, she fought congressional attempts to weaken nutrition standards for school lunch programs nationally. It was one of her rare direct moves as first lady to affect a major and controversial policy. She had advocated for lower levels of fat, sodium, and sugar in school lunches that are offered to children, as part of her efforts to fight childhood obesity. And she felt that weakened standards would jeopardize the progress that had been made.

Her effort to improve nutrition in school lunches was opposed by some in the food industry and by legislators who said this was a local or state decision and that the first lady's policies were proving to be too costly and resulting in too much food being thrown away.[28]

The School Nutrition Association (SNA), a group representing 55,000 cafeteria workers, shifted its position from supporting the 2010 Healthy Hunger-Free Kids Act backed by the first lady, which required schools to serve more fruits, vegetables, and whole grains and use less sodium in school lunches in exchange for more federal money for meals. Officials of the SNA, in alliance with congressional Republicans, concluded that the program was force-feeding kids foods they didn't like and wouldn't eat, resulting in more waste and lower rates of participation in the school lunch program, costing the schools money. The SNA and the GOP came out in favor of amending the law to grant waivers to schools if they were losing money and, beyond that, to relax some of the standards.[29]

Opponents of the rollback said the SNA and the Republicans were responding to food-industry interests that made more money when the kids were served less-nutritious dishes such as pizza, fries, and burgers. Mrs. Obama fought back and said it would be best to maintain the standards but to help the local school districts to meet them rather than weakening or voiding them. "We have to be willing to fight the good fight now," she said. She got support from a group of retired generals and admirals who argued that young people weren't fit enough and supported her goal of improving nutrition and encouraging exercise. But a Republican-controlled House committee rejected her arguments and weakened the standards in June 2014. The fight over the law has not been resolved, and more battles seem inevitable.

Still, the jump into politics didn't reduce Michelle Obama's popularity. On average, her favorable ratings have been higher than those of Laura Bush and Hillary Clinton, her immediate predecessors. Two-thirds of the public maintained a positive view of Mrs. Obama, according to a Gallup poll and the Pew Research Center. Her average Pew favorable rating was 69 percent, somewhat higher than Laura Bush's average of 65 percent and markedly higher than Hillary Clinton's 55 percent during Bill Clinton's second term in office.

"Unlike other recent first ladies, her popularity has not fallen or risen with her husband's. . . . In short, more so than other recent first ladies, the public views Michelle Obama as her own person, and her image has not been tied closely to swings in judgments about her husband," writes independent pollster Andrew Kohut.[30]

Regarding her sense of fashion—always a fascinating topic for the media when reporting on a first lady—Michelle Obama made a commitment to "affordable glamour," says Democratic pollster Geoff Garin, and this added to her appeal. And the Obamas take seriously their positions as role models for other parents and spouses "in a way that's not always been true of others," according to Garin.[31] Part of the reason is that the Obamas choose to show themselves to the media as parents far more than, say, Bill and Hillary Clinton did because the Clintons were very concerned about protecting their daughter's privacy. "We didn't see President Clinton as a father or Hillary Clinton as a mother as we do Barack and Michelle Obama," Garin says. "For all the talk that he [President Obama] is too elitist, people really relate to them. And the first lady personally is very accessible."[32] This contributes to her star power.

* * *

OTHER FIRST LADIES had an impact on popular culture, even if it wasn't as extensive as that of Michelle Obama.

Abigail Adams was the spouse of the second president, John Adams, who served one term from 1797 to 1801. She advocated equal legal status for women and men and the emancipation of African American slaves. But her ideas didn't gain much traction, even with her husband, and her own lack of public approval limited her historic role. However, she was ahead of her time and historians have treated her kindly.[33]

Mamie Eisenhower appealed to everyday women to such an extent that her favorite color—"Mamie Pink"—soared in popularity during her husband's presidency, from 1953 to 1961, in everything from clothes to bathroom fixtures and kitchens.[34] When Mrs. Eisenhower wore bangs, she inspired requests to hairdressers from women across the country to have their hair "just like Mamie's," according to clothing designer Arnold Scaasi. Beyond this, Scaasi said, "Barbara Bush made a statement by having gray hair, and suddenly gray-haired grandmothers were chic."[35]

Lady Bird Johnson launched a program for highway beautification that improved the look of roadways around the country. And Barbara Bush and Laura Bush made the encouragement of literacy their special projects.

Betty Ford had a PR coup when she helped popularize citizens' band radios after she used a CB under the nickname "First Mama" during the 1976 presidential campaign. An electronics-industry trade association named her "CB Radio's First Mama."[36] On a far more important level, Mrs. Ford inspired many American women to have breast exams when she openly discussed her breast cancer and surgery. She underwent a mastectomy on September 28, 1974, and decided to use her experience to inform women about the disease and demystify it. "There had been so much cover-up during Watergate that we wanted to be sure there would be no cover-up in the Ford administration," she said.[37] A decade later, Nancy Reagan discussed her own breast cancer and helped many women cope with it in their lives.[38]

CHAPTER TEN
PRESIDENTS AND TELEVISION
PRIMAL FORCES

Television has propelled the American presidency into celebrity culture more deeply than any other factor, fundamentally reshaping the presidency as an institution and putting it squarely in the middle of the information-entertainment world. Today the average American watches thirty-four hours of TV a week, nearly five hours per day.[1] During the past half century, television has become nearly ubiquitous.

Television was a novelty during Harry Truman's presidency from 1945 to 1953.[2] Even though he delivered the first presidential address ever televised from the White House on October 5, 1947, and even though he was the first chief executive to have a TV set in the White House, relatively few Americans had TVs in their homes at that time and Truman's use of the medium was minimal.

This changed as TV became more popular during the administration of Dwight Eisenhower, who succeeded Truman and served from 1953 to 1961. During Eisenhower's first term, TV ownership increased from about 30 percent of the population to 70 percent, and it rose to about 90 percent during his second term in the late fifties.[3] Ike, in fact, became a big TV fan, along with his wife Mamie. They enjoyed *I Love Lucy*, the hit sitcom of the period, and they made a habit of eating their dinners from tray tables as they watched variety shows such as *Arthur Godfrey's Talent Scouts*, *The Fred Waring Show*, and *The Lawrence Welk Show*. Mamie also watched soap operas during the afternoons, as did many American women.[4]

But Ike was an awkward and uncertain TV performer, and as president in 1954 he invited actor Robert Montgomery to coach him, as Montgomery had done during Eisenhower's successful 1952 campaign. Montgomery, as the first official media consultant in the White House, encouraged Eisenhower to relax and to speak more conversationally, which softened his image and made him seem avuncular and approachable.[5]

Montgomery got along well with Ike, and the president followed his advice carefully. He stopped using a teleprompter; Eisenhower hated the machine, which gave his speeches a stilted, insincere quality. Montgomery persuaded Ike to base his talks on cue cards, which was more natural for him. Montgomery also vastly improved Ike's stagecraft. He positioned the TV lights during Oval Office addresses at a high angle to minimize the prominence of the president's bald head. And he got Ike to dress for television in flattering dark suits and light-blue shirts. He also persuaded Ike not to wear eyeglasses on camera whenever possible and to allow Montgomery to choose the eyeglass frames if Ike needed visual help.[6] Eisenhower's TV performances got much better.

Newly confident in his TV skills, Ike held the first televised cabinet meetings and press conferences.[7] But over time he soured on the televised press conferences, considering many reporters' questions silly and designed to embarrass him. (This opinion has been shared by most of Ike's successors, including President Obama.) The number of press conferences Ike held declined from 100 during his first term to 50 in his second term.[8]

Still, Ike understood that television could greatly expand the reach of the president and he encouraged the networks to carry some of his speeches live or use extensive excerpts. It was a step toward recognizing the power of television to create superstardom in public life.

"There is no doubt that in the creation and dissemination of language, nothing in day-to-day life plays a more significant role than television," writes public-opinion analyst Frank Luntz. "But the real question for those who seek to understand and then apply the power of words is whether television mirrors society or leads it. . . . We know so much about things that don't really matter because we see them on television—and therefore it matters to us—yet we are so remarkably ignorant about what should matter—our own national heritage, culture, and traditions—because no one ever explained why we should care. *Relevance* sells—and seeing it on television makes even the most obscure and trivial seem relevant."[9]

*   *   *

JOHN F. KENNEDY, who succeeded Ike, wasn't a great fan of TV. He didn't have a television in his Hyannis Port, Massachusetts, home before the 1960 presidential debates (although he did have a set at his home in Washington, DC). To watch JFK's jousting with Vice President Richard Nixon in 1960, Mrs. Kennedy had to rent a sixteen-inch TV at Hyannis Port.

When they arrived in the White House, President and Mrs. Kennedy started to pay more attention to The Tube as it became increasingly popular around the country, and they enjoyed *The Judy Garland Show*, *The Jack Benny Program*, and *Maverick*—two variety shows and one lighthearted Western.[10]

But beyond his personal taste in entertainment programming, Kennedy understood that he could use TV to his great advantage as a political leader. "In the television age, poise and physical attractiveness became even more important for a politician—especially a president," writes historian Tevi Troy. "And youthful good looks were Kennedy's most outstanding quality. Television elevated these aesthetic advantages at the same time that it minimized the importance of extended persuasive and logical skill. Kennedy's performance in the 1960 televised debates against Nixon was crucial to his victory. . . . Nixon was at his worst on the screen. His fair skin revealed the barest five o'clock shadow and his propensity to sweat created distracting rivulets—all of which got in the way of his over-rehearsed, encyclopedic responses. It is an established part of American political lore that among those who listened to the debate over the radio, Nixon prevailed, but TV viewers thought that Kennedy, with his charm and relaxed demeanor, walked away the winner. Kennedy defeated him not on the substance but by looking like a man ready to take command."[11]

Kennedy mastered TV as Franklin Roosevelt had mastered radio, but Kennedy went further than FDR by cultivating his image in a more methodical and comprehensive way. As a consequence, a special JFK persona emerged—the president as an icon of glamour, vigor, and grace under pressure.

A large part of Kennedy's success came from his simple recognition of the power of TV. He understood that, with the onset of world crises and increasing news coverage of domestic affairs, the president would be in America's living rooms with growing frequency. Kennedy realized that he needed to be a star to have the most impact, and he liked the personal notoriety.

Writes cultural historian Fred Inglis, "The first and most obvious way to follow this making of celebrity by television is to tell the tale of politicians as they perform the dance of power between 1960 and the present day. John F. Kennedy was the first president imaginatively to grasp the momentousness of television, and his remains the most gripping moral fable of celebrity politics. His thousand-day creation of a television president and his combination of exhilarating and energetic charm, flagrant sexual allure, fixity of will, and the delighted possession of absolute political power is a fearful object lesson. Later politicians have to be judged by his lights."[12]

Kennedy held sixty-four news conferences during his three years in office, roughly two per month, including thirteen that were carried live, an unheard-of practice because a president could so easily make a mistake on live TV. And he commanded a vast audience, with 90 percent of Americans saying they had watched one of his first three news conferences.[13] What they saw was a witty, charming, intelligent leader who was quick with a quip and had a reassuring manner—all conveyed directly to the viewers without media filtering. The news stories would come later; but by then Kennedy's image was already set by his live performance.

A measure of the deference given to the president in those days could be seen in the decision by NBC executives to remove a comedy sketch about the Kennedys from *The Art Carney Show* because it seemed "improper to have performers actually portraying the president and his wife," an NBC spokesman said.[14] How times have changed. Not only are presidents portrayed regularly on TV today; they are often pilloried and ridiculed.

But TV gave Kennedy overwhelmingly positive coverage. By the time of his assassination in November 1963, he was so familiar and so popular that many viewers felt they had lost a close friend or even a member of the family when he died.

* * *

LYNDON B. JOHNSON, Kennedy's successor, wasn't nearly as adept at performing on TV and he shied away from it. The Johnson "treatment"—an in-your-face approach that involved cajoling, threatening, and intimidating—worked in one-on-one meetings but wasn't effective on TV, which made LBJ look like a bully who used strong-arm tactics. Lady Bird Johnson, his wife, once remarked, "Television was not his friend; it was his enemy."[15]

For starters, Johnson was insecure about how he looked on TV. It deepened the wrinkles on his face and the circles under his eyes. Compared with JFK, he seemed oafish. Johnson also became increasingly bitter about how TV was covering the Vietnam War. He felt the correspondents and the networks were biased against the conflict.

The Tet Offensive by anti-American forces in Vietnam severely damaged Johnson's credibility with the media and the country in 1968. It came as a surprise that the enemy could do so well despite official American optimism about how the war was going. After the bloody offensive, which was graphically covered on TV's prime-time news shows night after night, influential CBS anchorman Walter Cronkite gave a very negative assessment of the war, which prompted LBJ to say, "If I've lost Cronkite, I've lost middle America." Military officials pointed out that the Americans and their South Vietnamese allies actually won most of the battles associated with Tet, although it took a long time and cost many casualties. But the media's patience with the war had run out, and Johnson knew it. He would soon announce that he wasn't running for reelection in 1968.

* * *

RICHARD NIXON had an even worse time with TV than Johnson did. And this was ironic because Nixon, although he lost the famous televised debate with John F. Kennedy in 1960, had benefited from TV in the past. In his televised "Checkers speech"—named after his family dog, which he used to create sympathy—Nixon successfully defended himself against charges of having a political slush fund that could have blocked his path to the vice presidency. And his lighthearted appearance on the hit comedy show *Laugh-In* in 1968—when he repeated the program's signature line "Sock It To Me"—gave voters the impression that perhaps Nixon had a sense of humor and was likable after all.

But as president, Nixon became so frustrated by criticism on TV and elsewhere in the media that he had his staff draw up an "enemies list" of foes who were to be somehow punished. One goal was to isolate critical news organizations and deprive them of access to senior administration officials and the kind of news stories that were their lifeblood. Those on his enemies list included CBS commentator Daniel Schorr, the *Washington Post*, the *New York Times*, *Time*, and *Newsweek*.

Nixon wanted it known that he didn't watch much TV. He preferred to seem highbrow in his tastes in entertainment. He did tune in to *Kojak*, a cop show, most Sunday evenings, but not much else.[16] He said TV was superficial and was diverting Americans from reading, which was an accurate observation. "I must admit to a lifetime personal prejudice for reading," he wrote. "My mother taught me to read before I went to school, I was fortunate to have had outstanding teachers who inspired me to love books. Except when my favorite teams are playing, I always prefer reading to TV."[17]

Just as important, he wanted to avoid seeming overly concerned about negative news coverage on TV because he thought his critics would be emboldened if they thought they were getting under his skin. As his presidency proceeded, Nixon felt that the media were becoming more liberal and would never give him fair coverage. This was at least partially true because the media and most Americans were turning against Nixon's escalation of the Vietnam War. However, he made things worse for himself by adding to the stereotype that he was an overly secretive, isolated politician, and he increasingly became an object of scorn.

* * *

GERALD FORD also showed how damaging TV could be to a president if the chief executive failed to master the television arts and make the medium work to his advantage. Ford had been a solid athlete during his years playing football at the University of Michigan, and he prided himself on his physical abilities throughout his political career. But as president he endured a series of embarrassing mishaps that created the impression that he was a klutz, all captured by the cameras. He fell down the steps of *Air Force One* during a rainy arrival in Austria. He took tumbles while skiing in Vail, Colorado. He was hit on the head by a moving chairlift. He beaned a bystander while playing golf. And weekend after weekend, he was mocked by the comedian Chevy Chase, who impersonated Ford and portrayed him as a nincompoop on the hit TV show *Saturday Night Live*. Ford tried to counter the ridicule. Ron Nessen, his White House press secretary, actually appeared on *SNL* and played along, but he ended up inadvertently adding to the mockery.

There was a later parallel. In the 2008 presidential campaign, comedian Tina Fey did a hilarious and devastating impression of Republican vice presidential candidate Sarah Palin, depicting her as another nincompoop. This did lasting damage to Palin's image by distilling what many voters felt were her weaknesses as a candidate and a leader.

The lesson is clear: if a president or another prominent public figure has vulnerabilities, and if the country is concerned about them, TV can magnify those vulnerabilities and intensify the concerns more effectively than any other force.

Ford got another lesson in the power of TV when he mangled his response to a question about foreign affairs during a televised debate with Democratic challenger Jimmy Carter in 1976. Ford said, "There is no Soviet domination of Eastern Europe and there never will be under a Ford administration." What he meant to say, apparently, was that the USSR did not dominate the will of the people in Eastern Europe as they continued to seek freedom and democracy. But his actual words made him seem ignorant, adding to his reputation as an intellectual lightweight.

Politicians of both major parties have run into the TV buzz saw. Sen. Edward Kennedy (D-MA) had his presidential ambitions damaged by a televised interview with CBS's Roger Mudd in late 1979. This came as Kennedy was preparing to challenge Jimmy Carter in the Democratic presidential primaries of 1980. But Kennedy couldn't answer the simple question of why he wanted to be president. His meandering, nonsensical reply made his ambition seem like simply an ego trip. "The reasons I would run," Kennedy said, "are because I have great belief in this country; that is—there's more natural resources than any nation in the world; there's the greatest educated population in the world. It just seems to be that this nation can cope and deal with the problems in a way it had done in the past . . . and I would basically feel that it's imperative for the country to either move forward, that it can't stand still or otherwise it moves backwards."[18]

Senator Kennedy's problem with TV was all the more remarkable because his brother John F. Kennedy had been so deft on television. Edward went on to lose the Democratic nomination to Carter, and he never ran for president again.

*   *   *

RONALD REAGAN made television work greatly to his advantage. He was a brilliant performer, and it helped him sell his policies. Reagan also understood the dangers of overexposure and wearing out his welcome, so he tried to limit his TV presence to when it really counted. He knew how much attention he could draw as a political star, having already been a movie and television star, and he used it to dramatize his administration, his policies, and his persona.

His larger-than-life image was greatly enhanced when he displayed grace and a sense of humor in the aftermath of an assassination attempt that almost took his life shortly after he assumed office in 1981. It became clear that he hadn't simply portrayed heroic or upbeat characters in the movies; he actually showed heroic qualities in real life by joking about the attack and, from the start, demonstrating optimism that he would survive.

Reagan was amused when commentators and critics wondered how a former movie actor could have been elected president in the first place. When TV journalist David Brinkley asked Reagan if being an actor had helped him be president, Reagan replied, "There have been times in this office when I've wondered how you could do the job if you hadn't been an actor."[19] Jack Valenti, former adviser to President Johnson and later chairman of the Motion Picture Association of America, said, "Politicians and movie stars spring from the same DNA. Both hope for applause, read from a script and hope to persuade audiences."[20]

Frank Donatelli, former White House political director for Reagan, told me, "Issues do matter but people want to know about their presidents [personally]. Today, you have to tell your story as president."[21] And Reagan was a brilliant storyteller.

Donatelli traces this development to President Kennedy. "The personality dimension of the presidency blossomed under Kennedy," Donatelli said. "When you are a celebrity, people want to learn more about you. You have a leg up in that way." And Reagan knew how to feed the media beast, running an administration that was organized like a TV show, with a theme every day and Ron in the middle of the action trying to master the crises of the moment and thriving in the process.

Reagan, who had hosted TV shows *Death Valley Days* and *General Electric Theater* in his earlier years, genuinely liked TV for both news and entertainment. Among his favorite shows, which he watched with his wife Nancy, were *Dallas* and *Dynasty*, two prime-time soap operas about rich and powerful families; *The Waltons*, a show about a frontier family; *Family Ties*, another evening sitcom revolving around the life of a young conservative played by Michael J. Fox; *Jeopardy*, a long-running game show; and *Murder, She Wrote*, a murder mystery series. In the news category, he liked to watch the Sunday talk shows, especially *This Week with David Brinkley*.

His viewing helped him keep up with popular culture and gain the information needed to enhance his own status as a celebrity. One of his main advantages was understanding the nature of television itself. Advised by brilliant media experts such as Michael Deaver and David Gergen, he and his staff arranged events to emphasize compelling images that would override what TV reporters were saying about Reagan. They created a "message of the day"—hardly more than a phrase or a sentence such as "creating jobs," "fighting crime," or "peace through strength"—and arranged administrationwide events, as well as presidential activities and comments, around this theme.

I covered the Reagan White House and vividly recall the Reaganites' ability to dominate the agenda using these techniques. They knew how to come up with powerful or beautiful images and backdrops that TV, with its emphasis on the visual, couldn't ignore.

Even *Saturday Night Live*, the scourge of Nixon and Ford, gave Reagan relatively positive treatment. Its most memorable skit about Reagan, played by comedian Phil Hartman, depicted him as an amiable but slow-witted dunce in public but a tough, smart, detail-oriented manager in private. Neither part of the parody was true, but Reagan remained such a celebrity that the portrayal helped to maintain public interest in him at a high level.

* * *

GEORGE H. W. BUSH, Reagan's vice president and successor, lacked Reagan's TV skills. He had never paid much attention to TV during his political career and wasn't a natural visual performer, a skill that has become vital for a successful president. Bush mangled his syntax and his staff was undisciplined and lacked creativity in devising a narrative for his presidency.

Bush lacked confidence on TV and it showed. Weeks after taking office, he told me in an interview that he would never be the communicator or the television performer that Reagan had been. He added that he had been over six feet tall since he was eighteen years old, but after seeing him on TV many people thought he was "a little guy." It was as if, in his mind, his stature had literally been diminished by television.

Bush lost his bid for reelection to the culturally connected and TV-savvy Bill Clinton, the former governor of Arkansas and a baby boomer who grew up with television and closely followed popular culture throughout his life. Clinton's appearance on *The Arsenio Hall Show*, wearing sunglasses and playing a saxophone, was a sensation, indicating that he would be a different kind of president, more hip and connected to popular culture than ever before.

*   *   *

BILL CLINTON'S family had purchased its first TV set in 1956, when Bill was ten years old, making him the first president to have grown up with The Tube. He said TV intensified his fascination with politics as he watched the Democratic and Republican National Conventions that year.

As president, Clinton tried to replicate the Reagan White House's emphasis on clever staging of made-for-TV events. But he got off to a messy start and nothing seemed to go correctly. Congress refused to pass his plan to overhaul the health-care system, and he slid further in public approval when he focused on a policy to allow gays to serve in the military instead of emphasizing ways to fix the economy, which was voters' top concern. *Time* magazine published a cover story on June 7, 1993, entitled "The Incredible Shrinking President," and a reporter at a news conference asked Clinton if he was becoming irrelevant. Annoyed, he said no, because a president has so many powers that he really can't become irrelevant.

Faced with multiple setbacks, Clinton hired David Gergen, one of Reagan's media gurus, as a senior adviser. At the same time, Clinton agreed to focus more clearly on setting priorities and moving closer to the center politically so he wouldn't be pigeonholed as being too far to the left. But things were getting more complicated. The media world had changed in the four years between the end of Reagan's presidency and the start of Clinton's. The three broadcast networks of ABC, CBS, and NBC were losing influence and viewership, and twenty-four-hour cable news coverage, led by CNN, was gaining traction.

When the Monica Lewinsky sex-and-lies scandal hit during Clinton's second term, in 1998, Clinton got some of the most negative coverage in history, a situation that lasted for a full year. He was impeached by the House of Representatives for perjury and other offenses but acquitted by the Senate. Clinton complained that he was being unfairly treated, that his private life was being scrutinized like no other president's had ever been.

But in a sense it was a matter of living by the sword and dying by the sword. He had become a target of the same celebrity culture that had enabled him to thrive as a candidate. His presidency became a lurid soap opera, full of salacious details about his affair with former White House intern Lewinsky, how he behaved sexually, and his lies about the episode. Details were supplied by a hard-charging independent counsel. And the news media, especially the TV networks, were fascinated by this titillating scandal involving the fate of the most powerful person on Earth, one who suffered from what classicists would call tragic flaws—an overly active libido and a powerful sense of self-indulgence.

Not surprisingly, the scandal changed Clinton's TV viewing habits in a fundamental way. He and his wife Hillary started avoiding news shows (a common response of presidents and first ladies when they come under attack), which featured a never-ending series of reports on his escapades. They were too painful for the first couple to watch. From then on, President Clinton concentrated on sports shows and live coverage of football and basketball games.

*   *   *

GEORGE W. BUSH was also easy to caricature. Although he was a baby boomer brought up on TV and popular culture, he wasn't as adept at using television as Clinton was. He was not a natural performer and resented the need to use stagecraft to get his ideas across, sharing this attitude with his father, George H. W. Bush. He also was often inarticulate, as was his father, and the media depicted him as an intellectual lightweight.

Bush enjoyed high job-approval ratings and overwhelmingly positive coverage in the immediate aftermath of the terrorist attacks of September 11, 2001. He offered just what the country wanted—strong, decisive leadership at a time of calamity. But as time went on, he lost his aura of positive celebrity, and stories about his lack of intellectual depth returned. The wars he launched in Iraq and Afghanistan became increasingly costly, and by the end of his eight years in office, he was extremely unpopular and was not so much a celebrity as a political pariah, especially with Democrats and independent voters.

*   *   *

AS FOR BARACK OBAMA, he started off as a historic figure—the first African American president. Television was instrumental in his rise. He catapulted into the national consciousness with a brilliant nationally televised speech to the Democratic National Convention in 2004. Then unknown nationally, he emphasized themes of hope, change, and the need for national unity that impressed millions of Americans and many in the media.

Obama today is the most famous person in America, and quite possibly the world. He has become a divisive figure, with millions of Americans supporting him but millions also detesting him. Yet despite his polarizing qualities in terms of policy, Obama projects an easygoing, approachable persona on TV, even though in private he is often detached and distant. This public persona and the endless attention he receives from TV and the rest of the media have made Obama into more of a celebrity than any president in history.

Obama, brought up as a TV fan all his life, also can bond with many in the country because of their shared tastes in TV fare. Obama has said, for example, that his all-time favorite TV show is *M.A.S.H.*, the irreverent and immensely popular show about military doctors and other medical personnel trying to cope with the Korean War. His recent favorites have included *House of Cards*, a dark tale of Washington insiders.

The first lady is similarly a celebrity and cultural icon. Michelle Obama has led a campaign to fight childhood obesity and to encourage proper nutrition, and gets lots of attention for her White House fruit and vegetable garden.

*   *   *

TELEVISION BOTH REFLECTS and shapes our perceptions of presidents and politicians of all kinds, as it does with so many other aspects of our culture. And those perceptions can change over time, sometimes rapidly.

Take the contrast between *The West Wing*, a popular series about a fictional president that had a successful run starting in 1999, and *House of Cards*, the brooding political drama about Washington politicians that gained popularity more than a decade later.

Sometimes the entertainment industry will make a genuine effort to research the presidency in order to best reflect the realities of the job. This happened with NBC's Emmy-winning *The West Wing*. The producers and writers hired a number of Washington insiders as consultants, including Dee Dee Myers (former White House press secretary for Bill Clinton) and Marlin Fitzwater (former press secretary for Ronald Reagan and George H. W. Bush). Partly because of this, the plots of *The West Wing* were often based on real situations and had the ring of truth, even if the president and his aides were idealized. Other Washington-based TV shows had a much harder edge and demonstrated a cynical attitude about politicians and government.

"Part of what has made 'House of Cards' so successful—and what sets it apart from its political-snake-pit brethren—is how [series creator] Beau Willimon's personal obsession about power, and the freedom Netflix grants him to explore it, dovetails so perfectly with our collective impressions of the current political arena," wrote Adam Sternbergh in the *New York Times Magazine*. "You can make the case that 'House of Cards' will one day seem as instructive about our current political moment as 'The West Wing' was of its political moment. The latter show appeared in 1999 as a kind of late-Clinton-era liberal *cri de coeur*, full of dedicated, snappily literate bureaucrats who would always win their debates, serving under an unimpeachable President-Dad whose moral compass never wavered from true north. Aaron Sorkin's 'West Wing' was a vision of American government, presided over by a morally righteous liberal leader, unfolding each week even as Bill Clinton was assailed for abandoning liberal principles and subsuming important issues in his own moral messiness. Jed Bartlet was the kind of president, albeit fictional, we could believe in."

Sternbergh continued, "The politicians in 'House of Cards,' by contrast, are morally bankrupt and endlessly opportunistic. The show is no *cri de coeur*, but a cold dissection of the post-Obama (or post-the-Obama-many-hoped-they'd-elected), post-hope political landscape. It's a vision of American government not as we wish it were, but as we secretly fear it is. Good old Jed Bartlet wouldn't last a single news cycle here."[22]

*   *   *

ANOTHER KEY DEVELOPMENT in TV is partisan polarization. Fox News has become the network of the right and MSNBC has become the network of the left. In addition, innumerable websites and media outlets cater to political ideologues. All this means that partisans at both ends of the spectrum can constantly get their views reinforced on television without considering alternatives in the middle ground. Networks that are less partisan, such as CNN, ABC, CBS, and NBC, are struggling to find a way to hold and build their audience shares.

*   *   *

OVERALL, presidents who master TV as performers and who learn from it as viewers do better than those who don't. Presidents who minimize the importance of TV do so at their political peril.

George Washington:
The Original Celebrity President

Illustrating his unique status as "the father of his country," George Washington was chosen by the Electoral College without dissent for each of his two terms as president.

George Washington had been commander in chief of the Continental Army during the Revolutionary War and was one of the founders of the United States, presiding over the convention that drafted the Constitution. Many Americans thought he was the only person capable of uniting and leading the fractious new nation in its early days. He was widely revered, and was known to virtually everyone as the premier American of his time. This positive celebrity gave him a special ability to set precedents that would guide the United States for many years, including the tradition of a president serving only two terms and his rejection of the trappings of monarchy. Washington served as president from 1789–1797. When he died, he was eulogized by Congress as "first in war, first in peace, and first in the hearts of his countrymen." (Library of Congress, www.loc.gov)

A Parade of Celebrity Presidents

Celebrity has helped American presidents to govern, enabling them to capture the nation's attention and make the case for their agendas.

Theodore Roosevelt was an advocate of what he called "the strenuous life," a philosophy that called for him to be a man of action and excel at everything he did. A big-game hunter, TR is pictured here with a rhinoceros that he shot during an expedition to Africa in 1909, shortly after he left office. (Bettmann/Corbis/AP Images)

Roosevelt delighted the country with his athletic feats and sporting activities. One of his favorites was riding horses and jumping fences. It was a dangerous hobby, and occasionally Roosevelt would return to the White House from a ride scraped and bruised from a fall. But he wasn't averse to risk and would try harder to get it right the next time. This is the kind of persistence he hoped to inspire in Americans as celebrity in chief. (Bettmann/Corbis/AP Images)

Franklin D. Roosevelt is shown giving a "fireside chat" to the nation to explain his job-creation programs as he tried to lift the country out of the Depression. He mastered a dominant medium of his time—radio—and his voice became widely known. His optimistic message was that the economy would get better and his leadership would make the difference. His celebrity was such that he was one of the most popular and consequential presidents in history. (Franklin D. Roosevelt Presidential Library & Museum, www.fdrlibrary.marist.edu)

Eleanor Roosevelt, Franklin's wife, was one of the most traveled first ladies. Because her husband never recovered the use of his paralyzed legs from polio, she served as his "eyes and ears" and became an advocate for government relief for everyday people during the Depression. During her dozen years in the White House, she became a celebrity in her own right. Eleanor is pictured here at a music festival at White Top Mountain in Virginia. (Franklin D. Roosevelt Presidential Library & Museum, www.fdrlibrary.marist.edu)

Jacqueline Kennedy was one of the most glamorous and popular first ladies, which enhanced her husband's celebrity. She is shown on horseback with children John F. Kennedy Jr. and Caroline Kennedy in a photograph released by the White House in 1962. White House officials used public-relations photos such as this to create an image of the Kennedys as icons of family values and youthful vigor. (Cecil Stoughton. White House Photographs. John F. Kennedy Presidential Library and Museum, Boston)

John F. Kennedy was popular among show-business personalities, and he used their celebrity to intensify his own. Here, he laughs as comedian-actor Bob Hope makes remarks after receiving the Congressional Gold Medal, presented by Kennedy in a Rose Garden ceremony, for entertaining US troops around the world. (Abbie Rowe. White House Photographs. John F. Kennedy Presidential Library and Museum, Boston)

Kennedy was at home in the world of style and glamour, and enjoyed the company of entertainment stars such as singer-actor Frank Sinatra, shown here at Kennedy's inaugural ball on Jan. 20, 1961. (AP Photo)

Ronald Reagan was unique—
a former movie star who became
celebrity in chief as president.
One of his most famous roles was
playing Notre Dame halfback
George Gipp in the 1940 movie,
Knute Rockne—All American.
He is shown posing in football
gear while making the film. The
movie provided an inspirational
slogan that Reagan later used
in politics—"Win one for the
Gipper." (Courtesy Ronald
Reagan Library)

Reagan was associated with the
entertainment industry because
of his movie and television
background, and he tapped into
the celebrity of others to expand
his own fame. Here, he walks out
onto the South Lawn of the White
House with iconic singer Michael
Jackson, who is in full regalia, on
May 14, 1984. Reagan presented
Jackson with an award for his
role in a campaign against
drunk driving. (Courtesy Ronald
Reagan Library)

Reagan was known for his affability and likability, traits he honed as a Hollywood actor in which he often played genial everyman types. In addition to movies, he became widely known to Americans as the gracious host of General Electric Theater on television from 1954–1962. Reagan presented a drama to the country every week, and for a while the show was a hit. It brought Reagan into America's living rooms on a regular basis, serving as a springboard for his later political career as governor of California and president of the United States. He is shown here seated in a director's chair during the period when he hosted GE Theater. (Courtesy Ronald Reagan Library)

Bill and Hillary Clinton become a celebrity couple during his presidency from 1993–2001. Both were larger-than-life personalities in personal and policymaking terms. They are shown dancing at an inaugural ball in 1993. (Official White House photograph, Library of Congress)

Bill Clinton loved to mingle with the nation's top entertainers, and his critics said he sometimes became too enamored of a glamorous show-biz lifestyle. Here, he poses with singer-actor Will Smith at his inaugural gala in 1993. Clinton followed popular culture to stay in touch with the country; he was a devoted fan of movies, TV shows, and pop music. (AP Photo)

Barack Obama was a political superstar from his first day in office as the first African American president of the United States. He was awarded the Nobel Peace Prize during his first year even though he had at that point done little as a peace maker to justify the honor. Instead, the award was based on his rhetoric about bringing a new spirit of international understanding and harmony to US foreign policy and his promises to bring hope and change to the United States. Here, he examines the Peace Prize medal after the award ceremony in Oslo, Norway, on Dec. 10, 2009. (Official White House Photo by Pete Souza)

Obama made history as the first African American president, and many Americans felt he would usher in a new era of racial conciliation, but the results have been disappointing. Obama is pictured at the Henry Ford Museum in Dearborn, Michigan on April 18, 2012, sitting in the same vehicle where civil rights advocate Rosa Parks defied Alabama law in 1955 and refused to sit in the back of the bus with other black riders in Montgomery. (Official White House Photo by Pete Souza)

Adding to Barack Obama's celebrity is the fame and popularity of his wife Michelle and his reputation as a devoted husband and father. The president and first lady are shown in a personal moment as they ride a freight elevator from an inaugural ball on Jan. 20, 2009. The president has given the first lady his coat as Secret Service agents and aides look on awkwardly. (Official White House Photo by Pete Souza)

First Ladies

Some first ladies achieved cultural stardom, advising their husbands on policy or shaping popular tastes in fashion and in other ways.

Jacqueline Kennedy sits on a camel with her sister, Princess Lee Radziwell, during a goodwill visit to Karachi, Pakistan on March 1, 1962. Mrs. Kennedy had a way of drawing attention wherever she went, including on her foreign tours. (AP Photo)

President Bill Clinton placed his wife Hillary Clinton in charge of overhauling the health-care system during his first year in office, making her the most influential policy maker of any first lady in history. Her plan failed to clear Congress, however. She is shown holding a copy of her health-care plan during a visit to Baltimore on Oct. 28, 1993. (AP Photo/ Joe Marquette)

Michelle Obama has become widely known for her signature "Let's Move" initiative, which promotes exercise and good nutrition. Here, she leads children in a fitness routine during a visit to Des Moines, Iowa, on Feb. 9, 2012. (AP Photo/Carolyn Kaster)

Non-Celebrity Presidents

Most presidents, while famous, never achieve true celebrity status, or lose that status because of their unpopular policies or lack of likability.

Lyndon B. Johnson became extremely unpopular when Americans turned against the Vietnam War, which Johnson had escalated, and when many whites rejected the civil rights movement, backed by Johnson, for moving too far, too fast. Here, LBJ confers with the Rev. Martin Luther King Jr., one of the era's top civil rights leaders. (LBJ Presidential Library, photo by Yoichi Okamoto)

Richard Nixon was far from hip but he did try occasionally to connect with popular culture, such as when he met with rock-and-roll star Elvis Presley at the White House on Dec. 20, 1970, shown here. Presley wanted a law-enforcement badge because he had long admired police, and he got it. Nixon got this picture. (Richard Nixon Presidential Library and Museum, U.S. National Archives and Records Administration)

Presidents and the News Media

The tug of war between presidents and the Fourth Estate has persisted for many years. Some presidents used the media to successfully shape perceptions and add to their celebrity. Other presidents were targeted relentlessly by the media for criticism and ridicule.

Lyndon B. Johnson felt that the media turned against him over the Vietnam War, and he blamed negative news coverage in part for his unpopularity. Here, he announces a bombing halt and declares his intention not to seek re-election in an Oval Office address in 1968. (LBJ Presidential Library, photo by Yoichi Okamoto)

Ronald Reagan was a master of stagecraft and getting good news coverage, especially from television. He projected a sunny personality and eternal optimism, which enhanced his celebrity. He is shown meeting with retiring CBS anchor Walter Cronkite on March 3, 1981. (Courtesy Ronald Reagan Library)

PRESIDENTS AND THEIR PETS

Presidents have valued the companionship of their
pets. Many used their beloved animals to connect with
millions of Americans who are also pet owners.

*One of the best-known presidential
pets was Franklin D. Roosevelt's
Scottish terrier Fala. Here,
FDR enjoys a picnic with his
pal, four months old at the time,
near Pine Plains, New York, in
1940. (Franklin D. Roosevelt
Presidential Library & Museum)*

*Bill Clinton found a devoted
companion in his Labrador
retriever Buddy. A presidential
spokesman said Clinton got the
canine because "It's the president's
desire to have one loyal friend
in Washington." (www.media.
nara.gov)*

*Barack Obama cavorts on
the South Lawn of the White
House with Bo, his Portuguese
water dog, on May 12, 2009.
(Official White House Photo by
Pete Souza)*

PRESIDENTS AND MUSIC

Many modern-day presidents have kept up with popular culture partly through their knowledge of and appreciation for music. A few have been talented musicians in their own right.

Harry Truman loved to play the piano to relax or to entertain family members and friends. As Franklin D. Roosevelt's vice president, he got into hot water with his wife when he played at a public function while actress Lauren Bacall sat provocatively on the piano, shown here. Bess Truman said Harry looked a bit too captivated by the beautiful starlet. (Harris and Ewing, Courtesy of Harry S. Truman Library)

John F. Kennedy wasn't a big fan of classical music but his wife Jacqueline was, and she arranged a series of concerts at the White House that made JFK seem to be a classical aficionado. Here, the first lady and the president greet violinist Isaac Stern in the East Room. (Robert Knudsen. White House Photographs. John F. Kennedy Presidential Library and Museum, Boston)

Bill Clinton has played the saxophone since high school, and used his knowledge of pop music to bond with fellow baby boomers. His appearance on "The Arsenio Hall Show" on June 3, 1992, during which he played "Heartbreak Hotel" wearing sunglasses, caused a sensation during his presidential campaign. (AP Photo/ Reed Saxon)

THE OBAMA FACTOR

President Obama has entered deeper into popular
culture than any other president.

*Obama uses a wide variety of methods to show he is in touch and to communicate
with the country, including social media, the White House website, the mainstream
media, late-night comedy shows, and daytime TV. Here, a photo of candidate Obama
is matched with the iconic "hope and change" poster that became popular during his
successful 2008 campaign. (AP Photo/Mannie Garcia/Shepard Fairey)*

CHAPTER ELEVEN
PRESIDENTS AND THE NEWS MEDIA
TUG OF WAR

In past decades it was considered essential for presidents to stay in the public eye through the "mainstream media," such as major newspapers and the TV and radio networks. That's much less important today because presidents have learned to communicate with vital segments of the country and maintain their celebrity in different, nontraditional ways.

It's still constant warfare, as it has been since the beginning of the republic. But now it's even more hostile. The White House and the news media have entered an era in which neither side trusts the other in almost any way.

Both Democrats and Republicans have contempt for the "mainstream media," and the public is very distrustful of traditional providers of news. I have observed these trends firsthand as the White House correspondent for *U.S. News & World Report* since 1986. As I pointed out in my 1996 book *Feeding the Beast: The White House versus the Press*, we in the news media have become too cynical and have lost touch in some important ways with our readers, viewers, and listeners. Part of the reason is cultural. At the upper levels of the media establishment in Washington, journalists don't live like ordinary middle-class Americans. They make far more money than average citizens and operate in a world that is dominated by politics and government. Too often, Washington journalists—including members of the White House press corps—think that by talking to one another they are really talking to America. Of course they aren't.[1]

"One fundamental fact affecting the relationship between the media and the presidency," I wrote in *Feeding the Beast*, "is that both institutions are changing so drastically that we will hardly recognize either of them within a generation. The media are more competitive than ever, and reporters are trying to set themselves apart by adding opinion or 'edge'—often in the form of a derisive tone or smart-aleck attitude—to their stories or by rushing to judgment about the people, trends, and events they cover. Adding to the problem is that today's news cycle never ends. The traditional morning- and afternoon-edition newspaper and evening-news-show deadlines have been supplanted by round-the-clock internet and televised news capability and coverage: Anything that happens around the world can be shown on America's television and computer screens instantaneously, at any time of day or night. This means the mainstream media are constantly groping for ways to move a breaking story forward by breaking a tidbit of news or quasi-news rather than dealing with a story in depth, and too often the result is sensational, superficial or negative coverage. Just as important, television has greatly accelerated the velocity of White House decision-making and increased the difficulty of governing."[2]

Unable to get what they consider fair treatment from the mainstream media, presidents have become more interested in making their cases to the American people directly. Lately, the White House has been communicating increasingly through the Web and social media. President Obama has taken this trend to a new level, and his successor will certainly adopt his techniques of bypassing the mainstream media. Today, it's easier than ever for a president to circumvent the media and convey to the country what amounts to propaganda about what he is doing and what his policies mean.

A huge shift occurred during Abraham Lincoln's presidency. The Civil War created a massive appetite for news about the conflict between the North and South and the politics behind it. Lincoln came to personify the Union war effort and he therefore drew endless attention, and he used it to good effect to shape public opinion. He also moved aggressively to limit newspaper coverage he didn't like, such as by restricting reporters' access to the telegraph so officials could better control the flow of information about battles.

"Public sentiment is everything," Lincoln once said. "With public sentiment, nothing can fail; without it, nothing can succeed."[3] He devoted much of his presidency to manipulating that sentiment in his favor, as presidents have done ever since. The public's desire for information about the war added to the power of newspapers, which people turned to for news about the conflict, the president, and the government.

"By the end of the Civil War, the press was beginning to cover the White House regularly," writes historian Vicki Goldberg. "Reporters expressed a strong sense that American democracy gave them a right to be in and report on the White House. . . . As mass readership and illustrated publications continued to increase in number, human interest, gossip, and sensationalism increased along with them and extended to the White House."[4]

The press's focus on the personal life of the president greatly expanded. By 1886, when Grover Cleveland got married to a much younger woman, Frances Folsom, newspapers gave the wedding exhaustive coverage and sent reporters to follow the president and his bride on their honeymoon. The newspapers filed an estimated 5,400,000 words of copy over five and a half days. The Clevelands considered all this an outrageous invasion of their privacy, and the incident deepened the president's scorn for the press.[5] I discuss this more fully in Chapter 9, on first ladies.

During Theodore Roosevelt's presidency from 1901 to 1909, reporters got a space in which to work within the West Wing of the White House as they gave the nation's leader more and more coverage. The president set aside a small room for the press in 1902. This encouraged the formation of a permanent White House press corps. Roosevelt believed the owners of the big newspapers didn't like him or his progressive policies limiting the power of big business, but he befriended the reporters and generated good coverage from them.[6]

He pioneered the use of the press to promote himself and his causes. He called the presidency his bully pulpit, and he mastered the art of creating news that was favorable to his administration. He hired a press secretary, as President Grover Cleveland had done in the 1880s, and provided reporters with a large helping of salty remarks, policy pronouncements, and criticisms of big business and greedy corporate executives, a strategy designed to give him the image of an activist and aggressive leader who was looking out for everyday Americans.[7]

Roosevelt would invite half a dozen White House correspondents to watch his 1 p.m. shave every afternoon, and he would entertain them with his observations about issues and people. He brought in individual reporters once or twice a week and would frequently host small groups of journalists in his office for briefings.[8] He understood the importance of showmanship and dramatization in governing. He knew that, with the rise of newspapers as truly mass media accessible to Americans as never before, being a celebrity could help a president hold and maintain the country's attention. This was a lesson that the most effective of his successors would absorb and use to good effect.

Writes Goldberg, "As the technology and reach of the media swelled in the twentieth century, and as the president became ever more the center of government and news, presidential attention to media coverage and ways to obtain and influence it mounted steadily. It is easier, and more likely to intrigue a reader, to focus a story on a man, his actions and personality, than on a policy, particularly one that is complex. Presidential campaigns ultimately became primarily and predominantly media events, and presidencies lean in the same direction. The media and the president frequently have different goals and reciprocal enmities, but they have played with and upon one another as often as against. The media wants both news and stars; the president qualifies on both counts."[9]

* * *

JOHN F. KENNEDY MADE reporters feel as if they were almost partners in governing, showered them with presidential attention, and, in some cases, gave them private access to the president, sometimes over dinner and drinks. That seems extraordinary today.

Kennedy's strategy of granting access resulted in lots of fawning coverage, just what he wanted. "It was Kennedy's show," wrote journalist Richard Reeves. "He was the man in the arena—charming, informed, caring, and witty—gracefully drawing reporters into his cape and even pricking them with his sword on occasion. His dominance in that arena changed the journalism of Washington and, to a large extent, that changed the Presidency and government itself. When Kennedy took office, there had been only a few dozen men and women regularly covering the White House full-time. There were hundreds now as 1962 began. One after another, news organizations shifted their men and women to where the action was. Reporters like Peter Lisagor of the *Chicago Daily News* or Sander Vanocur of NBC News had begun covering the Kennedy administration in the traditional way, checking in daily with the big departments; but within the year, they were covering only Kennedy. The President was gaining more and more control over information going out of the government, information that used to be distributed by Cabinet secretaries, appointees, and civil servants with their own agendas. Reporters and editors, and Republicans, grumbled periodically about 'news management,' but for the gentlemen and ladies of the press it was fair exchange, a lovely affair. And many White House regulars were becoming celebrities themselves."[10]

* * *

LYNDON JOHNSON felt that the media were out to embarrass him. He believed he could never charm them as the urbane and handsome Kennedy had done, and he resented them. Johnson even made a point of complaining about reporters to their bosses, which guaranteed hard feelings.

In 1967 Johnson told NBC President Bill McAndrew that the networks were prejudiced against the administration and he was watching them "like a hawk." This was troubling to TV executives and journalists because TV stations were licensed and regulated by the government and there was concern about retribution. Writes historian Tevi Troy, "Johnson may have been peevish with the press and their network bosses, but that doesn't mean he was wrong about their intentions. They gave him a hard time, and not all of it was of his own making. Reporters had enjoyed their close ties with Kennedy, whom they treated more favorably than the hectoring and often undignified Johnson. As a result, Kennedy was an impossible act to follow, especially after his tragic death. The escalation of the Vietnam War made matters worse, as journalists soured on both the war and on Johnson."[11]

As the Vietnam War intensified, more Americans turned against him, and the media followed public opinion. I remember the chants at antiwar rallies that were widely reported, and therefore magnified, on TV—"Hey, hey, LBJ, how many kids did you kill today?" Seeing the tide of opposition, Johnson didn't seek reelection in 1968.

* * *

RICHARD NIXON, Johnson's successor, made the media–White House relationship even more hostile. As the Watergate scandal unfolded in the early 1970s, it became clear that Nixon had betrayed the nation's trust and poisoned the White House's relationship with the journalism community. Nixon and his men hated the press. From the start, they considered the

Washington and New York media to be overwhelmingly liberal, an enemy to be openly attacked, undermined, and isolated.[12]

Nixon was about as far from a media celebrity as one could get. He made matters worse and seemed ever more cloistered when he created an Office of Communications under former newspaper editor Herbert Klein. This office was designed to carry Nixon's message directly to the regional and local media, which Nixon and his aides felt would be more favorable to him than the national journalists in Washington and New York. Meanwhile, White House press secretary Ron Ziegler jousted with and stonewalled the White House press corps.

Over the years, the communications office would be retained by Nixon's successors, who concluded that it did make sense to bypass the White House press corps. But Nixon and his aides coupled their use of this bypass operation with escalating attacks on the national media, making the president appear overly hostile, defensive, and preoccupied with payback.

"The Nixon administration also was determined to draw attention to mistakes and distortions in the news whenever they occurred," wrote James Deakin, former White House reporter for the *St. Louis Post-Dispatch*. "By itself, this was an entirely legitimate activity. But the Nixon people were not satisfied with merely correcting the record. They set out to convince the American people that the media were distorting the news *deliberately*. It was a conspiracy. Not just the derelictions but the *conspiracy behind them* must be exposed."[13]

Nixon even authorized his vice president, Spiro Agnew, to undertake a nasty series of attacks on the media, which Agnew called the "nattering nabobs of negativism." Agnew also attacked opponents of the Vietnam war as "an effete corps of impudent snobs." (Agnew later resigned in a political scandal.)

With his enemies list, which included journalists that the White House considered anti-administration, Nixon brought the adversarial relationship to a new low. He became widely distrusted and disliked by people in the media, and his public image became thoroughly negative.

*   *   *

RONALD REAGAN and his senior advisers focused day after day on enhancing his image as the celebrity in chief using the mainstream media, mainly television, the dominant medium of the era.

As an actor, Reagan had been trained to operate from a script. He preferred to make news under carefully controlled circumstances, mostly in speeches or brief announcements. Even at news conferences, his staff would anticipate virtually every question, benefiting from the fact that reporters are predictable and would focus on whatever was in that day's news. The president would rehearse his answers carefully. It was the perfect style for TV.

"I have always believed that impressions are more important than specific acts or issues, especially with the president," Michael Deaver, Reagan's chief media strategist, said to me in 1994. "Ronald Reagan used to tell me, 'The camera doesn't lie.'" Deaver tried to place Reagan in interesting, patriotic, or beautiful settings to provide the networks with images they couldn't resist putting on the air, with Reagan front and center as the lead actor in each minidrama.

Often the administration's goal was to create memorable visual moments with Reagan cast as the nation's master of ceremonies, a celebrity whose affable personality and homespun values made him welcome in America's homes through TV. Even though Reagan and his aides believed the news organizations were run by liberals who opposed his conservative agenda, as often as not the administration managed to manipulate the media into providing the coverage they wanted through the use of dramatization and imagery.

In his first inauguration address in January 1981, Reagan set forth a bold call for American optimism and offered the nation his historic conservative agenda. Among the many other telegenic moments orchestrated by Reagan and his aides was his speech honoring the US soldiers who stormed Normandy on D-Day in 1944. On the fortieth anniversary of the Allied invasion in 1984, Reagan delivered one of the most memorable speeches in the history of the presidency when he spoke movingly of the "boys of Pointe du Hoc" who scaled the cliffs in the face of withering fire from Nazi defenders. It was the perfect use of his own celebrity to bestow fame on these former soldiers, who sat before him as greying, balding, and in some cases frail old men. Reagan also gave a brilliant speech to honor the seven astronauts killed in the *Challenger* space-shuttle explosion in January 1986.

It was celebrity in the service of a larger cause, and these moments revealed Reagan as perhaps the best showman who has ever occupied the White House.

*   *   *

GEORGE H. W. BUSH made a fundamental mistake in dealing with the news media: he disdained the idea that he was a celebrity and didn't give journalists or the country a compelling or particularly interesting narrative of his presidency. He held more than 250 press conferences and was a master of the details of policy. But many reporters found him boring, and the country largely agreed.

Bush told aides that his mother had always warned him against "the great 'I am,'" and he took her advice to heart. He kept things low-key and understated, and this was quite a letdown after eight years of glamour and excitement under Reagan. During his first twenty-two months in office Bush made the evening news only one-third as often as Reagan had.[14]

Marlin Fitzwater, Bush's press secretary, set the tone during a speech at the National Press Club in March 1989 when he described his boss's minimalist approach to the news. "There are not enough stories out of the White House to keep one honest person doing an honest day's work," Fitzwater said. "What's happened is this: An exaggerated preoccupation with the White House has forced stories to come from the president that should be coming from the secretary of state, the secretary of defense, or any one of the other cabinet officials who help run the government. And so one of my pieces of advice to those who really want to improve the quality of White House journalism is, back off! Let real people do real work."[15]

This was an admirably candid assessment, but it described a communications philosophy that diminished Bush's presidency by lowering expectations too much. This doesn't work well in the era of the twenty-four-hour news cycle when a president is expected to be engaged and entertaining, not just quietly competent.

Bush brilliantly presided over the unraveling of the Soviet empire and the Persian Gulf War, but by 1992, when he was up for reelection, the country had moved on from its earlier focus on foreign policy. Voters wanted the president to emphasize domestic issues, especially the troubled economy, but Bush didn't have the answers and held little celebrity appeal. He lost his bid for reelection to Democratic challenger Bill Clinton.

*   *   *

PRESIDENT BILL CLINTON had a rocky relationship with the news media. He would give reporters and editors plenty of access, then would get angry at negative coverage and go through a phase when he would limit access. But he always returned to court his media adversaries because he felt that, on balance, it was best not to keep them at arm's length for too long because they would punish him with negative stories.

Mike McCurry, his White House press secretary, set an important precedent when he allowed live television coverage of his daily briefings. This turned the sessions into TV shows, with network reporters trying to show off for their bosses and their viewers by attempting to entrap, embarrass, and tangle with the press secretary on live TV. The daily briefings became a form of theater, and the press secretary became more of a celebrity in his own right.

McCurry has apologized to his successors for allowing the live coverage in the first place. He told me the briefings were more civil and intelligent when the cameras were turned off. Televised briefings have become next to useless as a way to inform the country because they are so adversarial and so dominated by preening TV reporters. But no press secretary has dared to end the practice of live coverage because the outrage of the networks and their payback would be too hard to bear.

One of the most important developments in presidential press relations that occurred during the Clinton administration was an unfortunate and destructive one—the coarsening of presidential coverage brought on by the Monica Lewinsky sex-and-lies scandal. Clinton at first denied, and then admitted, having an affair with Lewinsky, a former White House intern. He was under investigation for another matter at the time and, when asked about the affair, he lied about it under oath. Some members of Congress felt that this perjury was an impeachable offense, and the House of Representatives proceeded to impeach Clinton for it. The Senate acquitted him, but the yearlong story of the affair plunged the media and the nation into a soap opera of salacious details, denials, and revelations about the most private aspects of the president's life.

I covered all of this as the White House correspondent for *U.S. News & World Report*, and I found myself, along with other journalists, reporting and writing about things I never expected to deal with, such as the president's most intimate predilections. Clinton's conduct, paraded through the judicial system, dragged everyone involved through the muck and in many ways brought out the worst in everyone.

It also, in a strange way, added to Clinton's celebrity. He was considered a rascal with a flawed character. But his efforts to fight the charges and stay in office revealed a remarkable lack of shame and an amazing persistence in defending himself, and spawned endless jokes about his personal life from comedians and among everyday people. In the end, Americans decided that while Clinton had many personal faults, his policies were sound and he was a good president. His popularity actually increased over the course of the Lewinsky revelations and the many investigations by Congress, the independent counsel Kenneth Starr, and the news media.

*   *   *

PRESIDENT GEORGE W. BUSH got the benefit of the doubt from the news media and the country after the terrorist attacks of September 11, 2001. That's when two US airliners were hijacked and crashed into the World Trade Center towers in New York City, and a third plane was commandeered and flown into the Pentagon. Three thousand people died in New York alone and the images of the planes hitting the towers were played and replayed endlessly on TV, becoming etched in the nation's psyche. These acts shocked the country and had a rally-around-the-commander-in-chief effect most common during international crises. Bush's job-approval ratings soared and people at first liked his bravado and his relentless pursuit of a global "war on terror."

But over time, especially after Bush ordered the invasions of Iraq and Afghanistan as payback for the attacks and amid a deteriorating economy, public opinion about him turned negative. Afghanistan was the site for terrorist bases, so that invasion made sense even if the US and allied troops initially deployed were inadequate and had to be beefed up later. However, the Iraq invasion was a different story.

Bush argued that Iraqi leader Saddam Hussein had weapons of mass destruction that threatened his neighbors and the United States, and his brutal regime had to be deposed. The US news media were criticized, in retrospect, for giving too much credence to Bush's shaky claims, and no such weapons were found after the invasion, to the embarrassment of Bush and the media.

Most major news organizations initially went along with Bush's reliance on machismo and swagger in waging war, and this reflected public opinion in the first months after 9/11. Americans wanted retribution, and they wanted their president to, above all, keep them safe. For a while Bush's strong leadership and decisiveness matched the country's mood. After his first eight months in office, during which he appeared to be floundering, he suddenly became a celebrity—portrayed in the media as a man of fierce conviction who would go all out to decimate America's mortal enemies and protect the homeland. When he addressed firefighters and other first responders with a bullhorn from the smoking rubble of the World Trade Center towers a few days after the attacks, it was an iconic moment aired again and again on television. He seemed to speak for the country when he expressed defiance toward what he called the "evildoers" and promised a powerful response. The media covered him in an almost totally positive way and the nation turned to the president for leadership in this time of trouble. For months, 80 percent of Americans approved of his job performance.

When he threw out the ceremonial first pitch at a Yankees playoff game in New York not long after 9/11—from the pitcher's mound and in full view of the crowd—he got a huge ovation. He said privately that he felt his standing was amazingly high. Even when his motorcade sped through the streets of New York on official visits, he got applause and cheers from bystanders even though he had not won the city or the state in the 2000 election.

The predictions of an easy US victory in Iraq came true in the first phase of the war, which involved defeating the badly outmatched Iraqi military. But with the removal of strongman Hussein, the age-old antagonisms in Iraqi society—largely among the Shiites, Sunnis, and Kurds—began to erupt again.

Still, the media gave Bush the benefit of the doubt in a surge of patriotism. It was "us against them," and the media sided with Bush and America's men and women in uniform. "Confronting unfathomable horror, the press largely abdicated its watchdog role," wrote media critic Rachel Smolkin.[16]

On May 1, 2002, Bush flew to the USS *Abraham Lincoln* as a passenger aboard a Navy jet, walked across the aircraft carrier's deck in a form-fitting flight suit, and gave a victory speech in front of a sign that read, "Mission Accomplished." The mission had assuredly not been accomplished, but some in the TV networks and with other major media outlets gave Bush's performance rave reviews. John Gibson, a host on Fox News, the most conservative of the cable networks, said Bush showed up on the carrier in "historic, spectacular fashion." Newsman John Elliott of MSNBC, then evolving into a liberal network, said the event was "cool" and "history in the making." Various cable networks gave live coverage to Bush's *Top Gun* moment, elevating its importance and adding to his celebrity as a macho leader.[17]

Throughout Bush's eight years in office, the media strategy of Bush's high command, which senior Bush advisers described to me and other White House reporters, was based on the idea that news about the administration and the president was a valuable commodity that could improve the bottom line of news organizations who received and used it. So White House officials felt they were doing news organizations a big financial favor by providing information. This was partly true, but it was a remarkably cynical and materialistic way of looking at the media. It didn't account for the First Amendment stipulation that the media are essential for effective and democratic governance.

*   *   *

BARACK OBAMA'S RELATIONS with the mainstream media started off well. The media shared his goal of spreading favorable stories about the young and vigorous new president, who was a historic figure from day one because he was the first African American to hold that office.

But the relationship gradually deteriorated and tensions grew with members of the White House press corps, who complained about lack of access to the president and to his senior staff. This wasn't of as much concern to Team Obama as it had been to previous administrations. Obama and his advisers didn't think they needed the mainstream media as much as their predecessors, and they didn't much like reporters and their "gotcha" ways. They believed, accurately, that they could bypass the traditional media of broadcast networks and big newspapers and magazines, and communicate directly with the public, especially the president's supporters, through the Internet and social media. Obama was able to sell himself and his programs, at least for the first four years of his presidency, through email, YouTube, Flickr, the White House website, Facebook, MySpace, LinkedIn, and other new media, and by carefully feeding positive information to the mainstream media.

Adding insult to injury, the president said he didn't watch much television news, an avoidance he shared with many other Americans. He conceded, though, that he read some magazines and newspapers such as the *New York Times* and the *Washington Post*.[18] Many reporters complained about receiving angry and sometimes abusive phone calls and emails from White House officials criticizing their stories. As a White House correspondent for *U.S. News*, I was on the receiving end of some of these unpleasant broadsides. So was Bob Woodward of the *Washington Post*, who helped to break the Watergate scandal that led to the resignation of President Richard Nixon. Woodward got into a much-publicized fuss with Obama's economic adviser Gene Sperling, and the reporter took offense when Sperling told him in an email that he would "regret" criticizing the White House over a budget battle in 2013.[19]

The Obama White House also declared war on Fox News for being too conservative and biased against the Democratic president. Obama had ample justification for reaching this conclusion, but the administration may have let the problem get too personal, causing Fox to become even more critical. Anita Dunn, who was a White House spokeswoman at the time, said, "What I think is fair to say about Fox—and certainly it's the way we view it—is that it really is more a wing of the Republican Party."[20]

A survey of White House correspondents by *Politico* in April 2014 showed how much the relationship between the White House and the press corps had deteriorated. Half the reporters surveyed said a White House official had lied to them, and 42 percent agreed that Obama had the "most secretive" White House they had ever encountered; 39 percent said at least one White House official had sworn at them.[21]

Obama added to the frustration of the regulars in the White House press corps by granting much-sought-after interviews not to them, but to TV anchors and famous media personalities—including comedian Jon Stewart, host of *The Daily Show*, where Obama drew 3.6 million viewers, far more than the 2 million who usually watched the program.[22]

Obama did try to keep lines of communication open to journalists he thought could help him. He sometimes met with them privately and off the record, as he did on May 27, 2014, when he talked with a handful of foreign-policy specialists and other journalists, including Thomas Friedman of the *New York Times*, Fareed Zakaria of CNN, and Gerald Seib of the *Wall Street Journal*. They met for ninety minutes over lunch in the Roosevelt Room of the White House.[23] But these sessions were unusual. In general, Obama kept his distance from the mainstream media.

Chapter Twelve
Presidents and the Movies
Cinema Stars

It was inevitable that as America became more of a visual culture, our presidents would realize the need to connect with a key industry of visual entertainment—movies.

"It's hard not to acknowledge the staggering impact of visual imagery on modern life," writes public-opinion analyst Frank Luntz. "We are all overstimulated—or is it narcotized or lobotomized—by film, television, billboards, and now, the Internet. The amount of information we consume grows ever greater, even as our collective attention span shrinks."[1]

Cultural historian Fred Inglis writes, "Political leaders and cinema stars are intensely familiar (one of the family) by way of the cinema screen, and (at first) by way of their voices on the living room radio, but physically and in terms of how we all need to feel the directness of experience, they have the remoteness of the supernatural. This is the compound which makes for the sacredness of celebrity and may suggest the reason why people both worship *and* vilify the famous. The invention of stardom and the instantaneous mass publicity it released by way of the new media from 1919 onwards twined together in a strong rope of meaning some of the strongest and strangest passions of modern society. The irresistible shine of money was added to the new emphasis given by the advertising industry to physical desirability and youthfulness. . . . All these ingredients come together in the compulsion of the new value, *glamour*. Our nineteenth-century history prepares the ground, and the twin forces of propaganda and stardom join in completing the manufacture of celebrity as it will be constituted from the 1920s to the present."[2]

Film has become a central part of American culture, and the presidents' tastes in movies reveal a lot about their characters and values. Making these tastes known to the public also shows the kind of image they want to present to the world as they try to stay in touch with their constituents and shape their own celebrity.

And the way in which presidents are portrayed on film provides many insights into the way Americans see their top leader. Author Gene Healy writes, "The Clinton era saw a burst of big-screen portrayals of the president, at least half of which reflected a post-Watergate sensibility, depicting the officeholder as worse than the ordinary run of humanity. In *Clear and Present Danger* (1994), for example, top CIA official Jack Ryan (Harrison Ford) battles with Colombian drug lords and his own crooked commander in chief, who has caused enormous bloodshed by ordering covert actions in defiance of Congress. . . . In the 1997 thriller *Absolute Power*, the president's taste for rough sex leads to an elaborate cover-up after a resisting paramour gets shot by the Secret Service. And in *Mars Attacks* (1996), *Murder at 1600* (1997), *Wag the Dog* (1997), *Primary Colors* (1998), and *Dick* (1999), the Hollywood president was a criminal, a fool, or—as often as not—both."

Healy continues, "Yet, even amid the silver-screen cynicism the yearning for *Camelot* persisted. Several of the more popular presidential movies of the 1990s enthusiastically embraced the heroic presidency. Rob Reiner's 1995 romantic comedy *The American President* featured Michael Douglas as President Andrew Shepherd, a Democrat and widower who falls in love with an environmental lobbyist (Annette Benning) and discovers his inner Bobby Kennedy. . . . In the hit films *Independence Day* (1996) and *Air Force One* (1997), our superhero president fights all enemies foreign, domestic—and extraterrestrial. . . . Ivan Reitman's 1993 comedy *Dave* didn't offer the cathartic violence of *Air Force One*, but it captured Americans' conflicting attitudes toward the office perhaps better than any other presidential movie of the era. In a twist on the familiar 'evil twin' genre, *Dave* gave Americans two presidents, the corrupt William Harrison Mitchell and his noble doppelganger Dave Kovic, both played by Kevin Kline."[3]

*   *   *

PRESIDENTS HAVE REFLECTED popular tastes in their preferences for films, which helped them keep in touch. And several presidents, in the privacy of the White House residence, enjoyed adult-rated fare.

Author Meriah Doty writes, "By and large when it comes to screening films in the White House theater, presidents for the most part play to their type-casting. George W. Bush watched a lot of war films including *Black Hawk Down*. The Obamas have shown historical dramas including [the] Jackie Robinson biopic '42,' and that film about living and working inside the White House itself, *The Butler*."[4]

A key moment came in 1915 when Woodrow Wilson became the first president to screen a film at the White House. It was D. W. Griffith's racist epic about the post–Civil War era, *Birth of a Nation*. The film is considered a landmark in popularizing cinema, but it also presented a bigoted view of African Americans after the Civil War, with a positive portrayal of the Ku Klux Klan. Wilson had been brought up in Virginia and had racist attitudes, and during his administration he resegregated much of the federal government in Washington. Wilson's screening of the film at the White House helped legitimize the movie for the viewing public.[5]

*   *   *

BUT THE FIRST PRESIDENT to truly understand the power of motion pictures was Franklin D. Roosevelt, who grasped that films could unite the nation with a shared cinematic experience. He also saw that film stars were becoming celebrities whose endorsements could help him politically.

In September 1932, just before the election that would place FDR in the White House, Hollywood producers and stars honored the Democratic presidential nominee with a huge Motion Picture Electrical Parade and Sports Pageant at Olympic Stadium in Los Angeles. Roosevelt sat in a flag-draped box seat and watched contentedly as the major stars of his day showered him with praise or greeted him warmly, one by one. Those attending included Wallace Beery, Charlie Chaplin, Claudette Colbert, Marion Davies, Irene Dunne, Clark Gable, Boris Karloff, Stan Laurel and Oliver Hardy, Tom Mix, William Powell, and Loretta Young. Humorist Will Rogers was master of ceremonies, and 75,000 people attended. Money raised at the event went to help down-on-their-luck actors, actresses, and other employees in the movie industry, and disabled children.[6]

By 1940, as he was seeking a third term, the Hollywood elite was more committed to Roosevelt than ever. In September a variety of show-business folks formed the official Hollywood for Roosevelt Committee, with Pat O'Brien as chairman and Joan Bennett as vice chairwoman. Among the members were Humphrey Bogart, James Cagney, Henry Fonda, Betty Grable, Katharine Hepburn, and Dorothy Lamour.[7] "Roosevelt's outreach to Hollywood, both to the stars themselves and to the increasingly powerful studio heads, proved fantastically fruitful," historian Tevi Troy writes. He was depicted favorably in various films.[8]

During his first few years in office, Roosevelt often saw four or five movies a week. On a five-week goodwill tour of South America in 1936, he had his staff bring twenty-six films and he watched most of them to relax. He liked to have a newsreel and cartoon shown before a feature, as was the custom in movie theaters at the time, and he got a good laugh from the adventures of Walt Disney's Mickey Mouse. His moviegoing decreased, however, when the United States entered World War II in 1941 and the conflagration absorbed his attention.[9]

FDR's rules for moviegoing were to screen only films that were not "sad" and that weren't "too long," his wife Eleanor reported. He saw them as a means of escape. Among the movies he particularly enjoyed were Disney's 1937 animated classic *Snow White and the Seven Dwarfs* (twice); *I'm No Angel*, a 1933 comedy starring Cary Grant and Mae West; 1940's *Abe Lincoln in Illinois*, starring Raymond Massey; and 1934's *Judge Priest*, starring humorist Will Rogers.[10] In 1942 FDR installed a movie theater in the White House's East Wing residential quarters to make it easier for him to host screenings, and it's still used today.

*   *   *

HARRY TRUMAN wasn't a fan of films, and he had no interest in or sensitivity to Hollywood culture or movie stars themselves. At first, he didn't realize how his association with a movie personality could be an embarrassment. This became clear in 1945, while Truman was still vice president and only a few weeks before he succeeded to the presidency upon Franklin Roosevelt's death. The twenty-year-old starlet Lauren Bacall climbed on top of a piano that Truman was playing at the National Press Club, where both of them were attending a function. News photographers captured the image, which ran in newspapers across the country. The grinning president, wearing his conservative wire-rimmed glasses, looked a bit too delighted in the presence of the sexy actress, whose legs were exposed provocatively on the piano right in front of his face. First lady Bess Truman was miffed, and told her husband that the photo was undignified as well as inappropriate during wartime. From then on, Truman and his handlers were more careful about avoiding such embarrassing situations.[11]

*   *   *

DWIGHT EISENHOWER, who followed Truman as president, was a movie fan. He watched more than 200 films in the White House screening room during his eight years in office. He loved Westerns, especially *High Noon* with Gary Cooper, which featured a brave lawman fighting an evil gang even though the local townspeople refused to help.[12] (This theme and Cooper's heroic portrayal appealed to other presidents, too, including Ronald Reagan, George W. Bush, and Bill Clinton. Perhaps they saw themselves as the film's hero.)

Ike, who grew up in the Western town of Abeline, Kansas, once said he loved Westerns because they were fun to watch and took his mind off his duties. Others weren't impressed with his cinematic tastes. To the consternation of some of his visitors, Ike liked the 1958 Western *The Big Country,* starring Charlton Heston and Gregory Peck, so much that he showed it several times to guests. British prime minister Harold Macmillan attended one screening at Eisenhower's farm in Gettysburg, Pennsylvania, and said later that he couldn't even remember the film's title. He called it "*The Great Country* or some such name."[13] The film left a lasting negative impression on the British leader. He wrote in his diary, "It lasted three hours! It was inconceivably banal."[14]

Ike also had some strong personal feelings about what he was watching. He would stalk out of screenings when actor Robert Mitchum was on screen because he couldn't abide Mitchum's marijuana use and the fact that he had served time in prison for possession in 1948.[15] In dealing personally with Hollywood stars, however, Eisenhower did well, although he was not as successful as several of the Democrats who followed him into the White House, such as John F. Kennedy. Among Eisenhower's supporters in the film industry were performers Fred Astaire, Gary Cooper, Clark Gable, Mary Martin, Ethel Merman, Jimmy Stewart, Ronald Reagan, and John Wayne, and studio executive Jack Warner.[16]

* * *

ALTHOUGH JOHN F. KENNEDY was no great fan of movies, he liked to have them shown periodically in the White House theater as a way for him to relax and escape the duties of office. He particularly enjoyed films about the rakish British spy James Bond, starring actor Sean Connery, and he screened the 1963 Bond hit *From Russia with Love* on the evening before he was assassinated in November 1963. He told friends he liked *Goldfinger*, the book, but he died before the film version came out in 1964.[17] On October 23, 1963, a month before he was killed, he slipped out of the White House with journalist Ben Bradlee and saw *Dr. No*, another Bond thriller, at a local theater. "Kennedy seemed to enjoy the cool and the sex and the brutality," Bradlee recalled.[18]

Among the other films JFK liked were *Red River*, a 1948 Western starring John Wayne as a cowboy hero; *Bad Day at Black Rock*, a 1955 offering starring Spencer Tracy as an FBI agent dealing with a racist murder; and *Casablanca*, the 1942 classic starring Humphrey Bogart as a jaded nightclub owner who decides to resist the Nazis.[19]

Kennedy tried to give the impression that he was up to date on films in an effort to seem connected to popular culture. Among the forty-eight films he watched as president, according to the White House projectionist and others, were macho movies such as *From Here to Eternity* (1953) and *Bridge on the River Kwai* (1957), Alfred Hitchcock movies, and on a less serious, escapist level *Expresso Bongo* (1959). He watched 1953's *Roman Holiday*, starring Audrey Hepburn, one of his favorite actresses, during the Cuban Missile Crisis to take a break and clear his mind.[20]

JFK's favorite movie, though, was *Spartacus*, a 1960 epic starring Kirk Douglas as a slave who leads a revolt against the Roman Empire. Kennedy couldn't see it in the White House because the projector there was for 35-millimeter films and *Spartacus* was in 70 millimeter, so he went to a downtown Washington, DC, theater with a friend and some Secret Service agents and slipped in when the lights went down. He said it was the best film he had ever seen, which boosted attendance around the country.[21]

Kennedy had strong dislikes in films, and he wasn't reluctant to show his feelings. A friend said, "If he becomes bored he may order that the last reel be shown so he can see how everything turned out, or leave without a word." Biographer William Manchester listed three movies that Kennedy had walked out on: *Butterfield 8* (1960), starring Elizabeth Taylor;

One, Two, Three (1961), featuring James Cagney; and *The Misfits* (1961), starring Marilyn Monroe and Clark Gable.[22]

His bad back made it uncomfortable to sit for long periods of time. One White House guest recalled Kennedy watching Kirk Douglas in 1962's *Lonely Are the Brave*, with the president lying on a bed placed in the front of the family theater, his head propped up on pillows.[23]

*   *   *

LYNDON B. JOHNSON didn't like movies at all. They bored him and he could rarely sit through one. But he did screen a film at the White House a few times, a documentary about the Texas hill country where LBJ was raised and about Johnson's boyhood. He considered the film quite flattering.

*   *   *

RICHARD NIXON saw a wide variety of movies as president—in the White House, at Camp David, and at his retreats in Key Biscayne, Florida, and San Clemente, California. He liked historical epics, Westerns, war movies, musicals, and romantic comedies. His favorite actor was John Wayne but he also appreciated action hero Clint Eastwood. His favorite movie, aides said, was *Around the World in Eighty Days*, based on the novel by Jules Verne and released in 1956, and he saw it repeatedly. He also saw the 1970 film *Patton*, starring George C. Scott as the famous US general George Patton, several times. He enjoyed *The Grapes of Wrath* from 1940, *Citizen Kane* from 1941, *War and Peace* from 1956, and *A Man for All Seasons* from 1966.[24]

This list reveals a sophisticated appreciation for the best in cinema, but if Nixon drew from movies any broader understanding of American culture, it didn't show. One indication of his political philosophy and his resentments came when he walked out on 1961's *West Side Story*, the famous musical about gangs in New York, because, an aide said, "he couldn't stand the propaganda." Presumably the film's theme of the need for interracial understanding and its sometimes lighthearted view of gangs ran counter to his tough-minded views about the need for law and order, one of his favorite political themes.

*   *   *

JIMMY CARTER ENJOYED movies more than most other presidents. He watched 480 films during his four-year presidency, an average of 120 a year, or 10 films a month. In his typically systematic way, he asked an aide to give him a list of the films he most needed to see to keep up on popular culture or simply for relaxation. Then he would proceed to methodically watch them. Two days after his January 1977 inauguration, he saw *All the President's Men*, released the previous year, about the Watergate scandal. The film reinforced the notion during the 1976 campaign that the Nixon administration was corrupt, a perception that Carter was also trying to convey. Carter didn't have time to see it until after he took office.[25]

He was a devout Christian, but his desire to stay in touch with popular culture led him to see the titillating *Midnight Cowboy*, an Academy Award winning film released in 1969 about a male prostitute in New York City. The movie was initially rated X, but later changed to R.[26]

Other movies that gave Carter a respite from his duties were 1974's *The Longest Yard*, starring Burt Reynolds; and Woody Allen's *Manhattan* (which Carter saw twice in May 1979, the month after its release). He also viewed two controversial movies about the Vietnam era, *The Deer Hunter* and *Apocalypse Now* (released in 1978 and 1979, respectively). He wasn't sure how to interpret *Apocalypse Now* but felt "deeply moved" by *The Deer Hunter* and its depiction of how the war had scarred many of the American soldiers who fought it.[27]

*   *   *

RONALD REAGAN HAD a unique connection to the film industry. He was the only president who had been a movie star.

He had specialized in playing likable average fellows, as he did in *Knute Rockne, All-American* in 1940, *Kings Row* in 1942, and *Bedtime for Bonzo* in 1951.

"Movies helped shape Reagan's presidency," writes historian Paul F. Boller Jr. "He brought the style, manners, gestures, attitudes, and even ideas he'd learned in movie-making to his work as President. In his speeches he liked to quote from movie dialogue, referred to episodes in films that he believed taught lessons, and sometimes discussed some of the events portrayed in movies as if they had actually happened. Movies, moreover, became one of the chief sources of entertainment for Reagan and his wife Nancy (who had made films, too, including one in which the two appeared together), when they spent their evenings together. The

Reagans were both avowed film addicts. At Camp David on weekends, and sometimes during evenings at the White House, they watched movies, mostly 'golden oldies,' and consumed popcorn before retiring for the night. Reagan's preference was for science fiction, westerns, and war movies, while his wife liked romantic comedies. They rarely picked films made after the 1960s, because they regarded the newer ones as vulgar and too sexually explicit."[28]

His critics were unsettled when it turned out that one of Reagan's own movies, *Murder in the Air*, from 1940, was based on the idea that a ray gun had been invented that could shoot down aircraft far in the distance. Reagan never forgot this premise and some believed it was what led him to promote the Strategic Defense Initiative (SDI), which was a theoretical system for shooting down enemy missiles after they had been launched. Fittingly, the nickname given to SDI by the media was "Star Wars," drawn from still another movie.

He was also impressed by the 1951 film *The Day the Earth Stood Still*, about a powerful alien and a giant robot who visit Earth. The alien warns humans to get along and end their fixation with nuclear weapons, or be destroyed. This seems to have partly motivated Reagan to offer to share SDI technology with the Soviet Union after reformer Mikhail Gorbachev took over the Kremlin.

Reagan, who celebrated traditional values such as commitment to family, loved the family-themed 1965 movie *The Sound of Music*, starring Julie Andrews. He once was asked by his chief of staff James Baker why he had fallen behind one evening in reading his paperwork. "Well, Jim," he replied, "*The Sound of Music* was on last night."[29] It was also reported that in 1985, when Reagan was serving his second term, five-year-old Chelsea Clinton, who would later live in the White House with her father Bill Clinton, referred to the musical in a letter to Reagan before he visited a German cemetery containing the graves of Nazis. "Dear Mr. President," Chelsea wrote, "I have seen *The Sound of Music*. The Nazis don't look like nice people. Please don't go to their cemetery." Reagan proceeded with the visit, which he said was designed to promote understanding.[30]

Reagan's values also were reflected in movies featuring patriotic themes and larger-than-life cultural heroes who often started out as everyday people but overcame great adversity to prevail. Among them were *Uncommon Valor* (1983), in which a father leads a mission to rescue his son held as a prisoner of war in Indochina, and *First Blood* (aka *Rambo*, 1982), in which Sylvester Stallone stars as a Vietnam veteran fighting the Establishment at home and, later, in a sequel, in which the action hero undertakes a mission to free hostages in Vietnam.[31]

Reagan loved to watch films in the White House, at Camp David, and at his ranch in Santa Barbara, California. He preferred to see movies accompanied by his wife, as if it were a date. They often would hold hands. But like other presidents, including George H. W. Bush and Bill Clinton, Reagan would also invite several people and sometimes more to join them. On those occasions, watching movies became a group event and a social experience.

Marlin Fitzwater, Reagan's White House press secretary, told me that the president sometimes wept during movies. He connected with them emotionally, and this personal reaction gave him a deep understanding of the power of film and television to influence people. Sometimes his emotional reactions took people by surprise. After a showing of *Bedtime for Bonzo*, in which Reagan had starred with a chimpanzee, the lights came on in the White House Family Theater, and a guest noticed that the president was crying. Reagan, noticing the man's concern, explained, "I loved that chimp."[32]

"Carter saw movies as an escape, while Reagan understood their ability to shape the American psyche," writes Troy. "The contrast between the two men was revealing. Reagan saw that America is more than just a country; it's an idea. So he understood how images captivate and transform Americans, who are always dreaming and aspiring. Carter saw art as the depiction of a mechanistic world that needs technocrats to repair it."

Troy explains, "Reagan's idealism meant that he was far less interested in the cutting-edge movies of his day than was Carter. The former actor understood the importance of culture in politics, and he liked films of a bygone era, when patriotic, hard-working Americans strove to make a better life for themselves. The films of the 1970s began to yield dark and morally ambiguous tendencies, calling into question the central aspects of the American character—and even the certainty that the good guys would prevail. When Reagan watched movies, and especially when he talked about movies, he had little interest in such ambiguity."[33]

Reagan described his elaborate movie-watching routine at Camp David this way: "I usually took a pile of homework and made my weekly radio broadcast during our weekends at Camp David. But there was almost always time to relax in front of a fire with a book. When the weather was right, we'd go swimming; during the summer, we often ate our meals on the patio. There were always a dozen or so members of the White House staff with us, and on Friday and Saturday nights we usually all got together to watch a movie with big baskets of popcorn in front of us. . . . At first, the movies we watched were new or recent releases from Hollywood. Then I began trying to sandwich in a few older movies from my generation. Before long, the staff, most of whom were relative youngsters, only wanted to see golden oldies; so each Saturday night we'd bring out an old movie featuring stars such as Clark Gable and Barbara Stanwyck, Humphrey Bogart and Jimmy Cagney, and occasionally a couple of actors named Reagan and [Nancy] Davis [who became Nancy Reagan]."[34] The staff took a different view. They said they asked to see the oldies because they thought the president wanted to see them, not because of their own preferences.

Reagan aides told me they hadn't been sure of the protocol when they attended their first screenings with the president. Should they sit silently? Was small talk allowed? How about making remarks about the movie itself? Was it proper to address the president during a screening? What they learned was that Reagan, ever the traditionalist, wanted to replicate the movie theaters of his youth, which meant whispering an occasional remark if someone felt moved to speak but largely watching the movie and keeping quiet.

Among the movies that Reagan watched as president were 1980's *Breaker Morant*; 1981's *Chariots of Fire*, *Gallipoli*, *The French Lieutenant's Woman*, and *Continental Divide*; 1984's *The Flamingo Kid* and *Places in the Heart*, and 1985's *The Purple Rose of Cairo* and *Witness*. The contemporary films he liked most often included inspirational stories of individuals standing up for what's right, showing courage, or overcoming the odds. This was certainly true of *Chariots of Fire*, *Gallipoli*, and *Witness*. But sometimes the screenings were a flop. Even though White House media adviser Michael Deaver recommended *Kiss of the Spider Woman* (1985), the president and first lady walked out. It apparently was too left-wing-oriented in Reagan's mind, and celebrated the kinds of revolutionaries that the Reagan administration was opposing in Latin America.

"For all the accusations that he conflated movies with reality, Ronald Reagan had a profound understanding of how the American people related to movies," Troy writes. "In his youth, motion pictures were a source of inspiration and pride in America. Reagan's presidency reflected that vision. And he also understood the unifying role of popular culture. Americans disagree about policies, but nearly everyone relates to the popular culture—an insight that contributed to Reagan's effective leadership. He built on the optimism of movies, the idea that the underdog can triumph and that good will overcome evil. He then used those ideas in his political life and succeeded by constantly conveying those themes to the receptive American people."[35]

There were, of course, dark and brooding movies during Reagan's era, but Reagan, ever the optimist, saw positives even in *The Deer Hunter*, a violent and often shocking film about the Vietnam War period. He lauded it as "a story of friendship among young men" that was "unashamedly patriotic." He expressed admiration for the boldness and bravery celebrated in the cartoonish and macho Rambo. After a plane was hijacked, Reagan quipped, "Boy, after seeing *Rambo* last night, I know what to do the next time this happens." On another occasion, attempting to confront members of Congress who wanted to increase taxes, he raised the threat of a veto by quoting Clint Eastwood as the title character in 1971's *Dirty Harry*, a movie about a tough rogue cop: "Go ahead—make my day."[36]

Ken Duberstein, former White House chief of staff for Reagan, said the president got support from many of his old friends from his Hollywood days, such as his former agent Lew Wasserman, as well as Bob Hope and Mickey Rooney.[37] He didn't do very well in gaining support from more-contemporary stars because Hollywood by that time had shifted well to the left.

Reagan also understood the limits of celebrity. He didn't want to highlight his connections to Hollywood too much because he thought his critics would use these affiliations and friendships to argue that he was still at his core a B-list movie actor playing another part and not a serious thinker.[38] Reagan's sensitivity about not being taken seriously was evident when an aide suggested that he should be awarded the Nobel Peace Prize, along with then–Soviet leader Mikhail Gorbachev, for their partnership that had eased Cold War tensions. Reagan ruefully dismissed the idea: "I have less of a chance of getting the Nobel Peace Prize than getting an Oscar," he said. He never got either.

*   *   *

GEORGE H. W. BUSH, who followed Reagan in the Oval Office, reached out to the Hollywood crowd during his successful 1988 presidential bid. His effort culminated in the last six weeks of the campaign, when his supporters held ninety events with entertainers and athletes. The seventy-seven actors and actresses who endorsed him included Arnold Schwarzenegger, Bob Hope, Charlton Heston, and Clint Eastwood as well as lesser stars such as Rick Schroder and Efrem Zimbalist Jr.[39]

But after he became president, Bush lost interest in the Hollywood stars. He was too conservative and straight-laced for them, and he realized any efforts he made to court them would be rebuffed. He also exhibited relatively little interest in the films they made.

* * *

BILL CLINTON was a movie buff ever since his younger days in Arkansas, when he enjoyed the 1950s *Flash Gordon* serials; biblical epics such as *The Robe* from 1953, *The Ten Commandments* from 1956 (which he saw twice), and *Ben-Hur* from 1959; and Bugs Bunny cartoons.

As president, Clinton said his favorite movie was 1952's *High Noon*, starring Gary Cooper (which several other presidents admired). Clinton watched *High Noon* twenty times, including a dozen times in the White House, he once said. He wrote in his memoirs, "Over the long years since I first saw *High Noon*, when I faced my own showdowns, I often thought of the look in Gary Cooper's eyes as he stares into the face of almost certain defeat, and how he keeps walking through his fears toward his duty. It works pretty well in real life too."[40]

The list of movies Clinton watched at the White House Family Theater, with screenings nearly every weekend, was enormous. It included classics such as *Casablanca* from 1942, contemporary comedies such as the *Naked Gun* comedy series, and dramas such as *Sling Blade* from 1996. The list also included *Blazing Saddles*, a comedy by Mel Brooks (1974); *Philadelphia*, starring Tom Hanks (1993); *The Hurricane*, featuring Denzel Washington (1999); and *Wolf* starring Jack Nicholson (1994). Moviegoing was a favorite part of his stays at Camp David, the presidential retreat in Maryland's Catoctin Mountains. During one Thanksgiving weekend there, the movies ran from 7 p.m. to 3 a.m. the following day, according to an attendee. The play list included *Space Jam* (1996), *Shine* (1996), *Midnight in the Garden of Good and Evil* (1997), *Shakespeare in Love* (1998), and *Billy Elliott* (1999).[41]

Sometimes Clinton would watch adult fare. *The Apostle*, a 1997 movie about a philandering preacher, was screened the Saturday after the Monica Lewinsky sex-and-lies story broke. Among those attending were first lady Hillary Clinton, actor Robert Duvall, and actress Farrah Fawcett. It was an awkward situation given that the film featured adultery as a major theme. Mrs. Clinton tried to break the tension by quipping, "Another quiet day at the White House." But the discomfort remained.[42]

Troy argues that "Clinton's success stemmed from his serious engagement with popular culture, yet he managed to avoid being tarnished by Hollywood's excesses. He understood that movies had an escapist quality but that they also allowed America to present an idealized version of itself to the world. Presidents, who must present an idealized version of themselves, have succeeded when utilizing movies to convey their best characteristics to the voting public."

Troy continues, "Watching films in the White House to stay up to date or to reward political allies is commendable, but there's a lot more to political power in the movies than only that. The most astute presidents of the cinematic era, such as Clinton and Reagan, have understood that movies tell stories about themselves and about the country that can reach voters with no interest in political speeches but who hold great interest in what is taking place on the silver screen. More than any other medium, the movies help presidents capture the American imagination."[43]

*   *   *

FOLLOWING IN THE FOOTSTEPS OF his father, George W. Bush was not much of a movie buff, but he enjoyed *Austin Powers: International Man of Mystery*, released in 1997, before he became president in 2001. Bush was a fan of several characters in the wacky film, especially "Dr. Evil," and he was known to do a fair impersonation of the character's signature gesture, with a pinkie finger raised to his lips.[44] But he was largely clueless about celebrity culture. During his 2000 campaign, he admitted he had never heard of Leonardo DiCaprio, a megastar from his 1997 film *Titanic*.

As president, Bush watched movies sporadically. He screened *Thirteen Days*, an uplifting film (released in 2000) about the Cuban Missile Crisis that was managed brilliantly by Kennedy, and invited members of the Kennedy family to the White House for the screening. Bush also watched *The Rookie* (2002), about a middle-aged man who becomes a major-league pitcher. This fit in with his background as a former owner of the Texas Rangers baseball team.[45]

*   *   *

BARACK OBAMA's list of favorite movies includes 1972's *The Godfather* and 1975's *One Flew Over the Cuckoo's Nest*, two classic films that critics loved. During his presidency he has shown an eclectic taste, viewing films ranging from *Slumdog Millionaire* to *The Wrestler* (both from 2008) to *Where the Wild Things Are* (2009).[46] His movie-watching habits reveal a curious and nimble mind and an interest in learning as much as possible about the country. These traits were discussed at length in Chapter 7.

CHAPTER THIRTEEN
PRESIDENTS AND READING
GRAVITAS ALERT

With all the new technologies available for instant communication, from the Internet to television, one might think that reading has become a lost art for presidents. It hasn't, and it still enables the nation's leaders to find a valuable link to the world of ideas and especially to history. They don't read newspapers as much as presidents used to, for several reasons: they don't learn much from the press, they feel that the print medium is in decline and they need to focus on other forms of communication such as the Internet and social media, and they don't like to read negative stories about themselves (which tend to be what the newspapers provide).

But books are a different story. The book-publishing industry has had its share of financial problems, but modern presidents still rely on books as a connection to the life of the mind, just as the early presidents such as John Adams and Thomas Jefferson did. President Obama appears to be a voracious reader of books, as were Presidents Truman, Clinton, and Kennedy. This was less true for other modern-day presidents, such as George H. W. Bush and Lyndon Johnson.

"To judge from their reading, the postwar presidents have for the most part been a remarkably serious group," writes historian Tevi Troy. "Presiding over the most powerful country on earth in what has arguably been the most perilous epoch in human history, they have taken their responsibility to heart by reading widely, especially in history and in biography.

However, some have read more widely, and more seriously, than others. And the great readers have not always been the ones you might expect."[1]

*   *   *

HARRY TRUMAN, old-fashioned and proud of it, read books to learn and to relax. He had never attended college but was on a lifelong mission to learn. As president, he loved history and biography, but also whodunits such as the *Perry Mason* series by Erle Stanley Gardner, who would send the president signed copies of his latest work.

"Readers of good books, particularly books of biography and history, are preparing themselves for leadership," Truman said. "Not all readers become leaders. But all leaders must be readers."[2]

Margaret Truman, Harry's daughter, wrote of her father, "He has always been able to read a book or a memorandum with the radio or the phonograph playing and my mother and me conducting a first-class family argument." If the world were about to end, Margaret wrote, "he could not look up until he got to the bottom of the page he was reading."[3]

Dwight Eisenhower liked to read Western novels, such as those of Louis L'Amour and Zane Grey, but he didn't devour books as Truman did. He also showed in other ways that he wasn't an inveterate reader. He wasn't interested in perusing lengthy staff memos or policy analyses unless he felt he had to. He preferred single-page summaries prepared by his staff.

John F. Kennedy was an avid reader, and of course he was the Pulitzer Prize–winning author of *Profiles in Courage*, a study of eight senators who made difficult decisions by staying true to their convictions. But as president his staff probably exaggerated the extent of his reading in order to project the air of an intellectual. This was designed to ingratiate him with influential academics, especially historians, and everyday Americans who wanted their president to be cerebral and in touch with the life of the mind.

One Kennedy reading habit that was probably genuine was his admiration for the books of Ian Fleming about the glamorous and sexy spy James Bond. This not only helped deepen the image of Kennedy as a celebrity who appreciated the cool and the sophisticated; it also aided the sales of Fleming's books. Historian Arthur Schlesinger Jr., a Kennedy White House adviser, later claimed that JFK's "supposed addiction to James Bond" was a "publicity gag."[4] Others suggested that it was a real preference of the president's. Regardless of how sincere it was, the tie to James Bond worked as a public-relations gambit to enhance Kennedy's celebrity.

Richard Nixon shared Kennedy's love of books. He read mostly histories and political biographies as president, often with a view to adding to his understanding of a problem he was dealing with. After a summit meeting with the Soviets, Nixon bought Winston Churchill's World War II analysis *Triumph and Tragedy* to reread the storied British leader's analysis of the historic Yalta conference in which he participated with Franklin Roosevelt and Josef Stalin.

Jimmy Carter was one of the most voracious readers ever to occupy the White House. Reading books had been a habit since he was a child, and he continued it as president. To increase his reading capacity he even took a speed-reading course with his daughter Amy while he was president. His choice of topics was extremely varied, including both nonfiction and fiction, suggesting a deep intellectual curiosity and a desire to stay in touch with life in the country he governed. Among the books he read were Richard Adams's *Watership Down*, Saul Bellow's *Herzog*, and John McPhee's *Coming into the Country*.[5]

Carter, however, didn't use as much common sense as he should have when it came to processing what he read. Pat Caddell, his pollster, knew how much Carter could be enthralled by intellectual arguments leavened by history and references to popular culture, and he wrote what amounted to a book for Carter's consumption about what was wrong with the country. Caddell argued that the United States was undergoing a crisis of confidence, and he spelled out his theory in compelling detail. Carter described his pollster's analysis as "penetrating" and brilliant, and Caddell's opus became the basis for the president's infamous "malaise" speech on July 15, 1979.[6] Other Carter aides nicknamed Caddell's school of thought the "Apocalypse Now" theory, but Carter adopted Caddell's downbeat concepts and entitled his address "Energy and the Crisis of Confidence." He didn't use "malaise," but that's the word that his critics attached to Carter's address. He urged Americans, facing severe problems with the economy, with energy supplies, with social frictions, and with challenges abroad, to begin an era of austerity and to scale down their expectations about the future. "All the legislation in the world can't fix what's wrong with America," Carter said. What was needed was a rebirth of "faith in each other, faith in our ability to govern ourselves, and faith in the future of this nation."[7]

Many voters thought he was blaming the country for his own failings, and his job-approval rating fell to 29 percent by October 1979, according to Gallup. This paved the way for the optimistic Ronald Reagan to defeat him in November 1980.

* * *

RONALD REAGAN had what might be called a hidden life of the mind. His liberal critics didn't think he was very bright and made fun of his intellect. Former Democratic presidential adviser Clark Clifford memorably called him "an amiable dunce."

But as so often happened, Reagan's critics misjudged and underestimated him. Reagan actually had been a reader of books and periodicals since his youth and he kept up the practice as president.[8] He just didn't want to share his reading list with the media because he thought his critics would only use it as fodder to second-guess his choices and find fault with his taste in printed material. He also preferred being thought of as a rugged outdoorsman rather than bookish. He liked volumes about the American West (he had been governor of California) and the outdoors, and nonfiction by conservative authors. One book he did praise publicly—Tom Clancy's Cold War–themed, right-of-center *The Hunt for Red October*, published in 1984—soared in sales after the president lauded it.

Reagan was unusual in that he drew many of his impressions of the world outside the White House from the vast number of letters he received from everyday citizens. He was serious about reading as many of them as he could, and the White House correspondence office would filter them and send him the ones they thought he would be most interested in. He frequently sent back responses and had pen-pal relationships with many Americans. In one such arrangement, he began corresponding with an elementary-school student in Washington, DC, named Rudy Hines, and they kept up their letter writing for years, well beyond Reagan's presidency.

* * *

GEORGE H. W. BUSH was right of center but not an ideologue, so he didn't share Reagan's fascination with conservative writing. In fact, Bush admitted that he wasn't much of a book reader at all. "Now I don't have time," he said during his presidency.[9] Asked about what he planned to do during a 1991 vacation, Bush said, "a good deal of golf . . . a good deal of tennis, a good deal of horseshoes, a good deal of fishing, a good deal of running—and some reading. I have to throw that in there for the intellectuals out there."[10] But he didn't seem serious about it and his aides didn't provide details on his reading material.

Bush did admit to reading one particular volume: *Truman*, David McCullough's 1992 biography of Harry Truman. He apparently did it to boost his own spirits about his prospects in his reelection bid that year. He got inspiration from "Give-'em-Hell Harry" and Truman's come-from-behind victory in 1948.[11] It didn't work. Bush lost.

During my four years covering the Bush presidency for *U.S. News & World Report*, Bush's aides told me repeatedly that he learned about the world, the nation, politics, and Washington not from reading but from the many people he knew personally. He also learned from his long experience in the capital as Ronald Reagan's vice president, director of central intelligence, chairman of the Republican National Committee, and a Republican member of the House, as well as from his years as US ambassador to the United Nations and US envoy to China.

*　*　*

IN CONTRAST, BILL CLINTON loved books, and his range of reading was very wide. He used books to learn about popular culture and issues facing him as president, and his reading was no abstract exercise. Books influenced his thinking on policy. Clinton's reading of Robert Kaplan's *Balkan Ghosts* gave the president insights into the depth of ethnic hatred in the former Yugoslavia and caused him to delay intervening in Bosnia. The author was surprised at his influence. "The idea that any policymaker would read it, I didn't even consider," Kaplan said. "I saw it purely as an entertaining journalistic travel book about my experiences in the 1980s."[12]

Among other books Clinton read while in office were Maya Angelou's *I Know Why the Caged Bird Sings*, one of his all-time favorites; Walter Mosley's detective story *White Butterfly*; Taylor Branch's *Parting the Waters: America in the King Years 1954–63*; Donald Fromkin's *The Way of the World: From the Dawn of Civilizations to the Eve of the Twenty-First Century*; and Gabriel Garcia Marquez's *One Hundred Years of Solitude*.[13]

There was a broader pattern. Clinton not only liked to read; he wanted Americans to know he was reading. It was an effort to expand his celebrity and impress different constituencies that he was paying attention to their history and concerns and taking a broad look at American culture, always trying to update himself. As a result, he and his aides frequently released the titles of the books he was reading or had read and the president often referred to his reading in speeches and interviews.

* * *

GEORGE W. BUSH, like Reagan, had the reputation of being an intellectual lightweight. But he read far more often than his critics imagined. His list of favorites included a biography of baseball great Joe DiMaggio by Richard Ben Cramer, *Joe DiMaggio: The Hero's Life* (Bush had been managing partner of a major-league team in Texas prior to his presidency) and a book by New York Yankees coach Don Zimmer, *Zim: A Baseball Life*. He also read Mark Kurlansky's *Salt: A World History* and Juan Williams's *Enough,* which examines the way African American leaders hadn't adequately addressed the problems in the black community, in addition to books about the Alamo (he had been governor of Texas) and about a key political compromise Henry Clay arranged in Congress prior to the Civil War.

His critics may have been surprised to learn that Bush read 186 books between 2006 and 2008, according to a friend. He was so concerned about the bioterror scenario raised in Richard Preston's *The Cobra Event* that he urged several of his cabinet officers to read it.[14] George W. Bush's aides said he had a book-reading contest in which he and political adviser Karl Rove competed in how many books they could read in a single year. Rove said Bush won.

But Bush didn't want much publicity for his reading habits because he felt that the media and his political critics would make fun of his choices and engage in psychobabble about what it revealed about his psyche.

* * *

FROM HIS DAYS in high school and through college and Harvard Law School, Barack Obama was a voracious reader, especially of the works of African American writers such as Maya Angelou, James Baldwin, W. E. B. Du Bois, Langston Hughes, Toni Morrison, Richard Wright, and Malcolm X.

Obama, a best-selling author before being elected president and a man who has prized formal education throughout his adult life, is one of the presidency's most consistent readers. Among the books he has read as president are Edmund Morris's *The Rise of Theodore Roosevelt*, Daniel Woodrell's *The Bayou Trilogy*, Ward Just's *Rodin's Debutante*, Jonathan

Franzen's *Freedom*, Kent Haruf's *Plainsong*, Richard Price's *Lush Life*, Joseph O'Neill's *Netherland*, and Taylor Branch's *The Clinton Tapes*. He has generally made his choices known and boosted sales of these books in the process.

Unlike other presidents, who rarely read fiction and preferred history and biography, fiction has been a staple of Obama's reading as president, especially during his vacations at Martha's Vineyard in Massachusetts. There, his reading has included Emma Donoghue's *Room*, David Grossman's *To the End of the Land*, and Abraham Verghese's *Cutting for Stone*.[15]

Over the years, and partly because of his readings, Obama has gained a reputation for being an intellectual, embellishing his celebrity in the world of ideas.

His staff makes clear that his interest in books hasn't faded, and they portray him as a man of sophisticated tastes. He has his bases covered— seeming in touch with pop culture through movies and TV, but also in sync with highbrow culture through his reading of books.

CHAPTER FOURTEEN
PRESIDENTS AND SPORTS
LINKS TO EVERYDAY AMERICA

Many presidents have associated themselves with sports, teams, athletes, and competitive activities as a matter of personal interest, to connect with popular culture, and to enhance their own celebrity. In fact, it's remarkable how many presidents have had backgrounds in sports and athletics.

In terms of their personal participation, presidents tend to prefer golf, a companionable game where participants can relax and enjoy each other's company in lush outdoor settings. It's far different from the endless meetings and tedious ceremonial events that make up a president's day at the White House, which makes golf extraordinarily appealing to a chief executive. "I think it's the camaraderie," said Gerald Ford, who loved to play. "You make friends and you expand friendships when you play golf." The disadvantage is that it takes a lot of time, Ford said, but he noted, "It's a good atmosphere for relaxation and escape." He added that golf "is competitive. And I think most presidents are competitive or they wouldn't be there."[1]

Presidents also make a habit of watching popular sports on TV, and promoting this to the country. For years the chief executive has held ceremonies at the White House to honor champions in major sports, ranging from professional baseball to football, basketball, and hockey and including collegiate teams. Presidents like to bask in the reflected glory of nationally or internationally known athletes. By tapping into sports, they also demonstrate their connections to pop culture, with a special goal of appealing to the fans.

*   *   *

NO PRESIDENT has identified himself with sports and athletic competition as thoroughly as Theodore Roosevelt, who made every effort to be larger than life and add to his celebrity.

Roosevelt wasn't shy about using sports to promote himself and his agenda, and in some ways he became America's athletic director. He used hunting and camping trips, which received extensive coverage in the newspapers, the dominant mass medium of his time, to draw attention to his goals of preserving federal land and protecting the environment. By the end of his presidency, he had declared millions of acres of federal land off limits to development, marking the start of the national forest system.[2]

"Sports enabled Roosevelt to keep himself front and center, a veritable Barnum of a three-ring governmental circus," writes historian John Sayle Watterson.[3] As his second term was nearing an end in January 1909, TR decided on one final and very ambitious public-relations gambit. It was a classic, combining a brilliant sense of what would capture public attention with a focus on the fundamental traits of Roosevelt's personality that made him a celebrity.

Roosevelt had been displeased for years at what he considered a decline in physical fitness among many military officers, especially those who were senior in rank. When General J. Franklin Bell suggested that the president invite senior commanders to go on a hike with him, Roosevelt jumped on the idea. During the subsequent hike in the capital's Rock Creek Valley, the president embarrassed many of the officers by leaving them behind and climbing a sixty-foot cliff that many of his companions avoided.[4]

After this experience, he issued an executive order requiring Army and Navy personnel to make a fifty-mile hike over three days and for mounted soldiers to make a ninety-mile ride in three days. And to set an example and perhaps shame some of the more portly officers, the president, who loved such acts of bravado, decided to make the ninety-mile ride himself.[5]

The goal was to reach the town of Warrenton, Virginia, about fifty miles from Washington, and return. It was tougher than he expected. He and his riding partners faced a gale, freezing and muddy roads, and barely adequate horses. Roosevelt was his typical exuberant self, shouting over the wind with stories of his youth, the Civil War, and other topics. Upon his arrival in Warrenton, he found many local residents there to greet him, and he gave them a quick speech, ate a fast meal, and then made the ride back to the White House. Nearly seventeen hours later, amid more sleet, snow, and wind, the ordeal was over.[6] Roosevelt had added another story to the many tales that illustrated his commitment to what he called "the strenuous life."

* * *

HIS SPORTSMAN'S experience led to an enduring tale that permeated popular culture. On a hunting trip in Mississippi in November 1902, about a year after he took over as president, he was so eager to kill a bear that his hunting guide took it upon himself to capture a small, lame black bear and present it for the president to shoot. Roosevelt was appalled at the unsportsmanlike conduct that was being suggested, and, according to the story, had the animal released into the woods.

This became the basis of the "teddy bear." A cartoonist for the *Washington Evening Star* published a drawing that showed TR, as a proud hunter, standing in front of a grateful bear that the president had spared. Over time, cartoonists depicted the bear as an adorable cub tied up at a campfire, and the president as the animal's kindly benefactor. A Brooklyn candy-store owner began selling cuddly reproductions of "Teddy's bears," creating a marketing phenomenon that added to TR's fame.[7]

By another account, a German dressmaker from Giengen, disabled by polio, was making toy bears from pieces of felt and sent some to the United States for sale. The president's daughter, Alice, liked them so much that she had the little bears imported from Germany as decorations for the main table at her wedding in 1905, in honor of her father. The German dressmaker asked the president's permission to use his name for her bears, and Roosevelt agreed.[8] Regardless of how the fad started, in 1907 nearly 100,000 teddy bears were sold in the United States, and they have been part of the toy market ever since.

TR was old-fashioned in his personal philosophy of displaying what he considered the manly virtues of nineteenth-century America, such as aggressiveness, bellicosity, and physical strength, but he was modern in his outlook on using the federal government to right society's wrongs and limit unbridled corporate power. "By Roosevelt's presidency," Watterson writes, "automobiles had begun to replace horses, though Roosevelt would remain a man on horseback who loved riding and insisted on traveling in horse-drawn carriages. Like his contemporaries, he played tennis (though not golf) and polo, and exercised daily on horseback. Yet TR never quite fit into the formal mold of an eastern aristocrat. Just as he had done in his father's house, Roosevelt would transform the White House into a sporting arena, while the District of Columbia and the wild spots in and around it became the equivalent of Roosevelt's backyard frontier. Although the media heard more than they saw of Roosevelt's sporting pursuits, they would use their growing capacity for image building to publicize the president's sporting exploits. Roosevelt's hunting and hiking trips across the West, mixed with political appearances, would create a sporting persona for the president. Politics and sports would forever be joined at the hip."

Watterson continues, "Presidents change and times change, but since the days of Theodore Roosevelt, sports as a central theme of presidential character has become a norm for presidential behavior as well as a vehicle for public relations. To be sure, TR's high energy approach to his sporting interests and to his politics has not yet been matched by any other president in its scope and intensity, but only reproduced in pieces of the whole. The Roosevelt revolution, though unique, is still representative of something at once new and enduring in presidential politics."[9]

TR loved what he called point-to-point hikes or obstacle walks at his estate in Sagamore Hill, New York. He chose an objective in the distance, often from the starting point of his front porch, and he would lead family members and visitors in a straight line to reach it. The goal was to go over or through any obstacle rather than around it, whether it was a stream, a ravine, a thicket, a briar patch, or a wall.[10]

He went horseback riding frequently, both in the Washington area and around Sagamore Hill, often taking jumps with his favorite horse, a big bay named Bleistein.[11] In October 1904, he took a nasty spill. "The President came in this morning badly bunged up about the head and face," Secretary of State John Hay wrote in his diary. "His horse fell with him yesterday and gave him a bad fall." Hay wrote later, "The President's fall from his horse, ten days ago, might have been very serious. He landed fairly on his head, and his neck and shoulders were severely wrenched. For a few days there seemed to be a possibility of meningitis." Hay added, "The President will, of course, outlive me, but he will not live to be old."[12]

He had a similarly bad experience boxing in the White House gym. Sparring with an Army officer, he was hit hard on the forehead and was partially blinded in his left eye. He reluctantly gave up boxing after that and took up wrestling and jujitsu.[13]

Living "the strenuous life," exemplified by working and playing as intensely as possible, he participated in an assortment of athletic endeavors, including hiking, horseback riding, boxing, wrestling, jujitsu, rowing, fencing, and swimming. He also loved tennis, and he had the first White House tennis courts installed in 1902.[14] But he thought the public considered it a rich man's game, so it was one of the few activities that he didn't call attention to, and he never allowed a photo to be published of himself in "tennis costume."[15]

As a man who had developed his body and stamina immeasurably from the time when he was a scrawny youth, Roosevelt believed that Americans were becoming too soft and lazy, and urged his fellow citizens to end their sedentary lifestyles and join him in vigorous pursuits. As one of the most sports-minded of all presidents, he had a fully formed and well-thought-out philosophy about where sports should fit in someone's life. Roosevelt once told Harvard undergraduates, "It is of far more importance that a man should play something himself, even if he plays it badly, than that he should go with hundreds of companions to see someone else play well." He also said, "I trust I need not add that in defending athletics I would not for one moment be understood as excusing that perversion of athletics that would make it the end of life instead of merely a means in life."[16] What he meant was that sports should be part of a well-rounded life, not the be-all and end-all, just as he derided men who devoted themselves solely to business, politics, or the law.

Roosevelt's interest in athletics led him to intervene in a major sports controversy of his time—the savagery of football. He became increasingly concerned about the rising number of serious injuries in the game. In the early 1900s, football was mainly a college sport and it was a brutal spectacle that left several people dead at colleges and prep schools every year. There was no forward pass and the only way to move the ball down the field was to use brute force, which in those days of little or no protective gear meant that severe injuries occurred regularly. The *Chicago Tribune* reported that in 1904 there were 18 football deaths and 159 serious injuries. Some wanted to ban the sport entirely.[17]

Roosevelt concluded that something needed to be done to save football from itself. He stepped in and on October 9, 1905, hosted at the White House a summit meeting of coaches and other representatives of the top football powers at the time: the teams from Harvard, Princeton, and Yale. TR actually loved the game because he believed it toughened the men who played it. "Football is on trial," he told the conference attendees. "Because I believe in the game, I want to do all I can to save it."[18]

His intervention didn't have an immediate effect, but after the brutal 1905 season and prodded by more demands from the president, reforms were accepted in 1906, including legalizing the forward pass, abolishing dangerous mass formations that caused lethal pileups, and creating a neutral zone between offense and defense.[19] TR's participation added to the perception that he would move aggressively to right society's wrongs and take action, even in the area of sports, which had previously been off limits.

*   *   *

WILLIAM HOWARD TAFT, TR's successor, was unable to capture the public's imagination as Roosevelt had. But Taft did earn a place in the history of presidents and sports. He became the first president to throw out the first pitch at a major-league baseball game. It happened on April 14, 1910, and Taft tossed the ball to Walter Johnson, a pitcher for the Washington Senators, in the team's opener against the Philadelphia Athletics. Johnson proceeded to blank the Athletics, 3–0. Taft got extensive coverage in the newspapers, and throwing out the first pitch has become a staple for presidents ever since, connecting the chief executive to millions of baseball fans, if only for a moment.[20]

*   *   *

HERBERT HOOVER was an expert fly fisherman. He purchased a mountain property in Virginia, about 100 miles from Washington, to serve as a presidential retreat and cast his line in the trout stream there on many weekends at the start of his single term in office. But with the arrival of the Depression, he felt it inappropriate to visit the retreat, which he called Camp Rapidan.

After he left office, Hoover went fishing with Dwight Eisenhower in Colorado, and a group of reporters showed up to watch them. This prompted Hoover to observe grumpily to his successor, "I used to believe there were only two occasions in which the American people had regard for the privacy of the president—in prayer and in fishing. I now detect you have lost the second part."[21]

Instead of fishing during the Depression, he resorted to throwing around a ten-pound medicine ball with friends and advisers on the White House lawn for a half hour at 7 a.m. each day except Sundays. The game got the nickname Hooverball. It never caught on with the public, but Hoover said he enjoyed it and felt it kept him in shape and diverted his attention from affairs of state, at least for a while.[22]

*   *   *

FRANKLIN ROOSEVELT was an excellent sailor and he loved both freshwater and deep-sea fishing, which he enjoyed often as president. He learned to swim without using his legs, which were paralyzed from polio, and performed therapeutic exercises in a thermal pool at a health resort in Warm Springs, Georgia. He purchased the resort for his own use and the use of children and others with polio. He enjoyed teaching the kids his techniques for swimming and for exercising in the water to improve his health. He never recovered the use of his legs, but his wife Eleanor said his struggles against polio taught him perseverance and gave him a powerful sense of empathy, one of his greatest strengths as president.[23]

Recognizing the importance of sports to the nation, he allowed professional baseball teams to continue playing during World War II, which was a widely popular decision. "Baseball provides a recreation which does not last over two hours or two hours and a half," he explained, "which can be got for very little cost." He estimated that 300 teams, including minor-league operations, employed 6,000 players who would entertain 20 million Americans in need of a break from wartime concerns.[24]

*   *   *

HARRY TRUMAN felt that the best thing for his physical and mental health was walking, and this form of recreation became his trademark. He treated it as a sport where he could outwalk everyone with him, often at a very brisk pace of 120 steps per minute. He would get up at 5 a.m., read some newspapers, shave, and get dressed, and then take a two-mile "constitutional" with his Secret Service bodyguards.[25]

"Well, you know," Truman said, "when you're on a job where you have to sit down all day, the best thing you can possibly do is to walk, especially after you're forty years old, because that exercises all the muscles of the body, a walk does. Legs were put on us to use. The present-day youngsters, and most people, will get in a car to go a block. They'd be much better off if they'd walk."[26]

Unlike other presidents, Truman didn't greet many athletes or teams at the White House. He had never been an athlete, partly because he was so near-sighted, and he had no experience in team sports. He never went to college and didn't have the opportunity to go out for organized athletics. He felt that he had better things to do than to associate with athletes, but he might have benefited from the publicity, as so many other presidents have.[27]

He went "fishing" when he vacationed at Key West, Florida, but showed more interest in simply being out on the water than in catching anything. He preferred to play poker, drink bourbon, and gossip with his pals. He followed the football teams of the service academies, though, especially the Army squad, mostly out of duty as the commander in chief.

Friends say he was somewhat interested in baseball, but he had an unfortunate experience at a game in 1951. This came a day after General Douglas MacArthur, a World War II hero whom Truman had fired for insubordination during the Korean War, addressed a joint session of Congress, gaining widespread praise and sympathy. When Truman threw out the first pitch at Griffith Stadium for the Washington Senators' opener, he was loudly booed. During the eighth inning, when the public-address announcer asked spectators to stay in their seats until the president and his entourage left the stadium, Truman was booed again.[28] It was a sign that the country was turning against him.

* * *

DWIGHT EISENHOWER was an athlete from boyhood in Abilene, Kansas, where he dreamed of becoming a professional baseball player. "It would be difficult to overemphasize the importance that I attached to participation in sports," he once said.[29]

At West Point, he boxed, ran track, and excelled at baseball and football, and he earned the nickname "the Kansas cyclone." He injured his left knee in a football game and was forced to give up both football and baseball, which deeply disappointed him.[30] But he took up golf and carried his commitment to it into the White House, where he became known for his near-obsession with the game. He started a trend, popularizing golf with many Americans. Since Ike legitimized it, most presidents in recent years have taken up golf as their sport of choice.

Not long after he became president in 1953, Eisenhower found time in his schedule to practice chipping balls on the White House lawn, and he was unsettled by the crowds that gathered at the gates to stare at him. But he wouldn't give up his avocation. From then on, when the people showed up he hid in a guard's shack until the unwanted audience departed, or he went back into a White House gym to hit golf balls into a net he had installed there.

In 1954, the US Golf Association installed a putting green, complete with a sand trap, on the White House grounds just outside the Oval Office, where Ike could practice without being observed by the public. The problem was that squirrels, which had inhabited the grounds for many years, began digging up the putting green to store acorns. Ike asked the Secret Service to shoot them, but his bodyguards said they weren't authorized to do that. He then told White House gardeners to trap the critters, but members of Congress thought the hero of World War II was going too far in his battle against the squirrels and the legislators protested. Finally, a fence was built to keep the squirrels away from the green, and Eisenhower said the trapping would end.

Ike played frequently at the Burning Tree Country Club near Washington, DC, sometimes twice a week, and he made frequent vacation trips to Augusta National Golf Club in Georgia, his favorite course. He also played nearly every day when he was at the presidential retreat in Maryland's Catoctin Mountains, which he renamed Camp David from Shangri-la (the name bestowed on the site by Franklin Roosevelt, who had created it).

Ike's Democratic opponents criticized him for taking too much time off and playing too much golf, but the president didn't change his ways. He said it improved his performance as president to relax on the links. His doctor, Major General Howard Snyder, agreed. "Golf is a tonic for the president," Snyder said. "It is good for his nerves and muscle tone, and it takes his mind off the anxieties that confront him daily. I say he should play whenever he gets the chance."[31] He did, usually shooting in the middle 80s. When he shot in the 90s he was distressed and angry, sometimes cursing under his breath.

Eisenhower took it upon himself to publicly promote the game of golf, playing with celebrities such as comedian Bob Hope and with professional golfers such as Bobby Jones and Arnold Palmer. He wrote an unusually glowing public letter to "golfers and fellow duffers" during his first term; it said, "While I know that I speak with the partisanship of an enthusiast, golf obviously provides one of our best forms of healthful exercise accompanied by good fellowship and companionship. It is a sport in which the whole American family can participate—fathers and mothers, sons and daughters alike. It offers healthy respite from daily toil, refreshment of body and mind."[32]

News and photographic coverage of President Eisenhower playing golf before and after his heart attack generated more public interest and participation in the game, according to officials in the golf business.[33] Media reports during Ike's first term in the mid-1950s, during which his passion for golf became well known, indicated that golf courses were proliferating. It was estimated that five million people played on 5,000 courses nationwide, and in 1954 alone 250 new courses were built. One business analyst said the sport was "bursting at the seams," and Eisenhower was a big reason for its growing popularity.[34]

Author Paul F. Boller Jr. writes, "During his eight years in the White House, Eisenhower played nearly eight hundred rounds of golf, and in so doing inspired millions of Americans to take up the game. . . . In 1953, when Eisenhower became President, there were some 3.2 million golf players in the country; in 1961, when he left the White House, there were twice that many."[35]

* * *

JOHN F. KENNEDY was a sports aficionado from boyhood, when his hard-charging father Joseph Kennedy instilled in him the values of competitiveness and a passionate desire to win. As president he followed college and professional football and listened to major boxing matches on the radio. He cultivated friendships with Ted Williams of the Boston Red Sox and Stan Musial of the St. Louis Cardinals, which added to his own celebrity as a man who appreciated the national pastime.

Despite his many physical ailments and chronic back pain, JFK played golf when he felt up to it and showed a talent for the game, scoring in the high 70s or low 80s. But after he became president, he was rarely photographed on the links; he feared being the butt of jokes or the target for criticism that he was goofing off, a fate that Eisenhower had endured. More seriously, in May 1961 he suffered a severe back strain when shoveling dirt during a tree-planting ceremony in Ottawa, Canada, and his doctors ordered him to give up golf. He waited until the summer of 1963 before he played again.

One of Kennedy's most popular and memorable initiatives echoed Theodore Roosevelt. Kennedy argued that Americans needed to improve their physical fitness, and this blended perfectly with his reputation as a man of vigor and action, who had campaigned on the promise to get the country moving again. He said, "Our growing softness, our increasing lack of physical fitness, is a menace to our security."[36] This was ironic coming from Kennedy because, counter to his image, he was not a healthy man; he suffered from Addison's disease, which caused failure of the immune system, gastrointestinal ailments, and severe and chronic back pain, and he used a variety of prescription drugs to ease his suffering and relieve his symptoms.

Kennedy wrote an open letter to the public in December 1960, the month after he was elected president, expressing concern about the level of America's physical fitness. The key part of the letter, published in *Sports Illustrated* magazine under the headline "The Soft American," read, "Physical fitness is the basis of all the activities of our society. And if our bodies grow soft and inactive, if we fail to encourage physical development and prowess, we will undermine our capacity for thought, for work and for the use of those skills vital to an expanding and complex America."[37]

Two years later, Kennedy emulated the 1908 directive from Theodore Roosevelt and challenged US Marines to show their fitness by marching fifty miles in twenty hours. Many of the troops accepted the challenge, and so did numerous other Americans. Boy Scouts, members of college fraternities, high-school students, politicians, and business leaders took up the fad of the fifty-mile hike. Attorney General Robert F. Kennedy, the president's brother, was one of them. He hiked the Chesapeake and Ohio Canal towpath in the Washington area in just under eighteen hours.[38]

President Kennedy himself never took the hike because of a painful back ailment, and some of his advisers had trouble living up to his challenge, as well. Pierre Salinger, Kennedy's White House press secretary, tried to lead a group of reporters on a long hike but gave up after six miles. "I may be plucky," the portly Salinger said. "But I'm not stupid."[39] The fifty-mile hike fad ended after Kennedy's assassination in November 1963.

During his presidency, Kennedy and his advisers used his image of vigor and achievement to enhance his celebrity, much as the press agents of Hollywood stars would create personas for their clients. A family friend once described how the Kennedys lived at their compound at Hyannis Port, Massachusetts. He called it "A Guest's Rules for Visiting the Kennedys," and it was revealing:

"Prepare yourself by reading the *Congressional Record, U.S. News and World Report, Time, Newsweek, Fortune, The Nation, How to Play Sneaky Tennis,* and the *Democratic Digest.* Memorize at least three good jokes. Anticipate that each Kennedy will ask you what you think of another Kennedy's a. dress, b. hairdo, c. backhand, d. latest public achievement. Be sure to answer 'Terrific.' This should get you through dinner. Now for the football field. It's *touch* but it's murder. If you don't want to play, don't come. If you do come, play, or you'll be fed in the kitchen and nobody will speak to you. Don't let the girls fool you. Even pregnant, they can make you look silly. . . . Run madly on every play, and make a lot of noise. Don't appear to be having too much fun, though. They'll accuse you of not taking the game seriously enough. . . . To become really popular, you must show raw guts. To show raw guts, fall on your face now and then. Smash into the house once in a while, going after a pass. Laugh off a twisted ankle, or a big hole torn in your best suit. They like this. It shows you take the game as seriously as they do. But remember, don't be too good. Let Jack run around you now and then. He's their boy."[40]

*   *   *

LYNDON JOHNSON was a workaholic who never placed much stock in athletics and was never much of a sports fan as president. He felt he was too busy for that. He did ride horses at his Texas ranch and was adept at it, but politics and government held far more appeal for him.

*   *   *

RICHARD NIXON had a hard time relaxing. One way he took a break from his duties was by following sports, especially by watching college and professional football games on TV. It was also a way for him to relate to sports fans across the country. When aides said he had a meeting or something else he had to do and it conflicted with a big game, he would protest angrily. He also liked to devise plays for his favorite teams and sometimes sent them to coaches he admired, although these plays generally flopped on the field. Immediately after watching a big game, he would sometimes phone winning coaches and managers to congratulate them on their victories. "Throughout his presidency, he contrived new ways to rub elbows with sports celebrities," says Watterson.[41]

On December 4, 1969, Nixon attended the football game between the University of Texas and the University of Arkansas in Fayetteville,

Arkansas, for the national championship. Texas won, 15–14. Afterward Nixon visited both locker rooms, which drew extensive news coverage.[42]

In December 1971 he offered a play to Washington Redskins coach George Allen, a Republican who had coached at Whittier College, Nixon's alma mater. Allen used the play—a flanker reverse—in a playoff game against the San Francisco 49ers. Washington lost three yards on the play and went on to lose the game, 24–20.[43]

Nixon tried again a month later for the Super Bowl, suggesting another play to Miami Dolphins coach Don Shula, this time a "down and in" pass to receiver Paul Warfield. But again it didn't work and the Dallas Cowboys won 24–3. As with his earlier play for Washington, Nixon was widely mocked in the press for his football adventures.[44]

Hoping to associate himself with millions of Americans who enjoyed bowling, Nixon made it known to the press in 1971 that he liked that sport. He even posed for photographers at the lanes donated by his friend Bebe Rebozo and installed under the Executive Office Building next door to the White House. "I usually bowl at about 10 o'clock at night," Nixon said. "When I'm here, I bowl alone. I bowl from seven to twelve games, one after another. That gives you a tremendous workout." He said his average was 152 and once he bowled an impressive 232.[45]

Nixon liked golf but didn't have the time to play very often.[46] And he believed it would hurt his image if he did play. "The average guy is not on the golf course, the tennis court or a speedboat because he doesn't have one," Nixon once told Vice President Dan Quayle. But Quayle, an avid golfer, disregarded the advice and played often.[47]

*   *   *

GERALD FORD became president when Richard Nixon resigned in August 1974 because of the Watergate scandal, and he was one of the most athletic of all presidents. He played tennis and golf and skied, and he had an impressive history as a football player at South High School in Grand Rapids, Michigan, and at the University of Michigan, where he was voted by his teammates as the most valuable player in his senior year and recruited by the Green Bay Packers and Detroit Lions to play professionally. He went to law school instead.

But his reputation suffered immensely as president when the media and his critics created the impression that he was a stumblebum and an intellectual lightweight. Once this image settled in, Ford was unable to use his celebrity to his advantage and he became somewhat of a laughingstock. He lost to Democrat Jimmy Carter in 1976.

*   *   *

JIMMY CARTER loved fishing, softball, and jogging as personal pastimes, and was a longtime fan of the Atlanta Braves baseball team and the Atlanta Hawks basketball squad in his home state of Georgia. But his connection to sports never bonded him with the country. There was too much about Carter that people came to dislike, such as his self-importance and, in policy terms, his failure to alleviate the nation's economic misery. He also suffered a huge setback internationally in the Iranian hostage crisis, in which religious zealots held scores of Americans hostage in Tehran during Carter's final year as president. Carter lost his bid for reelection to Ronald Reagan in 1980.

*   *   *

RONALD REAGAN, like so many other presidents, had connections to sports throughout his life. He liked baseball while attending Eureka College near Peoria, Illinois, but he couldn't see the ball well either as a hitter or a fielder because of his nearsightedness. He played football instead because in that sport his myopia wasn't as problematic.

He was also a strong swimmer. He often recalled that he had saved seventy-seven people from drowning while he was a lifeguard for seven summers at Lowell Park on the Rock River near his hometown of Dixon, Illinois.[48]

After graduation, he worked at WHO radio in Des Moines, covering the Chicago Cubs. He reported on many games remotely by using pitch-by-pitch reports from the telegraph wire and he made the games seem lively and interesting. Once, his "re-creation" was interrupted when the wire went dead. Reagan filled in the time for seven minutes with engaging patter and his listeners never knew about the interruption.

And as a movie star, Reagan had one particular role that cemented his link to sports. After he started making movies in Hollywood, his sports background came in handy. He sought the role of George Gipp, a halfback at Notre Dame, in the 1940 film *Knute Rockne—All-American*, and he persuaded the studio that his experience playing college football made him right for the part. Reagan's memorable line to his silver-screen teammates as he lay dying in the film—"Win just one for the Gipper"—became a rallying cry for fellow Republicans when he was president.

Writes Watterson, *"Knute Rockne, All American* was one of Reagan's first celluloid triumphs. Later, the first actor in the White House would use the media—and his imagination—to become the most visible and entertaining president in history; he was seen and heard via television by more of his countrymen than his one-time hero, Franklin Roosevelt. The Reagan mystique, born of legend and electronic legerdemain, exceeded all of his twentieth-century predecessors, especially the presidents who served in the pre-newsreel, pre-television era."[49]

As recreation, Reagan enjoyed horseback riding most of all, and he and his wife Nancy would ride as often as possible at Camp David and at their ranch near Santa Barbara, California. He explained to aides that "the best thing for the inside of a man is the outside of a horse." He had little interest in sports that other presidents loved, such as golf, tennis, or running. By the time he became president, Reagan was in his seventies and was beyond the point where he was interested in or would be very good at more vigorous forms of athletics.

*   *   *

PRESIDENT GEORGE H. W. BUSH was another lifelong sportsman. He tried to parlay his connections in the sports world into broader celebrity in 1988 by getting the endorsement of movie star and former bodybuilding champion Arnold Schwarzenegger. Schwarzenegger, campaigning for Bush in New Hampshire, uttered one of the most memorable lines of that campaign when he derided Bush's rivals with the putdown, "They all look like a bunch of girlie men, right?" The actor had picked up the line about girlie men from a series of hilarious *Saturday Night Live* sketches featuring comedians Dana Carvey and Kevin Nealon. They played bodybuilders from Austria, Hans and Franz—modeled on Arnold himself.[50] Bush won the 1988 election and Schwarzenegger accepted an appointment as chairman of the President's Council on Physical Fitness and Sports. He went on to become governor of California years later.

Aside from the Schwarzenegger connection, Bush's links to the sports world fell flat since his conservative policies weren't accepted by many athletes or everyday people, who felt they had little in common with this Brahmin from Yale. Still, he was a real athlete in his personal life. As president, he engaged in jogging, fishing, tennis, boating, horseshoes, and golfing at a breakneck pace he called "cart polo." He sped around the golf course in his motorized cart, sometimes covering eighteen holes in less than two hours when an average person played in about four hours. While I covered his presidency for *U.S. News & World Report*, he took me and my wife Barclay for a ride on his speedboat *Fidelity*, and it gave us insight into his frenetic lifestyle. He gunned the boat frequently, causing his surprised passengers to lurch in their seats or lose their balance. Rather than take a header, everyone grabbed for something solid, like handrails or the backs of chairs bolted to the floor. Part of his motivation might have been to use *Fidelity* as a control mechanism to show who was in charge. But it seemed more likely to me that he just loved the thrill of racing across the water, and he always wanted to move as quickly as possible to his next activity.

*   *   *

BILL CLINTON was a runner and golfer, but in a far different style than Bush. Clinton didn't rush; he used his athletic pursuits as a way to meet people and get to know them.

He would rise at 6 a.m., put on blue shorts (sometimes a bit too short), a red T-shirt, a blue baseball cap, and running shoes with "Mr. President" on the sides, and take off on a three-mile jog in Washington, with his Secret Service agents all around him. He often brought along members of the House and Senate, governors, mayors, movie and TV stars, and old friends, and he often kept up a patter throughout. He liked to end his jogs with spontaneous chats with people he'd meet on the streets or at a local McDonald's where he stopped for coffee. This contact with everyday people was why he kept running outside the White House grounds rather than on a jogging track his friends built for him on the South Lawn at a cost of $30,000 in donations. He got plenty of news coverage for his running and his delight in meeting people, including a favorable skit on *Saturday Night Live*, adding to his celebrity.

As Clinton's presidency proceeded, he took an interest in golf, as had so many of his predecessors, and played more and more. "He's like a great big jovial host," said a White House staffer who joined him on the links several times. "His golf game is an extension of him in the sense that he makes people enjoy being with him when he's out there." He loved the experience, and he took his time; sometimes his games would last five hours or more. And he would play in severe heat, in the rain, even when it was snowing. He would try to play at least once a week. He often took mulligans or second shots to improve his scores—so often, in fact, that his friends started to call them "Billigans."[51]

Typically, he analyzed the game in depth. "It really is a lot like life," he once said. "There is a lot of skill to it, but it's mostly a head game once you reach whatever level you are swinging. If you don't concentrate or get upset or you do all the stuff I did, you make mistakes and you pay for them. The other thing I like about it is, to some extent, it's an art, not a science. You do get breaks, both ways. You get some bad breaks, like when I hit the tree. And you get some great breaks—I hit another tree, and it went on the green. It's just a lot like life. I love it."[52]

*　　*　　*

GEORGE W. BUSH was one of the fittest presidents. His doctors said he was in great shape and he took a keen interest in exercise and nutrition. Formerly a problem drinker, he had given up alcohol many years earlier and prided himself on his self-discipline.

He created an exercise room on the top floor of the White House residence, which included a treadmill, an elliptical machine, and weights, and he made a daily habit of working out. He even had a treadmill installed on *Air Force One* so he could exercise when he traveled.

He loved to run outdoors, often on military bases in the Washington area and on the road. He liked to wear shorts and a T-shirt with running shoes, and photos of him running were widely disseminated. He told *Runner's World*, "For me, the psychological benefit is enormous. It helps me to clear my mind."[53] He also ran in the 100-degree heat at his Texas ranch, which he visited frequently, and, showing a bit of macho, he had T-shirts made up with the words "100 Degrees Club." He gave the shirts to staff members, Secret Service agents, and others who managed to keep up with him in the sweltering conditions for three-mile jaunts. None of this bonded him to the public, however, possibly because he was taking his exercise regimen so seriously that he was in a different category than recreational runners around the country.

Weakness in his knees forced Bush to give up running midway through his presidency, and he took up the arduous sport of mountain biking. He challenged himself so much that on one ride he spilled over the handlebars, bruising his face and hands, and showed up at the White House looking as if he had been in a bar fight. He was particularly eager to ride the bike at his Texas ranch, where he would also chop and burn cedar to stay fit while ridding his property of unwanted vegetation.

Bush was also an intense spectator-sports fan. He had been part owner of the Texas Rangers pro baseball team and he never lost his interest in that sport. He loved to throw out the first pitch to open the major-league season and was a diligent reader of the box scores each day to see how his favorite players were doing. He began the custom of tossing a coin at the White House to determine who would get the ball first in the initial game of the National Football League season, a moment carried live and shown on huge screens at a number of football stadiums.

Bush combined sports with his presidential duties in a very memorable way when he opened the third game of the World Series at Yankee Stadium by throwing out the first pitch in November 2001. This was two months after the infamous 9/11 terrorist attacks on New York and Washington, DC. Bush managed to throw a strike but, more important, his presence, choreographed in such a visible and vulnerable way, showed the nation it was okay to get back to normal and was an act of defiance to the terrorists. He got a huge ovation, and the pitch was carried on live television and broadcast many times across the country. It was Bush's biggest moment as a sports and political celebrity.

* * *

BARACK OBAMA has played basketball for recreation ever since his high-school days, when he was on the varsity team in Hawaii. He never lost his interest in the game and still plays occasionally as president, although he has minimized his time on the hard court because he doesn't want to get injured.

His sport of choice has become golf, and he tries to play at least once a week. He ran into trouble because he was on the links so often that his critics said he was loafing and showing insensitivity to Americans who were experiencing adversity. There was a crescendo of outrage in August 2014 when, during a vacation at the posh resort town of Martha's Vineyard, Massachusetts, he told reporters somberly that he was "heartbroken" at the shocking beheading of US journalist Jim Foley in Iraq. But a few minutes later he rushed to the links for another round.

As a sports fan, he has a ritual of trying to predict the winners in the major brackets of the college basketball playoffs each year. His picks often go astray, as do those of virtually everyone else, but he uses the occasion to commune with sports fans around the country. He often announces his picks on live TV, gaining a publicity windfall.

In early 2014 Obama recruited NBA superstar LeBron James to ask young people to sign up for health insurance under the president's controversial health-care law. White House officials said many did sign up, and James's appeals helped to persuade them to do so. It was a successful way to connect sports with policy and politics.

Obama solidified his attachment to sports in many other ways, such as following the tradition of his predecessors by hosting championship teams at the White House and congratulating them on their victories. He dropped in on a Little League baseball game in suburban Washington in May 2014, seeking an everyman appeal. And that same week he became the first sitting president to visit the National Baseball Hall of Fame and Museum in Cooperstown, New York, to promote tourism. And in times of crisis, he finds respite in sports on TV, as have some of his predecessors. He is a fan of ESPN, the all-sports cable network, and will watch it in the White House residence into the wee hours to relax.

He takes viewing of sports seriously. When he has guests at the White House, Obama has a rule: people are there to watch the game, not to schmooze with him. This even applies to his annual Super Bowl party, normally a jovial occasion that brings out the raucous side of football fans. But for Obama it's a time for serious deliberation on the fine points of the game.[54]

*   *   *

OBAMA TRIED to use his celebrity to improve safety in sports. On May 29, 2014, emulating Theodore Roosevelt's effort more than a century earlier to protect football players, Obama convened a White House Healthy Kids and Safe Sports Concussion Summit. He sought to use the White House "bully pulpit"—a concept popularized by TR—to call for "research on sports-related youth concussions" and to "raise awareness of steps to prevent, identify and respond to concussions in young people," a White House spokesman said. "Sports are one of the best ways to keep our kids active and healthy, but young people make nearly 250,000 emergency room visits each year with sport or recreation-related brain injuries," the spokesman added.[55]

Unlike Roosevelt, Obama didn't think he had all the answers, and he moved more cautiously. He used the conference to highlight the problem and gather information about what to do, not to force-feed the invitees his own prescriptions. Still, convening the meeting added to Obama's celebrity as a sports-minded leader and a good father. "We want our kids participating in sports," the president said. "I'd be much more troubled if young people were shying away from sports. As parents, though, we want to keep them safe and that means we have to have better information."[56]

Obama said he played football briefly when he was young and might have suffered mild concussions "a couple of times" but they weren't diagnosed and like so many other athletes, he didn't make a fuss about his injuries at the time. "We have to change a culture that says, 'You've got to suck it up,'" he argued.

He went on to say that as president he often played sports, such as golf and basketball, to relax, and that his daughters played basketball, soccer, and tennis and ran track. "Sports is also just fundamental to who we are as Americans and our culture," Obama argued, echoing TR and some of his other predecessors and countless coaches over the years. "We're competitive. We're driven. And sports teach us about teamwork and hard work and what it takes to succeed not just on the field but in life."[57] Teddy Roosevelt couldn't have said it better.

Chapter Fifteen

Presidents and Music
Sweet and Sour Notes

Music has played a little-known but important role in the lives of America's presidents. George Washington was an accomplished dancer, as were many American aristocrats of his time. John Tyler played the violin. Warren G. Harding played the cornet. Calvin Coolidge played the harmonica. Richard Nixon played piano. Other chief executives, such as Franklin D. Roosevelt and John F. Kennedy, showed an appreciation for music by hosting frequent concerts at the White House.

"Few edifices in the world can boast the variety and excellence of its music, yet few concert halls or opera houses have been so conditioned by changing political attitudes," writes music historian Elise K. Kirk. "No other single arts institution has been as progressive and at the same time as conservative as the great white mansion. No other aspect of White House life can define the presidential image quite like the music performed at the chief of state's residence."[1]

The entertainers the presidents have hosted at the White House reveal much about not only the leaders' musical tastes but also the cultural preferences they wanted to be known for and the demographic groups they wanted to be associated with.

Dwight Eisenhower hosted the "big bands" of Lawrence Welk and Guy Lombardo, who appealed to families and cultural conservatives, and stars from major Broadway shows who had similar mass popularity, such as ten-year-old prodigy Eddie Hodges from *The Music Man*.[2]

Kennedy liked to be known for bringing in classical artists such as cellist Pablo Casals. But privately he wasn't sophisticated about music. He liked show tunes and standards. Jacqueline Kennedy quipped that her husband's favorite song was "Hail to the Chief." Officially, his aides claimed that Kennedy's favorite was the mellow folk tune "Greensleeves." It was Jackie, twelve years younger, who introduced the president to musical fads of the time, such as the bossa nova and Chubby Checker's "The Twist."[3]

Lyndon Johnson preferred jazz musicians such as Dave Brubeck and Duke Ellington.

Nixon liked the straitlaced conservative performances of Up with People and the Carpenters, the smooth sounds of Frank Sinatra, and the down-home approach of Johnny Cash. In 1971 Nixon aides held a meeting to come up with a strategy for choosing entertainers on state occasions, such as dinners for royalty and heads of government, and it showed how politicized the decisions had become. A memo summarizing the meeting said, "We should concentrate on 'big' name stars—performers who will 'come out' for the president, and thereby influence a number of others to do the same. It stressed that we concentrate on entertainers who appeal to young people, i.e., Burt Bacharach, Ali McGraw, Flip Wilson and others." The memo urged that entertainers who weren't invited to actually perform because of "inappropriateness," such as Frank Sinatra and Elvis Presley, should be included as dinner guests.[4]

Gerald Ford liked glamorous stars, including Ann-Margret. Jimmy Carter enjoyed the diversity of country, jazz, and classical musicians.

Ronald Reagan chose singers of show tunes and Broadway hits, but he also hosted some of the biggest names in film, including musical stars Fred Astaire, Ginger Rogers, Gene Kelly, Frank Sinatra, and Dionne Warwick, all of whom attended a Hollywood party for Queen Elizabeth of Great Britain in 1983.

George H. W. Bush hosted country acts and easy-listening singers such as Johnny Mathis.

Bill Clinton liked rock stars such as Jon Bon Jovi and Eric Clapton, and African American performers including Michael Jackson, Aretha Franklin, Gladys Knight, and Lou Rawls. He also hosted Barbra Streisand, one of his staunch supporters.

George W. Bush wasn't much interested in performers at all and hosted few concerts at the White House, but those he invited included country singers Larry Gatlin and Toby Keith.

Barack Obama has hosted a wide array of artists, especially African Americans, including Aretha Franklin and Patti LaBelle.

But three chief executives stood out for their personal musical abilities—Thomas Jefferson, Harry Truman, and Bill Clinton. They found that music leavened their lives and gave them solace in times of trouble.

*   *   *

JEFFERSON, the nation's third president, was an accomplished violinist who said music was "the favorite passion of my soul," according to former Stanford music professor Sandor Salgo. His lifelong commitment to music was part of his search for excellence in nearly everything he did, from politics and government to architecture, agriculture, and his many hobbies.

During his youth in the wilderness of southern Virginia in the 1750s, Jefferson took up the violin at the suggestion of his older sister, Jane, who was a fine singer. Jane would often sing for family and friends, with adolescent Tom accompanying her on the violin. By the time he was nine years old, Thomas Jefferson could play from written music. When his father Peter died in 1757, fourteen-year-old Tom "immersed himself in his studies and his violin as a way of assuaging his grief," according to Salgo.[5]

While attending the College of William and Mary in the colonial capital of Williamsburg, Virginia, he continued his musical pursuits in an effort to become a well-rounded individual. "For example, during Christmas, 1760, at Colonel Nathaniel Dandridge's house in Hanover County, he met a young Virginian, classmate, and fellow violinist, one Patrick Henry," Salgo reports. "The house resounded with the music of violins all during the holiday."[6]

The aristocracy of Virginia, of which Jefferson was a member, attached considerable importance to music and dancing as social arts, and Jefferson was an accomplished dancer. He took dance lessons when he was a young man. There were many "assemblies" or dancing events in Virginia plantation society, mostly accompanied by fiddlers, and Jefferson was a full participant.

Jefferson became a law apprentice to George Wythe, an attorney, who introduced the future president to Royal Governor Francis Fauquier at the governor's palace in Williamsburg. Fauquier, it turned out, was also a violinist and he invited Jefferson to be a member of his weekly chamber-music group. They played at the governor's social events, focusing on the music popular at the time in America's high society, such as Haydn quartets and Corelli and Vivaldi sonatas and *concerti grossi*. Jefferson attended many performances of musical theater in Williamsburg. He particularly enjoyed English ballad opera such as Thomas Arne's *Thomas and Sally* and *Love in a Village* and John Gay's *The Beggar's Opera.*[7]

"The violin continued to play an important role in Jefferson's daily life as he began to practice law and travel out of Williamsburg on legal matters for his clients," Salgo writes. "He bought a 'kit violin' (or, simply, 'kit'), a small instrument with an extremely soft sound used frequently by the dancing masters. Jefferson, ever the innovator, designed a handsome but practical case for the instrument, so it could easily be attached to his saddle. The kit enabled him to practice in whatever room he had to spend the night without the risk of disturbing others."[8]

His musical pastime also helped his romantic life. He began courting Martha Wayles Skelton, a young widow who lived near Monticello, the Jefferson family estate a few miles south of Charlottesville, Virginia, that the young Jefferson inherited from his father. It turned out that Mrs. Skelton played the harpsichord and guitar and had a lovely singing voice. "According to Jefferson family tradition, Jefferson's violin playing and pleasant singing voice won Martha's heart; conversely, Martha's harpsichord playing and singing must have made a reciprocal mark on Thomas," writes Salgo. "It was their playing and singing together that contributed to Jefferson's success in courting her."[9] Martha and Thomas were married on January 1, 1772. One of his wedding presents to her was a fortepiano that he had imported from London.[10]

During his early marital years Jefferson increased his proficiency in the violin, hiring an Italian immigrant violinist-harpsichordist, Francis Alberti, to give lessons to him and Martha. Jefferson once estimated that he practiced the violin no less than three hours a day for a dozen years. And even if he exaggerated his estimate, it is clear that he continued his commitment to music. Isaac, one of his slaves, said later that Jefferson kept three fiddles in his home and played in the afternoons and sometimes after supper. He had a "fine clear voice," Isaac said, and was "always singing when ridin' or walkin'."[11]

Jefferson probably reached his peak as a violinist in the 1780s. His wife died of complications from childbirth in 1782 and grief pushed Jefferson to find solace in music, as had happened after his father died. While he was in Paris as the US envoy to France beginning in 1785 his interest in music deepened further as he was surrounded by the flourishing musical culture of Europe. He attended many concerts and kept up his playing, sometimes in the company of Maria Cosway, a married woman with whom he had a close friendship and a romantic interest.

In September 1786, the future president suffered a serious injury to his right wrist, probably a compound fracture, from a fall that he refused to describe, even to friends, other than to say it was a "folly." Those around him speculated that it resulted from a foolish act of physical prowess, possibly a tumble from a horse or an attempt to jump over a fence to impress Maria Cosway.[12] From then on, Jefferson's ability to play the violin was severely limited. (Cosway, by the way, moved to London with her husband, disappointing Jefferson. After that, their relationship was never as close as it had been during their Paris sojourn.)

During his presidential years (1801–1809), Jefferson missed the exciting cultural and musical world he had enjoyed in the temporary US capital of Philadelphia when he was vice president. The new capital, Washington, DC, was a backwater. But Jefferson participated in dancing assemblies and attended performances of the Philadelphia Opera Company when it played in Washington.

When he returned to Monticello after his presidency in 1809, Jefferson had the time and desire to return to his musical passion. He bought a Spanish guitar for his granddaughter Virginia, apparently had a harpsichord and a piano at his home, and frequently enjoyed evenings of music with his daughter Patsy and her family and friends. He kept several violins at Monticello.[13]

Jefferson scholars believe music was an important way for him to ease stress and escape from the pressures of his life. He called music, at various times, a "delightful recreation," and "an enjoyment, the deprivation of which . . . cannot be calculated." As Salgo writes, "Playing the violin gave comfort to Jefferson. He must have been closely attuned to his violin and, when it was at one with the beat of his heart, seen it as an extension of his body and spirit, a most personal and private form of expression. . . . Although Jefferson may not have performed at the level of a professional violinist, playing the violin almost certainly provided him tremendous emotional release and must have occupied a central place in his heart for much of his life. . . . Music unlocked the soul of this enigmatic and complex man. He had a compelling need to be surrounded by it."[14]

* * *

HARRY TRUMAN was a music aficionado all his life. Martha Ellen Truman, his mother, tried to instill in her three children, Harry, Mary Jane, and Vivian, an interest in music but only Harry displayed enough talent and commitment to pursue it, and Martha began personally giving him piano lessons at age eight and hired a local music teacher to provide the bespectacled boy with formal instruction. After a year Martha advanced Harry to a higher level and arranged to send him to Mrs. E. C. White, one of Kansas City's finest piano teachers. Harry got up at 5 a.m. each day to practice for at least an hour, and his mother called him "a young Mozart."[15]

In 1891, Mrs. White took Harry to a concert by Ignacy Jan Paderewski, a celebrated Polish pianist, and after the performance Mrs. White and Harry went backstage at Kansas City's Shubert Theatre. Paderewski gave young Truman a quick lesson on one of the master's compositions, "Minuet in G."[16]

Truman continued his piano lessons until he was fifteen years old, when he gave them up because he knew he would never be a concert pianist. "I wasn't good enough," he said later with typical candor, although he conceded that he had gained a good foundation in music.[17] Writes historian Brian Lingham, "It was this brief period of musical study early in Harry's life that laid the groundwork for his constant enjoyment of music. . . . Although Harry had ceased his study, he by no means had stopped his playing. All through his youth he played whenever he had the opportunity and attended every kind of musical and theatrical . . . that he possibly could."[18]

Lingham explains, "With his courtship of Bess [Wallace] beginning in earnest in 1910, Harry not only found a kindred spirit in his love for music and the theatre but also a willing audience for his own playing. Frequently making the trip to Independence from Grandview, Missouri to visit Bess, Harry would stay at the house of his aunt and uncle, Mr. and Mrs. Joseph Noland, who lived on Delaware Street. On a creaky upright piano, Harry frequently entertained Bess, the Nolands, and indeed the entire families of the Wallaces and the Trumans."[19]

After military service in Europe during World War I, Truman was discharged from the Army at Camp Funston, Kansas, on May 6, 1919. A bit more than six weeks later, he married Bess Wallace, who had shared his musical tastes for many years, in the Trinity Episcopal Church in Independence, Missouri. "Harry had proposed to Bess before the war while at a performance of 'The Girl from Utah,' which opened on Sunday, October 17, 1915," Lingham writes. "One song from that show, 'They'll Never Believe Me,' became a favorite of Harry and Bess, and there are frequent references to the song in Harry's correspondence with Bess in later years. Bess did not share Harry's talent for playing the piano, but she constantly remained a loyal and enthusiastic audience for Harry's playing and for his outspoken opinions on all musical matters."[20] Their daughter, Margaret, took her first music lessons from her father and developed a talent for singing.

After he became president upon FDR's death on April 12, 1945, Truman found more solace in music than ever during the course of his presidency, which ran from 1945 to 1953.[21] Truman kept a radio by his bedside so he could listen to classical music just before retiring, and a piano by his desk at his temporary presidential residence at Blair House (while the White House, across the street, was being renovated). Truman would often take a break from his duties and play the Steinway "O" grand piano for up to a half hour.

He also played publicly, and frequently. Throughout his adult life, he was asked to play "Missouri Waltz" and he generally obliged because so many people thought it was his favorite piece. It wasn't, but he felt it gave recognition to his home state, so he went along with the requests.

In 1946 and 1947, he held a series of concerts at the White House that revealed his strong preference for classical music. (He considered contemporary music mere "noise.") These Tuesday-night musicales followed white-tie state dinners and included performances by pianists Sylvia Zaremba on November 26, 1946; Oscar Levant on January 14, 1947; and violinist Carroll Glenn, pianist Eugene List, and accompanist Joseph Wolman on February 11, 1947.[22]

During the nearly four years that the White House was under reconstruction, from 1948 to 1952, Truman's opportunities for entertaining were limited. So he would sometimes organize "phonographic concerts" at his temporary residence at Blair House or at his vacation retreat in Key West, Florida, for friends or members of the White House staff. During these sessions he would play recordings of composers such as Chopin, Paderewski, and Lhévinne and lead discussions of their work. Lhévinne was his favorite, "the greatest pianist since Liszt," Truman said.[23]

One of the most famous incidents involving a president and music occurred while Truman was president. On March 16, 1947, his daughter Margaret, who took informal music lessons from her dad as a child, started her career as a coloratura opera singer when she sang with the Detroit Symphony Orchestra; the performance was carried live on the radio for an estimated fifteen million people.[24] She followed this with many performances around the nation and several on television. But Margaret's concert at Washington's Constitution Hall in December 1950 was panned by *Washington Post* critic Paul Hume. "Miss Truman cannot sing very well," Hume wrote. ". . . She is flat a good deal of the time. . . . There are a few moments during her recital when one can relax and feel confident that she will make her goal, which is the end of the song." Truman was furious. He sent a quick note to Hume on White House stationery, calling the critic "an eight-ulcer man on four-ulcer pay. . . . Someday I hope to meet you and when that happens, you'll need a new nose, some beef steak for black eyes, and perhaps a supporter below!"[25] The letter caused a sensation, but most Americans seemed to sympathize with Truman as an outraged father defending his child.

He played the piano for Soviet leader Josef Stalin and British prime minister Winston Churchill and, after Truman left office, for President John F. Kennedy and countless friends and acquaintances. He played a bit for thirty million Americans during a televised tour of the newly remodeled White House in the spring of 1952. Margaret Truman said his "thirst for good music sometimes drew him out of the White House." He attended numerous concerts in many venues, including Constitution Hall and Gadsby's Tavern in Alexandria, Virginia.

*   *   *

BILL CLINTON owed much to the saxophone. The instrument became an instant symbol of his unique qualities as a politician when he played it on *The Arsenio Hall Show* during his successful 1992 campaign. The performance left people with the impression that "he's hip, he's a real person," said Tom Burzycki, who was president of Selmer L.P., the Indiana company that made the saxophones Clinton played when he was a teen. "He's probably the most human president since Harry Truman played the Missouri Waltz on the piano," Burzycki added in 1993, shortly after Clinton was sworn in as president. "Someone who can put on sunglasses and play 'Heartbreak Hotel' has to be human."[26]

Clinton had used the instrument to gain popularity before—when he played it in his high-school band. He was overweight and a poor athlete, so he turned to the saxophone to get into the spotlight even if he wasn't proving himself as a player on the football team. The most popular instrument among "hip" teens in the 1950s, when rock-and-roll was gaining popularity and when Clinton was growing up, was the guitar. Clinton, however, knew he was good at playing the sax and he stayed with it during his high-school years in Arkansas. Playing sax became his favorite pastime. He practiced most days, played in jazz groups, and attended a band camp in the Ozark Mountains during the summers, according to a biography provided by his presidential library in Little Rock. "His hard work paid off when he became a top saxophone player at his school and won first chair in the state band's saxophone section," according to the bio.[27] He continued playing for relaxation all his life.

"His technique needs a little touching up, but he's got some soul," said Rickey Washington, band director at Hollywood High School in Los Angeles when Clinton started his first presidential term and performed in public. Washington, a sax player himself, added, "The sax is an instrument for solos, for the forefront, for the spotlight. Sax players are outgoing, they like to play fast, they are leaders. All these are good characteristics for a president . . . and if you play the sax you got to be pretty hip and, you know, being hip wouldn't be too bad a characteristic for a president either."[28]

In addition to helping to increase sales of and interest in the saxophone, Clinton deftly parlayed his musical skills into a larger PR advantage. He became known as a big fan of jazz, gospel, and rock and roll. If his favorite tunes and performers appeared designed to appeal to important political constituencies, such as baby boomers and African Americans, that seemed to be part of the larger plan.

"So much about him brought other people to the table, whether it was playing cards, watching movies, or playing games," Joe Lockhart, Clinton's White House press secretary, told me in an interview for this book. "But music seemed to me a more solitary thing." Clinton wouldn't listen to music in the Oval Office, which he considered a work zone, Lockhart said, but he would listen to his favorite recordings in many other settings. On

Air Force One, for example, he would send his staff out of his big office in the front of the plane and pop in a CD while he worked alone on a stack of papers. He often played jazz and occasionally gospel—rarely the rock and roll for which he was known publicly. Among his favorite musicians were jazz greats Miles Davis and Zoot Sims and singers Nina Simone and Mahalia Jackson. As with other presidents who loved music, it soothed him and gave him an escape from the tedium and pressure of his job.

Chapter Sixteen
Presidents as Trend Setters and Trend Spotters
Food, Fashion, Pets, and More

A president's cultural interests and predilections can shape the tastes and attitudes of the country, in addition to revealing much about the president as an individual. And the opportunities for presidents to have an impact on pop culture have expanded greatly over the years.

*   *   *

THEODORE ROOSEVELT was such a huge celebrity during his seven years in office that his effect on popular culture was strong. A good example was the creation of "Teddy's bear," a toy that became known as the "teddy bear." As recounted earlier in this book, it was based on a hunting incident in which the president spared a young bear that had been captured and presented to him to be shot. This was hardly fair, Roosevelt said, and he refused. The newspapers got hold of the story and it caused a sensation, adding to his fame as a sportsman and as a man of principle and good sense.

*   *   *

IN THE MASS-MEDIA AGE, presidents have been depicted many times in popular culture, especially on television, in ways that have both helped and hurt their images. Ronald Reagan's conservative policies were the inspiration for the character of Alex P. Keaton, played by Michael J.

Fox, on NBC's popular situation comedy *Family Ties*. Fox's appealing persona, both as a TV character and in real life, may have softened the rough edges of Reaganomics a bit. Bill Clinton's White House was the basis for *The West Wing*, another popular NBC series featuring an idealistic president, his strong and opinionated wife, and their aides. This depiction may also have conveyed a kinder, gentler perception of a polarizing president.

Saturday Night Live often sets the pace in characterizing politicians and establishing their roles in popular culture. Richard Nixon was seen as a conniving and unbalanced knave as portrayed by comedian Dan Aykroyd. Gerald Ford was relentlessly mocked by comedian Chevy Chase, adding to Ford's negative reputation. A brilliant *SNL* skit portrayed Reagan as a disengaged, avuncular figure in public but a hard-charging, hands-on manager in private, giving people another way to think of the "great communicator." George H. W. Bush, played by Dana Carvey, was a grammatically challenged Brahmin who was out of touch and didn't realize it. Clinton was caricatured as a good-hearted but self-indulgent fast-food junkie. George W. Bush, played by Will Ferrell, was, quite simply, a well-meaning dunce.

Comedians have had trouble impersonating or parodying Obama because he doesn't have a particularly distinctive and interesting speaking style, unlike John F. Kennedy, Ronald Reagan, Bill Clinton, George H. W. Bush, and George W. Bush. But his policies have been widely examined and used as themes that have appeared again and again in the media. "In Marvel's latest popcorn thriller, Captain America battles Hydra, a malevolent organization that has infiltrated the highest levels of the United States government," the *New York Times* reported on April 30, 2014. "There are missile attacks, screeching car chases, enormous explosions, evil assassins, data-mining supercomputers and giant killer drones ready to obliterate millions of people.

"Its inspiration?

"President Obama, the optimistic candidate of hope and change."

The *Times* went on to say that, "Five and a half years into his presidency, Mr. Obama has had a powerful impact on the nation's popular culture. But what many screenwriters, novelists and visual artists have seized on is not an inspirational story of the first black president. Instead they have found more compelling story lines in the bleaker, morally fraught parts of Mr. Obama's legacy."[1]

Obama's drone policy—the use of unmanned aircraft both for surveillance and to kill terrorists around the world—captured Hollywood's imagination, often in negative ways. "We were trying to find a bridge to the same sort of questions that Barack Obama has to address," said Joe Russo, codirector of *Captain America: The Winter Soldier.* "If you're saying with a drone strike, we can eradicate an enemy of the state, what if you say with 100 drone strikes, we can eradicate 100? With 1,000 we can eradicate 1,000? At what point do you stop?"[2]

The *Times* found that films, books, plays, comics, paintings, and TV shows had been stressing "the sometimes grim reality of Mr. Obama's presidency. The commando raid that Mr. Obama ordered to kill Osama bin Laden is the basis for the actions of the fictional President Ogden in the Godzilla comic books. Several episodes of CBS's 'The Good Wife' feature mysterious wiretaps of the main characters by the National Security Agency. Artists in California are protesting drones by sculpting a Predator out of mud. In New York, playwrights are exploring disappointment in the pace of societal change in Mr. Obama's America."[3]

Barack and Michelle Obama also try to affect the culture by example. "The president talks about the importance of fatherhood and the responsibilities of fatherhood," points out Democratic pollster Geoff Garin. He adds that the Obamas take seriously their positions as role models "in a way that's not always been true of others."[4]

One reason Obama has retained so much of his star aura for so long is because of his personal reputation as a good man who stands for hope and change. "Evocation of a compelling persona is critical in politics; voters must feel that a candidate speaks to them and is in touch with their personal concerns," says pollster and public-opinion analyst Frank Luntz. "It's one reason why the more 'likeable' presidential nominee almost always wins the election even when the opponent holds other important attribute advantages. This is not some breakthrough observation—it has been at the core of successful presidential campaign advertising since all the way back to the time of the first paid political ads, in 1952."[5]

Nixon and Acupuncture

One obscure fact is that Richard Nixon was indirectly pivotal in introducing Americans to acupuncture. It stemmed from Nixon's famous visit to

China in February 1972. Because of operations he witnessed in Beijing at that time, Dr. Walter R. Tkach, the president's personal physician, said he was impressed with the use of acupuncture needles and the application of electric current as a method of anesthesia. He passed along the information to American physicians when he got home, and the interest in acupuncture in the US medical field greatly increased.[6]

Acupuncture got another boost because of that same Nixon trip to China. *New York Times* columnist James Reston was on the trip and he was treated successfully with acupuncture for postoperative pain after an appendectomy in China. Reston's positive assessment of the treatment helped legitimize it in the United States.[7]

Presidents and Food

"Tell me what you eat, and I will tell you what you are," said French gastronome Jean Anthelme Brillat-Savarin. This is true of presidents as well as everyday people. John Moeller, author of *Dining at the White House* and chef for George H. W. Bush, Bill Clinton, and George W. Bush, said, "It's hard to beat the draw of food, politics and personality. . . . The food they eat at their own table tells the rest of us a little bit about who they really are."[8]

Marian Burros, longtime food critic for the *New York Times*, said presidents have both shaped and followed popular tastes in food for many years.[9]

Some early American presidents, especially Thomas Jefferson, had a strong preference for French cuisine. It was considered superior by educated Americans, and as American aristocrats several of the early presidents were influenced by the tastes of the elites at the time.

George Washington was eclectic. He expressed a fondness for simple foods but he made sure that his table was well stocked with all manner of dishes. A family member said, "He ate heartily, but was not particular in his diet, with the exception of fish, of which he was excessively fond. He partook sparingly of dessert, drank a home-made beverage, and from four to five glasses of Madeira wine."[10]

Add authors Poppy Cannon and Patricia Brooks, "Food reflects the man. In Washington, there is the interesting dichotomy of a man disinterested in the refinements of the table, yet anxious to offer as many refinements as possible to his guests, simple in his own tastes but generous toward others. . . . As food reflects the man, it also reflects the times. The food served at the President's table from 1789 to the end of Washington's second term, 1797, indicates the new nation's dependence on the land. Game, fowl, meats, plantation-grown fruit and vegetables, fish from local rivers or the Atlantic reveal the abundance of the land. Spliced throughout the menus are the remnants of Washington's English heritage—puddings, cream trifles, and taste for port and wine."[11]

Thomas Jefferson was probably the biggest admirer of French food of all the presidents. He had spent time in Paris as an envoy of the United States to France, and he developed an appreciation for French cuisine and wine. He even had a slave, James Hemings, brother of his consort Sally Hemings, trained in the French culinary arts so Hemings could cook for Jefferson at his home in Monticello near Charlottesville, Virginia.

The president's preference didn't catch on with the country at the time because most Americans weren't aware of their leader's culinary tastes. But Cannon and Brooks write, "Many of [Jefferson's] innovations are today an accepted part of our national diet. . . . [He had an] adventurous palate and active interest in a wide range of foods. . . . In his four years in Paris he sampled widely French cuisine, making copious notes of dishes he liked so he could serve them back home. . . . President Jefferson was particularly addicted to intricate dishes," and he returned from Paris with a taste for bouillabaisse, ragouts, gateaux, soufflés, ices, sauces, and wine-based recipes. Jefferson said he preferred French cooking "because the meats were more tender." He loved fresh vegetables, obtained from his plantation and local markets, and ate them often. He enjoyed olives, figs, mulberries, and, when they could be acquired, pineapples. He liked crabs, shad, oysters, partridge, and venison. He drank cider and malt drinks at his table and consumed large amounts of Madeira.[12]

Over the years, America's presidents have generally opted for comfort food or food from their younger years, Burros notes. Theodore Roosevelt had a big appetite, and even though his wife tried to limit his food intake to preserve his health, TR kept up his high-calorie diet. He particularly enjoyed fried chicken with white gravy, steak, hominy with meat gravy, game, coffee with as many as seven lumps of sugar in it, hot biscuits called "fat rascals," and cookies. He didn't drink alcohol very often, unlike many other presidents. His meals, especially supper, were occasions for lengthy conversations, with the president at the center of attention.[13]

William Howard Taft weighed more than three hundred pounds and was a voracious eater, especially when he was traveling outside Washington and could eat whatever he wanted and not what his health-minded wife recommended. On a trip to Savannah, Georgia, he had a breakfast of grapefruit, potted partridge, grilled partridge, broiled venison, bacon, waffles with maple syrup and butter, hominy, and rolls. He loved steak, including at breakfast, and a typical supper would include roast cold tenderloin with vegetable salad, lobster stew, salmon cutlets with peas, cold tongue and ham, frozen pudding, cake, fruit, and coffee.[14]

Woodrow Wilson was the opposite. As his presidency wore on and the pressures grew, his doctors thought he wasn't eating enough and feared he was growing too thin and frail. He said he liked chicken salad but when the cooks prepared it for him for lunch at his request, his plate was often untouched.[15] Food simply held no interest for him.

Franklin and Eleanor Roosevelt tried to steer clear of fancy foods that people of their background of wealth and privilege could have easily put on their menus. The Depression and the onset of World War II were times of sacrifice and the Roosevelts did their part. Eleanor had little interest in food, but Franklin did. He liked simple foods such as creamed chipped beef, corned-beef hash with poached eggs, fried cornmeal mush, Welsh rarebit, fish soups such as clam chowder, cheeses, and bread pudding. He also enjoyed doughnuts at breakfast and at teatime.[16]

On June 11, 1939, Eleanor even served the King and Queen of England hot dogs at the Roosevelt estate in Hyde Park, New York, a decision that shocked her straitlaced mother-in-law. Eleanor said she wanted to give them what everyday Americans ate, and King George VI was reported to have had more than one with a cold beer. The resulting publicity—including a front-page article in the *New York Times*—added to the frankfurter's popularity and gave people the sense that the president and first lady were doing their best to stay in touch with middle-class and working-class Americans.[17]

Harry Truman wasn't very interested in food and said he learned in the Army to eat what was placed in front of him and not complain.

Dwight Eisenhower was an able cook on the outdoor grill, a method of cooking that was already a trend among families in the suburbs.

Richard Nixon liked cottage cheese with fruit or ketchup, which never caught on. When it became known that he liked meat loaf, many Americans wrote to the White House for the recipe, according to chef Henry Haller.[18]

Jimmy Carter liked grits, and after a short time many people in Washington and around the country were serving them.

Ronald Reagan kept a jar of jelly beans on his Oval Office desk and had several jars distributed throughout *Air Force One*, his presidential jet. "You can tell a lot about a fella's character by whether he picks out all of one color or just grabs a handful," Reagan said in a bit of jelly-bean psychoanalysis. Even though his wife Nancy set an elegant table with fine cuisine, Ronald Reagan counted macaroni and cheese, meat loaf with mashed potatoes and gravy, roast-beef hash, osso buco, broiled swordfish, and a moist, buttery cake called "monkey bread" among his favorite foods.

An unintended effect of Reagan's partnership with Soviet leader Mikhail Gorbachev as they sought to reduce Cold War tensions was a boom in demand for heirloom tomatoes from Siberia. Opening up Soviet society to the outside world enabled Siberian farmers to market their excellent tomatoes, called the Galina, Sasha's Altai, Perestroika, and Glasnost, in the West.[19]

George H. W. Bush hated broccoli, and after I reported that he had banned the green vegetable from *Air Force One*, the broccoli growers of California sent ten tons of broccoli by truck from California to the White House in protest. But Bush never developed a taste for it.

Bush also said he liked pork rinds. In March 1988, this was publicized in an article in *Time* magazine and sales of pork rinds increased 11 percent. Bush was dubbed "Skin Man of the Year" by the pork-rind producers.

Even though first lady Hillary Clinton arranged for international foods to be served at the White House, Bill Clinton still loved to eat cheeseburgers and he ordered them often when he was outside the West Wing. His fondness for junk food was famously spoofed on *Saturday Night Live*, which depicted him going from table to table at McDonald's and eating from customers' plates.

George W. Bush enjoyed Tex-Mex fare and snacked on pretzels, but food held little interest for him; he was very committed to daily exercise and staying fit.

Obama says broccoli is his favorite food, a sign, no doubt, of the influence of his nutrition-minded wife Michelle, who is a strong advocate of healthy eating and is known for her White House garden of fruits and vegetables. But when President Obama leaves the White House to have lunch at a restaurant, he frequently orders burgers and fries. His wife also admitted that he often has a yen for chili.

* * *

A MAJOR EXCEPTION to the down-home preferences of most presidents was John F. Kennedy, under the strong influence of his wife Jacqueline.[20]

He enjoyed New England clam chowder and seafood chowder and baked beans, but overall he went along with his Jacqueline's desire for French cuisine, especially at official occasions or at other times when guests were present. She spoke the language and admired French culture, and since Americans emulated the Kennedys in many ways, their taste caught on. "They went big-time French and everybody wanted to do what they did," Marian Burros told me.[21]

Most important, the Kennedys brought in noted French chef René Verdon to cook for them and their guests at the White House. Spurred by both the Kennedys and celebrity chefs James Beard and Julia Child, who specialized in French food, French restaurants also became very popular as exemplars of fine dining and elegance.

Presidents and Fashion

John F. Kennedy probably had more influence on clothing, fashion, and style than any other president. His impact was more intense because the media, especially the relatively new mass medium of television, covered him so heavily. Many Americans were utterly fascinated by the handsome, charismatic new president, along with his equally attractive wife and their two children. TV made them welcome guests in America's living rooms. Peter Carlson, writing in *Gentlemen's Quarterly* in 1981, said Kennedy's "casual wear reflecting the Lacoste-loafer-chino syndrome, was a perfect expression of upper-class American aspirations of the time."[22]

Kennedy liked two-button suits instead of the more traditional three-button ones that his wealthy father and other rich business executives preferred. He had his suits tailored for a looser fit so he could wear a brace to relieve chronic back pain without detection. He also had his shirts custom-made. His taste was for solid colors, mostly blue and dark gray.

His famous disdain for hats reflected a generation of World War II veterans who preferred more informal looks to the regimented formality of the military. For them, not wearing a hat was a form of independence. JFK had his silk top hat with him at his inauguration and wore it while watching the inaugural parade. But he thought it made him look silly and he didn't wear it for his inauguration address. This gave the massive television audience the impression that he didn't wear it at all that day, which wasn't true. The hat industry, based in Connecticut, was not pleased with the president's hatless moments.[23]

"Every president has left a mark on American style, from Harry Truman's penchant for Hawaiian-style shirts to Dwight Eisenhower's cropped military jackets and Ronald Reagan's custom-made Hollywood glamour," writes social critic Kate Betts. "But it was the simple sartorial gestures of John F. Kennedy that really shaped 20th Century American style. The images are iconic now—a rolled-up sleeve, an untucked shirt, a shaggy head of hair—like something out of a J. Crew catalog or a Ralph Lauren advertisement. But in 1961, Kennedy's confident carefree style was a radical departure from the copycat boxy gray suits and felt hats that had defined men's fashion for previous generations."[24]

Betts adds, "Among other things, Kennedy . . . reintroduced the casual blue blazer both in the White House and on trips to Hyannis Port. Less well known is that for all the unself-conscious air that his wardrobe conveyed, JFK went to the trouble of having much of it made by a tailor in London, a sartorial standard he had come to appreciate as the son of U.S. Ambassador Joe Kennedy and one that his wife Jackie and sister-in-law Lee Radziwell thought should be the natural beginning point for a man of style."[25]

But Kennedy was perfectly capable of creating an image of cool all by himself. He wore Ray-Ban sunglasses, drove a convertible car at his Hyannis Port estate, and liked chinos, polo shirts, and those two-button suits. "He ushered in a whole new era of style—a convergence of Old World elegance and casual modernity," says fashion designer Michael Kors.[26]

*   *   *

RICHARD NIXON wasn't responsible for many fads, but he did start the trend of wearing a small American flag on the lapel of his suit jacket, a practice that presidents have used ever since as a gesture of patriotism. For Nixon it was also a way to embarrass his anti–Vietnam War adversaries. Wearing the American flag pin was also seen in conservative circles as an endorsement of the Vietnam War.[27]

Today, however, it's seen simply as a generalized patriotic display, not a statement on any specific policy. For a while President Obama didn't wear the pin, but when his patriotism was questioned he started wearing it again because he felt that it wasn't worth arguing over.

Theodore Roosevelt started a fad for the "Panama hat" when he donned the wide-brimmed, lightweight tropical headgear during a visit to the construction site of the Panama Canal, which he considered his greatest achievement as president.[28]

Dwight Eisenhower kicked off a trend before he became commander in chief when, as a well-known Army general, he wore a short jacket that became popular during World War II and was known as the Ike jacket.[29] He also pleased the hat industry by wearing a homburg on formal occasions. The hat industry reported in 1953 that Ike's preference had spurred sales of the homburg. After he wore one at his 1953 inauguration in January, sales jumped as much as 20 percent during the next month and such hats sold well through the spring.[30] One fashion expert said the homburg became "the distinguishing mark of the up-and-coming business and professional man." The trend didn't last very long, however.

Ronald Reagan, a former movie and television star, had an innate sense of style and glamour, as had Kennedy, and his tailor-made suits were of the finest quality. He liked brown suits, which he briefly brought into fashion, and, during a trip to Europe in 1982, he wore a patterned blue-and-gray glen plaid suit, a departure from the staidness of the worlds of diplomacy and Wall Street. This caused a "sartorial splash," *Time* reported, and showed that Reagan could make creative and somewhat risky fashion statements. Designers including Perry Ellis and Giorgio Armani in the mid to late 1980s, while Reagan was in office, used brown as a key color in their collections.[31] Ronald and Nancy Reagan also liked to dress up for formal occasions and they held many such events, which became a trend in Washington and around the country among the affluent.

Bill Clinton started in office as someone who didn't care about clothes or fashion. He appeared in ballooning suits and went casual too often, wearing bomber jackets and timepieces with plastic watchbands. He jogged publicly in very brief shorts, a baggy sweatshirt, and a baseball cap, and was pilloried by the media for looking unfit and unkempt. But over time Clinton had a makeover. He began wearing fine pinstripe suits and favored clothing designed by the respected Donna Karan. When Hillary Clinton, Bill's wife, bought him Jerry Garcia ties, this sparked a surge in popularity for the flashy neckwear inspired by the lead singer of the Grateful Dead rock band.

Clinton also showed the power of his celebrity when he began wearing colorful ties made by a New York designer for Save the Children, a children's advocacy group based in Connecticut. The neckwear often featured children's faces and hands amid unusual designs. A Save the Children spokeswoman said Clinton's use of the ties gave a "big boost" to mail-order sales of the neckwear.[32]

By the time he ran successfully for reelection in 1996, he was winning praise from fashion experts for his big navy-blue pinstriped suits, padded-shoulder suit jackets, cuffed pants with a full break, colorful ties, and elegant full-length overcoats. He succeeded in looking hip and youthful but not outlandish.[33]

*   *   *

OTHER PRESIDENTS' VENTURES into the world of style were less successful. By wearing cardigan sweaters for some of his activities, Jimmy Carter, who took office in 1977, tried to send the message that he was ending the "imperial presidency" of his predecessor Richard Nixon. Instead he came across like a retiree with no sense of style, according to one fashion critic. Another critic said the former Georgia governor's preference for jeans and chambray shirts resulted in "stylistic impotency."[34]

During the late 1920s and early 1930s, Herbert Hoover's use of starched detachable collars, similar to what had been popular two decades earlier, made him seem stuck in the past. This added to his image of haplessness in dealing with contemporary problems such as the Depression, and his sense of style never caught on.

Calvin Coolidge, who served in the mid-1920s, wore dull suits and ties and rigid collars. "I think the American people want a solemn ass as a president," he said, "and I think I'll go along with them." His old-fashioned garb made no stylistic headway, especially since many men were dressing more flamboyantly and colorfully during this period, known as the Jazz Age.

Even Franklin Roosevelt, who was influential in so many other areas of American life, was not a style setter. The fashion critics of his day considered him poorly dressed. Part of his challenge was that his legs were paralyzed from polio, and he had his suits made with extra width and length in the trousers to camouflage the leg braces that enabled him to move around. Those braces were often painted black to further disguise his disability.

Harry Truman, a former haberdasher in Missouri, knew his way around a fitting room and was familiar with fabrics and fashions. But a critic for

Life magazine said his lapels were too wide and his pants too long. He also liked bright ties, which some critics frowned upon. Over time, Truman wore a more subdued wardrobe to give himself a more dignified look. However, Truman liked to wear brightly colored and boldly patterned "Hawaiian shirts" while he was on vacation, especially in the subtropical environs of Key West, Florida. He never changed this approach, which inspired some men to wear similar outfits on the weekends for backyard barbecues and at the beach.

Presidents and Their Pets

Presidential pets have enabled the nation's leaders to bond with millions of other pet owners. And while presidents have had a variety of pets, ranging from Andrew Jackson's fighting cocks to Theodore Roosevelt's menagerie of dogs, horses, guinea pigs, a lizard, a hen, and a blue macaw he kept for his children, the presidential pet of choice has always been the dog, widely considered the most loyal and devoted of companions. How the presidents interacted with their canines and other pets has provided insight into their tastes and even their character.

"Our presidents show goodness of heart during their private and personal moments with the animals with which they have bonded," says Claire McLean, founder and director of the Presidential Pet Museum in Virginia. She adds, "If you doubt that White House pets have a powerful impact on the public, consider that the American Kennel Club's surges in breed registration closely track the types of breeds in the White House."[35]

The most memorable remark about presidential pets is attributed to Harry Truman: "If you want a friend in Washington, get a dog." Truman tolerated the Irish setter kept by his daughter Margaret, but despite his famous comment, he wasn't as much of an animal lover as other presidents.

Franklin Roosevelt's Scottish terrier Fala was one of the most famous presidential pets. The peppy little canine was a constant companion of the president, frequently photographed with him and adored by children and parents around the country.

When George H. W. Bush was president, first lady Barbara Bush published *Millie's Book*, a volume recounting a day in the life of the Bushes' English springer spaniel Millie. It became a big seller. The book was a publicity stunt, but it helped to humanize the president.

Bill Clinton and his family had Socks the cat but the president was partial to Buddy, his Labrador retriever. Buddy was reportedly the only member of the president's family that cared to be with him in the days after Clinton admitted having an affair with a White House intern.

George W. Bush's Scottish terrier Barney became famous when a White House staffer equipped him with a small camera—dubbed "Barney-Cam"—to record his life at the White House. These videos became popular on the Internet, especially among children.

President Barack Obama joined the dog owners' club with two Portuguese water dogs, Bo and Sunny. They were essentially the pets of his daughters, Malia and Sasha. But kids outside the family also loved them and they were often included in White House photos and allowed to romp among children at White House events.

It's rare that a president's association with his pets causes him problems, but it happened to Lyndon Johnson. The earthy Texan once stood before news photographers and pulled one of his beagles, named Him, off the ground by his ears. Many people reacted negatively to photos of the 1964 incident, which added to the impression that Johnson was ham-handed and insensitive. Hundreds of angry phone calls, letters, and telegrams poured into the White House, and Johnson issued a public apology.[36]

Chapter Seventeen
Consequential vs. Shallow Celebrity
All Stardom Is Not Equal

All celebrity is not created equal.

As shown in this book, some presidents have used their prominence to achieve great things, but some have failed miserably at parlaying their fame into positive results. It's the difference between consequential celebrity and shallow celebrity.

But it's inevitable that in our celebrity-driven culture an emphasis on fame has become a central part of the presidency, and future occupants of the office would do well to accommodate themselves to it.

* * *

OVERALL, the concept of celebrity has been important in the evolution of life in the United States, and not just in a political context. "Celebrity," writes cultural historian Fred Inglis, "is also one of the adhesives which, at a time when the realms of public politics, civil society, and private domestic life are increasingly fractured and enclosed in separate enclaves, serves to pull those separate entities together and to do its bit towards maintaining social cohesion and common values."[1]

During the years after World War I, Hollywood gave birth to what Inglis calls "the sacred infant of the century, the star. . . . The tale of the twenties and thirties is first of all . . . a story of how the great dictators and indeed the everyday victors of electoral politics—Mussolini, Hitler, and

Stalin, along with Woodrow Wilson and Lloyd George—made themselves into stars on the world stage of politics and corralled the public spectacles of celebratory propaganda—the rally, the armaments parade, the Olympic Games, the Cup Final, the ticker-tape drive through Manhattan, the state openings, the royal weddings, the Mayday march—which then became essential adjuncts of power. All such occasions lent themselves, with the help of newsreels and hugely amplified martial music and megaphone rhetoric, to the public dramatisation of power."[2]

This dynamic was intensified by the rise of television and the power of the mass media, which inextricably tied the political to the personal. Today Americans have become so immersed in celebrity culture that they expect their leader to be a superstar, and successful presidents must engage the nation, hold its interest, and exploit the mass media to promote their agendas. If this doesn't happen, the country tunes out and the result is a decline in a president's job-approval rating and an erosion of the ability to get things done. As a result, the most effective presidents—such as Theodore Roosevelt, Franklin D. Roosevelt, Ronald Reagan, and to some extent Bill Clinton—figure out ways to maintain and expand their celebrity as an essential part of governing.

President Kennedy's creation of the Peace Corps offers an example of a chief executive capturing the zeitgeist and affecting the culture in a major and positive way. Two big reasons for the volunteer agency's success in luring recruits were its embodiment of Kennedy's inspiring call for national service and its reflection of JFK's celebrity. Many young people felt that joining the Peace Corps was an admirable and fashionable thing to do because it was so closely associated with the charismatic young president, and they signed up in droves.

On November 2, 1960, as a candidate Kennedy proposed "a peace corps of talented men and women" who would provide their time, energy, and ideas to help people in developing countries. He quickly found that this call to service had great resonance, as he received 25,000 letters in response to his speech and he took action soon after assuming the presidency. Kennedy created the Peace Corps by executive order on March 1, 1961, and he named his brother-in-law Sargent Shriver, a capable administrator, to run the program.[3]

Congress approved the Peace Corps as a permanent federal agency and Kennedy signed the bill into law on September 22, 1961. It was the perfect program for the idealistic young president who, in his inaugural address, had said, "Ask not what your country can do for you. Ask what you can do for your country." Although some of its luster faded in succeeding decades—the victim of a lesser spirit of sacrifice, as well as growing cynicism about government—the Peace Corps was very popular for many years. Since its creation, 200,000 volunteers have served in 139 countries.[4]

There have been other examples of presidential celebrity leading to good works and positive developments. These include Franklin D. Roosevelt's rallying of the country behind his New Deal social safety-net programs and the massive effort to win World War II, Ronald Reagan's success in restoring public optimism and fostering patriotism, and Barack Obama's call for young African Americans to better themselves through education and perseverance.

Overall, perhaps the best examples of how a president enhanced his celebrity and used it effectively for good works were provided by Theodore Roosevelt, whose larger-than-life personality came to symbolize the rising America of the twenty-first century.

From the day he took office after William McKinley's assassination in 1901, having served as vice president for only a few months, Teddy Roosevelt captured the nation's imagination. His personality was bold and his policy ideas were audacious, such as his limiting the power of monopolistic trusts, including those running the steel, coal, and railroad industries. He argued that they were gaining too much influence over the economy. He arranged for the construction of the Panama Canal, one of the marvels of the era. He helped to end the Russo-Japanese War, which won him the Nobel Peace Prize. He set aside vast tracts of federal land and protected them from development. To marshal public support for himself and his programs, he understood that he needed to both entertain the country and create a sense of excitement, and this is what he did for two terms.[5]

He popularized phrases and concepts that still resonate today, such as the "bully pulpit," which makes the president's voice louder and more influential than anyone else's; his condemning greedy industrialists as "malefactors of great wealth"; and his use of the West African aphorism, "Speak softly but carry a big stick." He was imperialistic abroad and had racist attitudes about the superiority of whites, but in many cases he tried to use his celebrity for noble ends.

Most recently, Barack Obama has used today's diverse media to make himself into more of a celebrity than any of his predecessors. And he has expanded his celebrity by relying on entertainers and athletes to argue for his programs. In late 2014, for example, he turned out luminaries from sports and television for his campaign to end sexual assaults on America's college campuses. By that time such star-powered campaigns had become routine for the White House. Cleveland Cavaliers forward Kevin Love and actors Jon Hamm and Connie Britton were among the luminaries who urged their fans via an Internet video to support Obama's efforts to end rape among US college students.[6]

"Our purpose here [in the Obama administration] is to meet people where they are," White House adviser Valerie Jarrett said. "We're extremely strategic in how we engage and deploy validators, and we're very fortunate that people who have tremendous followings across the country are willing to be very effective messengers."[7]

*   *   *

BUT THERE IS a downside. Focusing too much on notoriety can add to the impression that fame is everything—even mindless, purposeless fame. This show-biz mentality encourages superficiality in public life and makes looking good and delivering memorable and provocative sound bites or tweets more important than serious thinking or sincere efforts to achieve compromise.

The dual nature of celebrity—consequential and shallow—also makes its overemphasis dangerous for presidents. People can be drawn to stars very quickly, as they were initially to Jimmy Carter and Lyndon Johnson. But Americans can turn against the stars abruptly, as happened to both of those presidents, depending on what the luminaries do and say and what the public mood might be. This fickleness is part of the nature of modern celebrity culture.

There's another cost to being celebrity in chief—loss of privacy. No matter what a president does, the public and the media pay attention, and a president can't escape from the scrutiny. Presidents today must deal with near-total visibility, near-total exposure, and near-total loss of privacy, and that's a big problem. Presidents need time to themselves, just as everyone else does. But being celebrity in chief puts them constantly under the microscope.

The celebration of celebrity for its own sake is illustrated by the annual White House Correspondents' Association dinner. This event was originally designed to allow reporters to get together with their sources on a friendly basis for one night a year, at a formal dinner that the president attended as a gesture of goodwill to those covering him. But the event has become a spectacle that has departed significantly from its roots. It is now an affair celebrating stardom and dominated in many ways not by government officials, the media, or even the president, but by Hollywood stars. Among those who have attended in recent years are David Arquette, Bo Derek, George Clooney, Kim Kardashian, Alicia Keys, Nicole Kidman, John Legend, Lindsay Lohan, Mila Kunis, Ozzy Osbourne, Martin Sheen (who was my guest), and Sofia Vergara. There has also been a proliferation of pre- and post-dinner parties and receptions, not only on the night of the dinner but in the days preceding and following it.[8]

The event's metamorphosis caused the *New York Times* to boycott it several years ago. Dean Baquet, the Washington bureau chief when the boycott started, explained, "It had evolved into a very odd, celebrity-driven event that made it look like the press and government all shuck their adversarial roles for one night of the year, sing together (literally, by the way) and have a grand old time cracking jokes. It just feels like it sends the wrong signal to our readers and viewers, like we are all in it together and it is all a game."[9]

Baquet had a point. In some ways the modern presidency operates like a game played by White House strategists to portray the chief executive in the best possible light while the media try to tear the president down. And celebrity is a very big advantage in trying to win that game.

* * *

IT'S LIKELY that future presidents will feel the need to tie themselves to popular culture and show they understand American life at least as much as Obama has. They will need to capitalize on their fame and make the most of their celebrity to most effectively communicate with the country in all of its complexity. This means reaching out to as many groups as possible, from mothers worried about their kids' health care to sports fans impressed that the commander in chief knows which college team is ranked number one. It means acknowledging that the fragmentation of our culture is a fact of life and finding ways to go directly to the people, even at the risk of embracing the shallowness and aimless glitz of show business.

A Pew Research Center poll released in 2014 showed that political polarization has deepened; Democrats and Republicans are hardening their positions and thinking badly of each other. The divide also is affecting how the American people live their lives, in what Pew called "ideological silos"; 63 percent of consistent conservatives and 49 percent of consistent liberals say most of their close friends share their political views, compared with 35 percent of the overall electorate. And the ideologues want to live in different places: 75 percent of consistent conservatives prefer communities where houses are larger and farther apart, with schools, stores, and restaurants a few miles away, while 77 percent of consistent liberals prefer smaller houses closer to amenities. Liberals prefer racially and ethnically diverse areas, while conservatives want to live among people who share their religious faith.[10] "If people living in 'deep red' (Republican) or 'deep blue' (Democratic) America feel like they inhabit distinctly different worlds, it is in part because they seek out different types of communities, both geographic and social," a Pew summary said.[11] And increasingly, Americans are looking to have their views reinforced rather than challenged by their media of choice.

Presidents have to deal with this polarization every day in making the case for their agendas and selling themselves. This means slicing and dicing the electorate and, as White House officials say, appealing to the voters where they are, whether it means on TV talk shows or ideological radio programs of various stripes, or through social media such as Twitter and Facebook. It's a far cry from the media environment of twenty years ago, when a relative handful of media outlets, led by the three broadcast TV networks of ABC, CBS, and NBC and including powerful newspapers such as the *New York Times* and the *Washington Post*, set the political agenda. Those days are long gone, swept away in a tide of mouse clicks, page views, and hardening ideology.

*   *   *

IT IS CLEAR THAT, despite the drawbacks, serving as celebrity in chief has become an essential function of the modern presidency. And if handled wisely, it can help a president govern more effectively, shape the country's perceptions of itself, and provide a narrative for where the United States is, where it is headed, and where it should be going.

Epilogue
The Future of Presidential Celebrity

Every modern president has been a celebrity to some extent, the subject of pervasive curiosity and able to command media and public attention almost at will. That's because every modern president, at least during the honeymoon period immediately following his election and during his first several months in office, has benefited from the essence of celebrity—fame, influence, and the insatiable interest of the mass media. The most successful presidents maintain or expand their star power; the least successful ones don't.

It's likely that future presidents will need to capitalize on their fame and make the most of their celebrity, to best communicate with the country in all of its complexity. This means reaching out to as many groups as possible. It means staying in touch with core supporters and remaining on good terms with them. It means standing for fundamental American values, defining themselves in positive and distinctive ways, and mastering the media of their times.

* * *

NEAR TERM, one of the biggest challenges for all the presidential candidates in 2016 will be how to deal with the celebrity factor. Hillary Clinton, the early favorite for the Democratic nomination, has a particular problem if she runs. She is probably the best-known woman in the world as former first lady, ex-US senator from New York, and former secretary of state. Her dilemma would be how to manage her celebrity. She must acknowledge her fame (and fortune), recognizing that the media have a voracious appetite for information about her and channeling their interest to areas that are beneficial to her and that put her ideas in the best light. At the same time, she needs to show that she is in touch with everyday people and doesn't take herself too seriously or feel entitled to the White House. This has been a bumpy road for her so far.

She also has a unique advantage and a major difficulty in her husband Bill. The former president is a superstar in his own right, one of the best-known people in the world and one of the most popular Democrats in the country. If she runs, it would be the first time that a celebrity couple without peer has sought the White House. (They weren't household names when Bill ran successfully in 1992.) As president emeritus, Bill could overshadow her or at least compete with her for attention. More than any other candidate in history, Hillary Clinton would have to reckon with celebrity culture because she has been in the public eye for so long and in such a dramatic way.

For other Democratic candidates and for Republican hopefuls, who are less familiar to voters and largely untested nationally, the problem is how to get better known in a positive way. Their challenge is to make the aura of celebrity work to their advantage by avoiding damaging mistakes and motivating people to learn more about them and their ideas.

All the candidates need to understand that celebrity, while it has its limits, can increase their effectiveness and their popularity and will be crucial to success in the 2016 election, as it will be to the success of the next president of the United States.

Notes

Introduction

1. Author's interview with Mark K. Updegrove, August 20, 2014.
2. Quoted in Gerald F. Seib, "Government by Celebrity?" *Globe and Mail* (Canada), September 18, 1999, p. C1.
3. Gene Healy, *The Cult of the Presidency: America's Dangerous Devotion to Executive Power*, Washington, DC: Cato Institute, 2008, pp. 2–3.
4. Ibid., p. 3.
5. Ibid.
6. Justin McCarthy, "Americans Losing Confidence in All Branches of U.S. Gov't," Gallup, June 30, 2014, http://www.gallup.com/poll/171992/americans-losing -confidence-branches-gov.aspx.
7. Healy, *The Cult of the Presidency*, p. 245. See also Kenneth T. Walsh, *Prisoners of the White House: Presidential Isolation and the Crisis of Leadership*, Boulder, CO: Paradigm Publishers, 2013.
8. Author's interview with Mike McCurry, June 9, 2014.
9. Quoted in Philip Galanes, "Table for Three: Oh, How They Like to Dish," *New York Times*, April 27, 2014, Sunday Styles, p. 1.
10. Ibid.
11. Thomas E. Cronin, *On the Presidency: Teacher, Soldier, Shaman, Pol*, Boulder, CO: Paradigm Publishers, 2009, pp. 39–40.
12. Quoted in Philip Galanes, "A Power Lunch, Times Two," *New York Times*, April 6, 2014, Sunday Styles, p. 12.
13. Ibid.
14. Cronin, *On the Presidency*, p. 41.

15. Alan Schroeder, *Celebrity-in-Chief: How Show Business Took Over the White House*, Boulder, CO: Westview Press, 2004, pp. 299–300.

16. John Sayle Watterson, *The Games Presidents Play: Sports and the Presidency*, Baltimore: Johns Hopkins University Press, 2006, pp. 91, 96–97.

17. Frank Luntz, *Words that Work: It's Not What You Say, It's What People Hear*, New York: Hyperion, 2007, p. 198.

18. Ibid., p. 115.

19. Tevi Troy, *What Jefferson Read, Ike Watched, and Obama Tweeted: 200 Years of Popular Culture in the White House*, Washington, DC: Regnery Publishing, 2013, pp. xvii–xviii.

20. This is a reference to the investigations launched by Sen. Joe McCarthy (R-MN) into alleged communist infiltration in America.

21. Russell Lynes, *The Tastemakers: The Shaping of American Popular Taste*, New York: Dover Publications, 1980, p. 350.

22. Author's interview with Geoff Garin, August 15, 2013.

23. Ibid.

24. Schroeder, *Celebrity-in-Chief*, pp. 3–4.

25. Ibid., p. 5.

26. Author's telephone interview with Bruce Reed, December 19, 2013.

27. Ibid.

Chapter 1

1. "The Inauguration of George Washington, 1789," http://eyewitnesstohistory.com/washingtoninaug.htm. Charles Thompson was his official escort and Col. David Humphries was his personal aide. See "The People's Vote: President George Washington's First Inaugural Speech (1789)," http://www.ourdocuments.gov/doc.php?flash=true&doc=11.

2. Ibid.

3. Ibid.

4. Thomas E. Cronin, *On the Presidency: Teacher, Soldier, Shaman, Pol*, Boulder, CO: Paradigm Publishers, 2009, p. 41.

5. Tevi Troy, *What Jefferson Read, Ike Watched, and Obama Tweeted: 200 Years of Popular Culture in the White House*, Washington, DC: Regnery Publishing, 2013, pp. 5–6.

6. Vicki Goldberg, with the White House Historical Association, *The White House: The President's Home in Photographs and History*, New York: Little, Brown and Company, 2011, p. 121.

7. Cronin, *On the Presidency*, p. 43.

8. Troy, *What Jefferson Read*, pp. 43–44.

9. Harold Holzer, *Lincoln at Cooper Union: The Speech that Made Abraham Lincoln President*, New York: Simon and Schuster Paperbacks, 2004, pp. 1–2.

10. Ibid., pp. 2–3.

11. Ibid., p. 179.

12. Ibid., pp. 218–219.

13. Ibid., p. 5.

14. Ibid., pp. 92–93.

15. Ibid., pp. 93–94.

16. Ibid., p. 99.

17. Ibid., pp. 243–244.

18. Paul F. Boller Jr., *Presidential Diversions: Presidents at Play from George Washington to George W. Bush*, Orlando, FL: Harcourt, 2007, pp. 109, 113.

19. Ibid., p. 109.

20. Ibid., p. 112.

21. Miller Center, "American President: Andrew Jackson," University of Virginia, http://millercenter.org/president/jackson/essays/biography/print.

22. Ibid.

23. Boller, *Presidential Diversions*, p. 62.

24. Miller Center, "American President: Zachary Taylor," University of Virginia, http://millercenter.org/president/taylor/essays/biography/print.

25. Kenneth T. Walsh, *From Mount Vernon to Crawford: A History of the Presidents and Their Retreats*, New York: Hyperion, 2005, pp. 7–8.

26. Ibid., pp. 7–8.

27. Miller Center, "American President: Rose Cleveland, Frances Cleveland," University of Virginia, http://millercenter.org/president/cleveland/essays/firstlady.

Chapter 2

1. Kenneth T. Walsh, *From Mount Vernon to Crawford: A History of the Presidents and Their Retreats*, New York: Hyperion, 2005, p. 65.

2. "Topics in Chronicling America—The Perdicaris Affair," Library of Congress, http://loc.gov/rr/news/topics/perdicaris.html.

3. Walsh, *From Mount Vernon to Crawford*, p. 79.

4. Ibid., p. 74.

5. Ibid., p. 75.

6. Theodore Roosevelt, *An Autobiography*, New York: Charles Scribner's Sons, 1913, p. 40.

7. "Theodore Roosevelt: President, Reformer, and Conservationist," United States History, http://u-s-history.com/pages/h959.html. See also "Theodore

Roosevelt," The White House, http://www.whitehouse.gov/about/presidents/theodoreroosevelt.

8. "Theodore Roosevelt Biography," Bio, http://biography.com/people/theodore-roosevelt-9463424. Accessed November 4, 2014.

9. Peter Collier, *The Roosevelts: An American Saga*, New York: Simon and Schuster, 1994, pp. 134–135.

10. Tevi Troy, *What Jefferson Read, Ike Watched, and Obama Tweeted: 200 Years of Popular Culture in the White House*, Washington, DC: Regnery Publishing, 2013, p. 56.

11. Roosevelt, *An Autobiography*, p. 336.

12. Ibid., p. 318.

13. Ibid.

14. John Sayle Watterson, *The Games Presidents Play: Sports and the Presidency*, Baltimore: Johns Hopkins University Press, 2006, p. 46.

15. Ibid., pp. 51–52.

16. Ibid., p. 58.

Chapter 3

1. This quote has been widely reported. See Mark Shields, "Elections Are Not About the Candidates," Creators.com, March 17, 2007, http://www.creators.com/opinion/mark-shields/elections-are-not-about-the-candidates.html. Also see Dorothy Rabinowitz, "Why Obama Is No Roosevelt," *Wall Street Journal*, November 2, 2010, http://online.wsj.com/articles/SB10001424052748704141104575588211544818170.

2. Fred Inglis, *A Short History of Celebrity*, Princeton, NJ: Princeton University Press, 2010, p. 174.

3. Ibid., pp. 174–175.

4. Robert E. Gilbert, "Franklin Delano Roosevelt," in William C. Spragens, ed., *Popular Images of American Presidents*, New York: Greenwood Press, 1988, p. 358.

5. Tevi Troy, *What Jefferson Read, Ike Watched, and Obama Tweeted: 200 Years of Popular Culture in the White House*, Washington, DC: Regnery Publishing, 2013, p. 81.

6. Quoted in Troy, *What Jefferson Read*, pp. 83, 84.

7. Gilbert, "Franklin Delano Roosevelt," pp. 358–359.

8. Ibid., p. 378.

9. Hedrick Smith, *The Power Game*, New York: Ballantine, 1988, p. 394.

10. Troy, *What Jefferson Read*, pp. 86, 87.

11. Alan Schroeder, *Celebrity-in-Chief: How Show Business Took Over the White House*, Boulder, CO: Westview Press, 2004, pp. 7–10.

12. Ibid., p. 10.

13. Ibid., p. 16.

14. Author's interview with Bob Clark, archivist at the FDR Library in Hyde Park, New York, August 18, 2013.

15. Ibid.

Chapter 4

1. Author's interview with Robert Dallek, September 3, 2013.

2. Thomas E. Cronin, *On the Presidency: Teacher, Soldier, Shaman, Pol*, Boulder, CO: Paradigm Publishers, 2009, p. 97.

3. Arthur Schlesinger, *A Thousand Days*, London: Andre Deutsch, 1965, p. 191.

4. Alan Schroeder, *Celebrity-in-Chief: How Show Business Took Over the White House*, Boulder, CO: Westview Press, 2004, p. 20.

5. Ibid., p. 20.

6. Ibid., p. 125.

7. Tevi Troy, *What Jefferson Read, Ike Watched, and Obama Tweeted: 200 Years of Popular Culture in the White House*, Washington, DC: Regnery Publishing, 2013, pp. 94–95, 96.

8. Paul F. Boller Jr., *Presidential Diversions: Presidents at Play from George Washington to George W. Bush*, Orlando, FL: Harcourt, 2007, p. 271.

9. Ibid., p. 272.

10. Ibid., p. 269.

11. Ibid.

12. Andrew Kohut, "JFK's America," Pew Research Center, November 20, 2013, http://www.pewresearch.org/fact-tank/2013/11/20/jfks-america.

13. Schroeder, *Celebrity-in-Chief*, pp. 289–290.

14. Author's telephone interview with Barbara Perry, November 4, 2013.

15. Ibid.

16. Cronin, *On the Presidency*, p. 94.

17. Schroeder, *Celebrity-in-Chief*, pp. 288–289.

18. Author's interview with Frank Donatelli, November 7, 2013.

19. Fred Inglis, *A Short History of Celebrity*, Princeton, NJ: Princeton University Press, 2010, p. 179.

Chapter 5

1. These are views expressed by many former Reagan aides, including Marlin Fitz-water, his former White House press secretary, in an interview with the author on August 3, 2013.

2. Jennifer Rosenberg, "Ronald Reagan Quotes," About Education, http://history 1900s.about.com/od/ronaldreagan/a/Reagan-Quotes.htm.

3. This point has been made frequently by scholars, political scientists, and journal-ists. For example, see Alan Schroeder, *Celebrity-in-Chief: How Show Business Took Over the White House*, Boulder, CO: Westview Press, 2004, p. 3.

4. Quoted in Tevi Troy, *What Jefferson Read, Ike Watched, and Obama Tweeted: 200 Years of Popular Culture in the White House*, Washington, DC: Regnery Publishing, 2013, p. 169.

5. Michael K. Deaver, *Nancy: A Portrait of My Years with Nancy Reagan*, New York: William Morrow, 2004, p. 31.

6. Author's interview with Grover Norquist, September 4, 2013.

7. Larry Speakes, *Speaking Out: Inside the Reagan White House*, New York: Charles Scribner's, 1988, p. 92.

8. Nancy Reagan, *My Turn: The Memoirs of Nancy Reagan*, New York: Random House, 1989, p. 106.

9. This story was recounted in Frank Luntz, *Words that Work: It's Not What You Say, It's What People Hear*, New York: Hyperion, 2007, pp. 28–29.

10. Thomas E. Cronin, *On the Presidency: Teacher, Soldier, Shaman, Pol*, Boulder, CO: Paradigm Publishers, 2009, p. 51.

11. Sidney Blumenthal, "Reaganism and the Neokitsch Aesthetic," in Sidney Blumen-thal and Thomas Byrne Edsall, eds., *The Reagan Legacy*, New York: Pantheon Books, 1988, p. 256.

12. Ibid., p. 261.

13. Ibid., pp. 262, 272–273.

14. Daniel Kurtzman, "Ronald Reagan Quotes," About Entertainment, http://politicalhumor.about.com/cs/quotethis/a/reaganquotes.htm.

15. Author's interviews with several Reagan advisers, including former White House chief of staff Ken Duberstein, June 11, 2014.

16. Schroeder, *Celebrity-in-Chief*, pp. 28–29.

17. Miller Center, "Interview with James Kuhn," University of Virginia, March 7, 2003, http://millercenter.org/president/reagan/oralhistory/james-kuhn.

18. Ibid.

19. Author's interview with Ken Duberstein, Reagan's former White House chief of staff, June 11, 2014.

20. Miller Center, "Interview with James Kuhn."

21. Ibid.
22. Cronin, *On the Presidency*, pp. 51–52.

Chapter 6

1. Transcript of William J. Clinton, Interview on MTV's "Enough Is Enough" Forum, April 19, 1994, http://www.presidency.ucsb.edu/ws/?pid=49995.
2. Author's interview with Mike McCurry, June 9, 2014.
3. Ibid.
4. Tevi Troy, *What Jefferson Read, Ike Watched, and Obama Tweeted: 200 Years of Popular Culture in the White House*, Washington, DC: Regnery Publishing, 2013, p. 135.
5. Ibid., p. 136.
6. Quoted in ibid., p. 111.
7. Alan Schroeder, *Celebrity-in-Chief: How Show Business Took Over the White House*, Boulder, CO: Westview Press, 2004, p. 29.
8. Ibid., p. 47.
9. Ibid., pp. 47–48.
10. Ibid., p. 48.
11. Ibid., pp. 48–49.
12. Ibid., p. 49.
13. Ibid.
14. Ibid., p. 51.

Chapter 7

1. Author's interview with Ken Duberstein, October 4, 2013.
2. Tevi Troy, *What Jefferson Read, Ike Watched, and Obama Tweeted: 200 Years of Popular Culture in the White House*, Washington, DC: Regnery Publishing, 2013, pp. 228–229.
3. Author's interview with Geoff Garin, August 15, 2013.
4. Alexander Mooney, "McCain Ad Compares Obama to Britney Spears, Paris Hilton," CNN, July 30, 2008, http://www.cnn.com/2008/POLITICS/07/30/mccain.ad/index.html?_s=PM:POLITICS.
5. Adam Goldberg, "Obama Celebrity Ad: American Crossroads 'Cool' Video Slams President over Fame, Economy," *Huffington Post*, April 26, 2012, http://www.huffingtonpost.com/2012/04/26/obama-celebrity-ad-american-crossroads-cool-video_n_1455413.html.

6. Catalina Camia, "Super PAC Ad Mocks Obama as 'Celebrity President,'" *USA Today*, April 26, 2012, http://content.usatoday.com/communities/onpolitics /post/2012/04/barack-obama-celebrity-president-american-crossroads-/1# .VGE4s747MkM.

7. Lucy McCalmont, "Karl Rove: Obamacare Rap Crosses Line," *Politico*, December 13, 2013, http://www.politico.com/story/2013/12/karl-rove-obamacare -rap-101121.html.

8. Peter Roff, "Obama's TV Connection," *U.S. News & World Report*, January 3, 2014, http://www.usnews.com/opinion/blogs/peter-roff/2014/01/03/breaking -bad-house-of-cards-and-what-republicans-can-learn-from-obamas-tv-choices.

9. Ibid.

10. James Warren, "President Obama on Zach Galifianakis' Funny or Die webseries 'Between Two Ferns,'" *Daily News*, March 11, 2014, http:// www.nydailynews.com/news/politics/president-obama-zach-galifianakis -funny-die-show-ferns-article-1.1717450.

11. Jim Acosta and Kevin Liptak, "LeBron, 'Ferns' Key to Enrollment Surge, White House Says," CNN Politics, April 1, 2014, http://politicalticker.blogs .cnn.com/2014/04/01/lebron-ferns-key-to-enrollment-surge-white-house -says/?iref=obinsite.

12. Jennifer Epstein and Carrie Budoff Brown, "Connie Britton, Mayim Bialik Help Obama Celebrate ACA," *Politico*, May 2, 2014, http://www.politico.com /story/2014/05/mayim-bialik-connie-britton-aca-106275.html.

13. David Jackson, "Obama Media Strategy Includes Meteorologists," *USA Today*, May 6, 2014, http://www.usatoday.com/story/news/2014/05/06 /obama-media-strategy-climate-change-meteorologists/8766075/.

14. Caitlin Dewey, "Reliable Source: Politicians, Reporters and Celebrities Took Lots of Selfies at the Correspondents Dinner. These Were the Most Excruciating," *Washington Post*, May 4, 2014, http://www.washingtonpost.com/blogs/reliable -source/wp/2014/05/04/politicians-reporters-and-celebritiestook-lots-of-selfies -at-the-correspondents-dinner-these-were-the-most-excruciating/.

15. "Celebrities, Athletes Swarm White House for ObamaCare Party," The Hill, May 2, 2014, http://freerepublic.com/focus/f-news/3151352/posts/May_2.

16. Carrie Budoff Brown and Jennifer Epstein, "Special Report: The Obama Paradox," *Politico*, June 1, 2014, http://www.politico.com/story/2014/06/the-obama -paradox-107304_Page2.html.

17. Tevi Troy, *What Jefferson Read, Ike Watched, and Obama Tweeted: 200 Years of Popular Culture in the White House*, Washington, DC: Regnery Publishing, 2013, pp. 229, 230.

18. Roger Runnigen, "Obama's Walk on the Outside," *Bloomberg*, May 21, 2014, http://go.bloomberg.com/political-capital/2014-05-21/obamas-walk-outside.

19. Ibid.

20. Katie Zezima, "Obama Takes an Unexpected Detour—to a Little League Game," *Washington Post*, May 19, 2014, http://washingtonpost.com/blogs/the-fix/wp/2014/05/19/Obama-takes-an-unexpected-detour.

21. "Presidential Flyby," *Washington Post*, June 11, 2014, p. B4.

22. Nikki Schwab, "The President Just Wants a Burger," *US News*, June 20, 2014, http://usnews.com/news/articles/2014/06/20/the-president-just-wants-a-burger.

23. Associated Press, "Obama Eats Ribs with 4 Kansas City Letter Writers," *Boston Herald*, July 29, 2014, http://www.bostonherald.com/news_opinion/us_politics/2014/07/obama_eats_ribs_with_4_kansas_city_letter_writers.

24. Timothy Stanley, "Obama Is No Superhero," CNN, May 14, 2014, http://cnn.com/2014/05/14/opinion/stanley-obama-hollywood-embrace.

25. Ibid.

26. Author's interview with Bill McInturff, December 12, 2013.

27. Ibid.

28. Maureen Dowd, "Is Barry Whiffing?" *New York Times*, April 29, 2014.

29. Howard Kurtz, "From Captain America to Maureen Dowd, Obama Is Losing the Media Culture War," Fox News, May 1, 2014, http://www.foxnews.com/politics/2014/05/01/from-captain-america-to-maureen-dowd-obama-is-losing-media-culture-war.

30. "A Conversation About Family," *Parade*, June 22, 2014, pp. 6–10, 13.

31. Barack Obama, *Dreams from My Father: A Story of Race and Inheritance*, New York: Crown, 2007, p. 62.

32. Michael Lewis, "Obama's Way," *Vanity Fair*, October 5, 2012, http://www.vanityfair.com/politics/2012/10/michael-lewis-profile-barack-obama.

33. Troy, *What Jefferson Read*, p. 219.

Chapter 8

1. Russell Lynes, *The Tastemakers: The Shaping of American Popular Taste*, New York: Dover Publications, 1980, p. 74.

2. Author's interview with Mark Updegrove, director of the LBJ Presidential Library, August 20, 2014.

3. Tevi Troy, *What Jefferson Read, Ike Watched, and Obama Tweeted: 200 Years of Popular Culture in the White House*, Washington, DC: Regnery Publishing, 2013, pp. 153, 155.

4. Paul F. Boller Jr., *Presidential Diversions: Presidents at Play from George Washington to George W. Bush*, Orlando, FL: Harcourt, 2007, p. 279.

5. Troy, *What Jefferson Read*, pp. 125–126.

6. Author's interview with Mark Updegrove.

7. Alan Schroeder, *Celebrity-in-Chief: How Show Business Took Over the White House*, Boulder, CO: Westview Press, 2004, pp. 31–32.

8. Ibid., pp. 32–33.

9. Ibid., p. 33.

10. Ibid.

11. Vicki Goldberg, with the White House Historical Association, *The White House: The President's Home in Photographs and History*, New York: Little, Brown and Company, 2011, p. 123.

12. Troy, *What Jefferson Read*, p. 127.

13. Quoted in ibid.

14. Schroeder, *Celebrity-in-Chief*, p. 58.

15. Ibid., p. 34.

16. Ibid., p. 35.

17. Ibid., pp. 69–73.

18. Troy, *What Jefferson Read*, p. 103.

19. Quoted in ibid., p. 106.

20. Ibid., pp. 159–160.

21. Quoted in Boller, *Presidential Diversions*, pp. 283–284.

22. Ibid., p. 286.

23. Quoted in ibid.

24. Rick Perlstein, *Nixonland: The Rise of a President and the Fracturing of America*, New York: Scribner, 2008, p. 747.

25. Ibid., p. 748.

26. Ron Nessen, *It Sure Looks Different from the Inside*, Chicago: Playboy Books, 1978, p. 173.

27. Troy, *What Jefferson Read*, p. 108.

28. Quoted in Rebecca Ritzel, "On the World Stage or in the Seats, Carter Is a Theater Guy," *Washington Post*, April 2, 2014, p. C3.

29. Jonathan Yardley, "Evangelist in Chief," *Washington Post*, May 18, 2014, p. B8.

30. Troy, *What Jefferson Read*, p. 177.

Chapter 9

1. "Dolley Madison," White House Historical Association, http://www.whitehousehistory.org/history/white-house-first-ladies/first-lady-dolley-madison.html.

2. S. J. Ackerman, "First Lady, First Celebrity," *Washington Post Magazine*, July 6, 2014, p. 12.

3. Kenneth T. Walsh, *From Mount Vernon to Crawford: A History of the Presidents and Their Retreats*, New York: Hyperion, 2005, p. 8.

4. Ackerman, "First Lady, First Celebrity," p. 13.

5. Ibid.

6. Ibid., pp. 13–14.

7. Walsh, *From Mount Vernon to Crawford*, p. 8.

8. "Biography of Eleanor Roosevelt," Franklin D. Roosevelt Presidential Library and Museum, http://fdrlibrary.marist.edu/education/resources/bio_er.html.

9. Kenneth T. Walsh, *Prisoners of the White House: The Isolation of America's Presidents and the Crisis of Leadership*, Boulder, CO: Paradigm Publishers, 2013, pp. 84–85.

10. Doris Kearns Goodwin, *No Ordinary Time: Franklin and Eleanor Roosevelt: The Home Front in World War II*, New York: Simon and Schuster, 1994, pp. 38–39.

11. "Jacqueline Kennedy in the White House," John F. Kennedy Presidential Library and Museum, http://www.jfklibrary.org/JFK/JFK-in-History/Jacqueline-Kennedy-in-the-White-House.aspx.

12. "Life of Jacqueline B. Kennedy," John F. Kennedy Presidential Library and Museum, http://jfklibrary.org/JFK/Life-of-Jacqueline-B-Kennedy.

13. Holly Hanson, "Jackie Kennedy's Pillbox Hat Inaugurated New Fashion Era," *Houston Chronicle*, March 7, 1991, p. 4.

14. Valerie Steele, ed., *Encyclopedia of Clothing and Fashion, Volume 3*, Detroit: Charles Scribner's Sons, 2005, pp. 240–242.

15. Quoted in Marion McMullen, "The First Lady of Fashion," *Western Mail*, May 14, 2014, p. 23.

16. Fred Inglis, *A Short History of Celebrity*, Princeton, NJ: Princeton University Press, 2010, p. 177.

17. Theodore H. White, "For President Kennedy: An Epilogue," *Life*, December 6, 1963, pp. 158–159.

18. Miller Center, "Interview with James Kuhn," University of Virginia, March 7, 2003, http://millercenter.org/president/reagan/oralhistory/james-kuhn.

19. Ibid.

20. "Just Say No 1982–1989," Ronald Reagan Presidential Foundation and Library, http://www.reaganfoundation.org/details_t.aspx?p=RR1005NRL&lm=reagan&args_a=cms&args_b=10&argsb=N&tx=1203.

21. Miller Center, "American President: Barbara Bush," University of Virginia, http://millercenter.org/president/bush/essays/firstlady.

22. Edward Klein, *Blood Feud: The Clintons vs. the Obamas*, Washington, DC: Regnery Publishing, 2014, pp. 189–190.

23. Amy Chozick, "It Takes a Village (and a Composer and a Writer): Hillary and Bill Clinton Inspire Musical Theater," *New York Times*, July 8, 2014, http://www.nytimes.com/2014/07/09/theater/hillary-and-bill-clinton-inspire-musical-theater.html.

24. Ibid.

25. Krissah Thompson, "A Vision of First-Lady Feminism from Obama, Bush," *Washington Post*, August 7, 2014, p. C1.

26. Luizze, Starnes, and Rothman were quoted in Helena Andrews and Emily Heil, "Michelle Obama's Bold Birthday Getup," The Reliable Source, *Washington Post*, January 23, 2014, p. C2. Michelle Obama's birthday was January 17; the party was January 18.

27. Edward-Isaac Dovere, "Obama Dance Video Blackmail?" *Politico*, July 23, 2014, http://www.politico.com/story/2014/07/obama-dance-video-blackmail-109317.html.

28. Tom Hamburger and Kimberly Kindy, "First Lady Vows Fight to Keep School-Lunch Standards," *Washington Post*, May 20, 2014, p. A3.

29. Helena Bottemiller Evich, "Behind the School Lunch Fight," *Politico*, June 4, 2014, http://www.politico.com/story/2014/06/michelle-obama-public-school-lunch-school-nutrition-association-lets-move-107390.html.

30. Andrew Kohut, "Barack Obama's Better Half: Why the First Lady Is So Popular," *Politico Magazine*, July 6, 2014, http://www.politico.com/magazine/story/2014/07/michelle-obama-popularity-108593.html#.VGE9dr47MkM.

31. Author's interview with Geoff Garin, August 15, 2013.

32. Ibid.

33. "First Lady Biography: Abigail Adams," National First Ladies' Library, http://firstladies.org/biographies/firstladies.aspx?biography=2.

34. 50s Pam, "Mamie Eisenhower: Unwitting Creator of THE Iconic Color of the 50s, 'Mamie Pink,'" Save the Pink Bathrooms, July 5, 2009, http://savethepinkbathrooms.com/mamie-eisenhower-unwitting-creator-of-the-iconic-color-of-the-50s-mamie-pink.

35. Quoted in Guy Trebay, "U.S. Fashion's One-Woman Bailout?" *New York Times*, January 8, 2009, p. E1.

36. Associated Press dispatch, May 1, 1978.

37. Ibid.

38. Nancy Gibbs, "Betty Ford, 1918–2011," *Time*, July 8, 2011, http://content.time.com/time/nation/article/0,8599,2082229,00.html.

Chapter 10

1. Tevi Troy, *What Jefferson Read, Ike Watched, and Obama Tweeted: 200 Years of Popular Culture in the White House*, Washington, DC: Regnery Publishing, 2013, p. 180.

2. "Biography: 33. Harry S. Truman," *American Experience*, http://PBS.org/wgbh/americanexperience/features/biography/presidents-truman/?flavour=mobile.

3. Troy, *What Jefferson Read*, p. 146.

4. Ibid., pp. 143–144.

5. Ibid., pp. 144–145. See also Alan Schroeder, *Celebrity-in-Chief: How Show Business Took Over the White House*, Boulder, CO: Westview Press, 2004, pp. 220–221.

6. Schroeder, *Celebrity-in-Chief*, pp. 220–222.

7. Troy, *What Jefferson Read*, p. 145.

8. Ibid.

9. Frank Luntz, *Words that Work: It's Not What You Say, It's What People Hear*, New York: Hyperion, 2007, pp. 114, 116.

10. Troy, *What Jefferson Read*, p. 146. See also Schroeder, *Celebrity-in-Chief*, p. 177.

11. Troy, *What Jefferson Read*, pp. 147–148.

12. Fred Inglis, *A Short History of Celebrity*, Princeton, NJ: Princeton University Press, 2010, p. 15.

13. Troy, *What Jefferson Read*, p. 148.

14. Ibid., p. 149.

15. Ibid., p. 152.

16. Paul F. Boller Jr., *Presidential Diversions: Presidents at Play from George Washington to George W. Bush*, Orlando, FL: Harcourt, 2007, p. 289.

17. Richard Nixon, *In the Arena: A Memory of Victory, Defeat, and Renewal*, New York: Simon and Schuster, 1990, p. 152.

18. Archive of American Television, "Interview with Roger Mudd," Maclean, VA, November 18, 2011, http://www.emmytvlegends.org/interviews/people/roger-mudd.

19. Schroeder, *Celebrity-in-Chief*, p. 299.

20. Ibid.

21. Author's interview with Frank Donatelli, November 7, 2013.

22. Adam Sternbergh, "The Post-Hope Politics of Beau Willimon," *New York Times Magazine*, February 2, 2014, p. 25.

Chapter 11

1. Kenneth T. Walsh, *Feeding the Beast: The White House versus the Press*, New York: Random House, 1996, pp. 14–15.

2. Ibid., p. 16.

3. Quoted in Harold Holzer, *Lincoln and the Power of the Press*, New York: Simon and Schuster, 2014, p. xxix.

4. Vicki Goldberg, with the White House Historical Association, *The White House: The President's Home in Photographs and History*, New York: Little, Brown and Company, 2011, p. 120.

5. Ibid.

6. Ibid., p. 121.

7. Walsh, *Feeding the Beast*, p. 32.

8. Ibid., pp. 32–33.

9. Goldberg, *The White House*, p. 121.

10. Richard Reeves, *President Kennedy: Profile of Power*, New York: Touchstone/Simon and Schuster, 1993, pp. 278–279.

11. Tevi Troy, *What Jefferson Read, Ike Watched, and Obama Tweeted: 200 Years of Popular Culture in the White House*, Washington, DC: Regnery Publishing, 2013, p. 154.

12. Walsh, *Feeding the Beast*, p. 43.

13. James Deakin, *Straight Stuff*, New York: Morrow, 1984, p. 284.

14. Michael Duffy and Dan Goodgame, *Marching in Place*, New York: Simon and Schuster, 1992, p. 46.

15. Walsh, *Feeding the Beast*, p. 92.

16. Rachel Smolkin, "Are the News Media Soft on Bush?" *American Journalism Review*, October/November 2003, http://ajrarchive.org/Article.asp?id=3406.

17. Ibid.

18. Troy, *What Jefferson Read*, p. 232.

19. Ibid., p. 234.

20. Quoted in Fox News, "White House Escalates War of Words with Fox News," October 12, 2009, http://www.foxnews.com/politics/2009/10/12/white-house-escalates-war-words-fox-news.

21. "The White House Beat, Uncovered," *Politico Magazine*, May/June 2014, http://politico.com/magazine/story/2014/04/whca-survey-the-white-house-beat-uncovered-106071.html#.VHIV7GePKJA.

22. Goldberg, *The White House*, p. 122.

23. Dylan Byers, "Obama Holds Private Lunch with Foreign Policy Journalists," *Politico*, May 27, 2014, http://www.politico.com/blogs/media/2014/05/obama-holds-private-lunch-with-foreign-policy-journalists-189236.html.

Chapter 12

1. Frank Luntz, *Words that Work: It's Not What You Say, It's What People Hear*, New York: Hyperion, 2007, p 28.

2. Fred Inglis, *A Short History of Celebrity*, Princeton, NJ: Princeton University Press, 2010, pp. 11–12.

3. Gene Healy, *The Cult of the Presidency: America's Dangerous Devotion to Executive Power*, Washington, DC: Cato Institute, 2008, pp. 276–277.

4. Meriah Doty, "9 Surprising Films Screened at the White House," October 20, 2013, https://movies.yahoo.com/blogs/movie-talk/surprising-films-screened-white-house-214820284.html.

5. Ibid.

6. Alan Schroeder, *Celebrity-in-Chief: How Show Business Took Over the White House*, Boulder, CO: Westview Press, 2004, pp. 116–117.

7. Ibid., p 117.

8. Tevi Troy, *What Jefferson Read, Ike Watched, and Obama Tweeted: 200 Years of Popular Culture in the White House*, Washington, DC: Regnery Publishing, 2013, p. 120.

9. Schroeder, *Celebrity-in-Chief*, pp. 178–180.

10. Ibid., pp. 178–179. See also Troy, *What Jefferson Read*, p. 120.

11. Schroeder, *Celebrity-in-Chief*, p. 80.

12. Doty, "9 Surprising Films."

13. Troy, *What Jefferson Read*, p. 122.

14. Thomas Powers, "He Got the Big Things Right," *New York Review of Books*, April 26, 2012, http://www.nybooks.com/articles/archives/2012/apr/26/he-got-big -things-right.

15. Doty, "9 Surprising Films."

16. Schroeder, *Celebrity-in-Chief*, pp. 122–123.

17. Doty, "9 Surprising Films."

18. Schroeder, *Celebrity-in-Chief*, p. 178.

19. Paul F. Boller Jr., *Presidential Diversions: Presidents at Play from George Washington to George W. Bush*, Orlando, FL: Harcourt, 2007, p. 270.

20. Troy, *What Jefferson Read*, pp. 124–125.

21. Boller, *Presidential Diversions*, pp. 270–271.

22. Schroeder, *Celebrity-in-Chief*, p. 175.

23. Ibid.

24. Boller, *Presidential Diversions*, p. 288.

25. Troy, *What Jefferson Read*, p. 129.

26. Doty, "9 Surprising Films."

27. Troy, *What Jefferson Read*, p. 131.

28. Boller, *Presidential Diversions*, p. 315.

29. Doty, "9 Surprising Films."

30. Ibid.

31. Sidney Blumenthal and Thomas Byrne Edsall, eds., *The Reagan Legacy*, New York: Pantheon Books, 1988, pp. 274–275.

32. Author's interview with Marlin Fitzwater, March 15, 2014.

33. Troy, *What Jefferson Read*, p. 132.

34. Ronald Reagan, *Ronald Reagan: An American Life*, New York: Simon and Schuster, 1990, pp. 397–398.

35. Troy, *What Jefferson Read*, p. 133.

36. Ibid.

37. Author's interview with Ken Duberstein, February 10, 2014.

38. Author's interview with Marlin Fitzwater, March 28, 2014.

39. Author's interviews with Rene Henry Jr., coordinator of the 1988 Bush campaign's "celebrity coalition," September 9 and 10, 2014.

40. Bill Clinton, *My Life*, New York: Alfred A. Knopf, 2004, p. 21.

41. Schroeder, *Celebrity-in-Chief*, pp. 172–173.

42. Doty, "9 Surprising Films."

43. Troy, *What Jefferson Read*, p. 137.

44. Doty, "9 Surprising Films."

45. Schroeder, *Celebrity-in-Chief*, p. 189.

46. Troy, *What Jefferson Read*, p. 219.

Chapter 13

1. Tevi Troy, *What Jefferson Read, Ike Watched, and Obama Tweeted*, Washington, DC: Regnery Publishing, 2013, p. 182.

2. Paul F. Boller Jr., *Presidential Diversions: Presidents at Play from George Washington to George W. Bush*, Orlando, FL: Harcourt, 2007, p. 244.

3. Kenneth T. Walsh, *From Mount Vernon to Crawford: A History of the Presidents and Their Retreats*, New York: Hyperion, 2005, p. 113.

4. Quoted in Troy, *What Jefferson Read*, p. 186.

5. Ibid., p. 193.

6. Kenneth T. Walsh, *Prisoners of the White House : The Isolation of America's Presidents and the Crisis of Leadership*, Boulder, CO: Paradigm Publishers, 2013, p. 175.

7. Ibid., p. 49.

8. Douglas Brinkley, ed., *The Reagan Diaries*, New York: HarperCollins, 2007, p. x.

9. Troy, *What Jefferson Read*, p. 197.

10. Michael Duffy and Dan Goodgame, *Marching in Place: The Status Quo Presidency of George Bush*, New York: Simon and Schuster, 1992, p. 42.

11. George H. W. Bush, *All the Best, George Bush: My Life in Letters and Other Writings*, New York: Scribner, 1999, p. 564.

12. Quoted in Troy, *What Jefferson Read*, p. 201.

13. "Bill Clinton's Favorite Books," *Huffington Post*, May 14, 2013 (based on information provided by the Bill Clinton Presidential Library), http://www.huffingtonpost.com/2013/05/14/bill-clinton-favorite-books_n_3274513.html.

14. Troy, *What Jefferson Read*, p. 200.

15. Email to the author from Tevi Troy, August 5, 2014.

Chapter 14

1. Don Van Natta Jr., *First off the Tee: Presidential Hackers, Duffers and Cheaters from Taft to Bush*, New York: Public Affairs, 2003, p. 92.

2. John Sayle Watterson, *The Games Presidents Play: Sports and the Presidency*, Baltimore: Johns Hopkins University Press, 2006, p. 51.

3. Ibid., p. 72.

4. Ibid., pp. 58–59.

5. Ibid., p. 59.

6. Ibid., pp. 59–60.

7. Ibid., p. 50.

8. Unbylined newspaper story available on the website of the Roosevelt Center at Dickinson State University, "Toy Claims T.R. Name," http://www.theodore rooseveltcenter.org/Research/Digital-Library/Record.aspx?libID=o274789&f= %2fSearch.aspx%3fsearchterms%3d%25e2%2580%259cToy%2520Claims% 2520T.R.%2520Name%2c%25e2%2580%259d.

9. Watterson, *The Games Presidents Play*, p. 46.

10. Kenneth T. Walsh, *From Mount Vernon to Crawford: A History of the Presidents and Their Retreats*, New York: Hyperion, 2005, p. 73.

11. Paul F. Boller Jr., *Presidential Diversions: Presidents at Play from George Washington to George W. Bush*, Orlando, FL: Harcourt, 2007, p. 181.

12. Ibid., p. 182.

13. Ibid.

14. Ibid., p. 181.

15. Jennie Cohen, "How the U.S. President Became the Nation's Star Athlete," *History*, May 25, 2011, http://history.com/news/how-the-u-s-president-became -the-nations-star-athlete.

16. Elting E. Morison, "The Strenuous Life of T.R.," *Sports Illustrated, SI Vault*, November 8, 1954, http://157.166.246.201/vault/topic/article/magazine /MAG1128690/index.htm.

17. Christopher Klein, "How Teddy Roosevelt Saved Football," *History*, September 6, 2012, http://history.com/news/how-teddy-roosevelt-saved-football.

18. Bob Greene, "The President Who Saved Football," CNN, February 5, 2012, http://cnn.com/2012/02/05/opinion/greene-super-bowl.

19. Klein, "How Teddy Roosevelt Saved Football."

20. Watterson, *The Games Presidents Play*, p. 84.

21. Boller, *Presidential Diversions*, pp. 255–256.

22. Ibid., p. 224.

23. Walsh, *From Mount Vernon to Crawford*, pp. 96–97. Also see Boller, *Presidential Diversions*, pp. 235–236.

24. Watterson, *The Games Presidents Play*, p. 168.

25. Boller, *Presidential Diversions*, p. 245.

26. Ibid.

27. Watterson, *The Games Presidents Play*, pp. 180, 182–183.

28. Ibid., pp. 184–185.

29. Boller, *Presidential Diversions*, p. 251.

30. Ibid., pp. 251, 252.

31. Ibid., p. 254.

32. Ibid., p. 255.

33. Associated Press, "Golf Interest Rise in Germany Credited to Ike," *Hartford Courant*, April 22, 1956, p. 8D.

34. Paul Gardner, "U.S. Has 5,000 Golf Courses: 4,000 Out of Date," *Nation's Business*, October 1954, p. 62.

35. Boller, *Presidential Diversions*, p. 255.

36. Ibid., p. 264.

37. Quoted in Lenny Bernstein, "President Kennedy's 50-mile Challenge Lives On," Charleston (West Virginia) *Daily Mail*, November 8, 2012, p. D5.

38. Ibid.

39. Associated Press, "50-Mi. Hiking Fad Tires Kennedy Fitness Council," *Chicago Tribune*, February 17, 1963, p. 1.

40. Quoted in Boller, *Presidential Diversions*, pp. 265–266.

41. Watterson, *The Games Presidents Play*, p. 234.

42. Ibid., p. 235.

43. Ibid., p. 237.

44. Ibid., p. 238.

45. Ibid., p. 241.

46. Ibid., p. 243.

47. Ibid., p. 300.

48. Ibid., p. 276.

49. Ibid., p. 277.

50. Peter Nicholas, "Schwarzenegger Deems Opponents 'Girlie-Men'—Twice," *San Francisco Chronicle*, July 18, 2004, http://www.sfgate.com/politics/article/Schwarzenegger-deems-opponents-girlie-men-2707461.php.

51. Boller, *Presidential Diversions*, p. 342.

52. Natta, *First off the Tee*, 2003, p. 223.

53. Boller, *Presidential Diversions*, p. 350.

54. Jodi Kantor, *The Obamas*, New York: Little Brown, 2012, p. 55.

55. "Healthy Kids Fact Sheet," White House press release, May 28, 2014.

56. Juliet Eilperin, "White House Conference Focuses on Concussions," *Washington Post*, May 30, 2014, p. A2.

57. Ibid.

Chapter 15

1. Elise K. Kirk, *Music at the White House: A History of the American Spirit*, Urbana: University of Illinois Press, 1986, pp. 21–22, 83–85.

2. Alan Schroeder, *Celebrity-in-Chief: How Show Business Took Over the White House*, Boulder, CO: Westview Press, 2004, p. 140.
3. Ibid., p. 177.
4. Ibid., p. 143.
5. Sandor Salgo, *Thomas Jefferson: Musician and Violinist*, Monticello, VA: Thomas Jefferson Foundation, 2000, p. 2.
6. Ibid., p. 3.
7. Ibid., p. 7.
8. Ibid., p. 8.
9. Ibid., p. 9.
10. Ibid., p. 10.
11. Ibid., pp. 10–11.
12. Ibid., p. 29.
13. Ibid., pp. 36–37.
14. Ibid., pp. 50–51.
15. Brian Lingham, *Harry Truman: The Man—His Music*, Kansas City, MO: Lowell Press, 1985, pp. 5–6.
16. Ibid., p. 6.
17. Ibid., p. 9.
18. Ibid.
19. Ibid., p. 10.
20. Ibid., p. 15.
21. Ibid., pp. 22–42.
22. Ibid., p. 30.
23. Ibid., p. 25.
24. Ibid., p. 35.
25. Ibid., p. 36.
26. Nancy Kruh, "The Saxophone Bandwagon; Clinton Is Just One Part of the Horn's Boom," *Dallas Morning News*, February 16, 1993, p. 1C.
27. "It All Began in a Place Called Hope," http://clinton4.nara.gov/WH/EOP/OP/html/Hope.html. Accessed November 4, 2014.
28. Miles Corwin, "Musician Clinton Gives Instrument a Note of Popularity," *Los Angeles Times*, January 21, 1993, p. 1B.

Chapter 16

1. Michael D. Shear, "The Rise of the Drone Master: Pop Culture Recasts Obama," *New York Times*, April 30, 2014, p. A1.
2. Quoted in ibid.
3. Ibid.

4. Author's interview with Geoff Garin, August 15, 2013.

5. Frank Luntz, *Words that Work: It's Not What You Say, It's What People Hear*, New York: Hyperion, 2007, p. 82.

6. Associated Press, "Nixon Doctor Says Acupuncture Is 'Very Superior' to Anesthesia," *Los Angeles Times*, April 12, 1972, p. A1.

7. Duston Harvey, "Acupuncture Shown to Medical Association," *Hartford Courant*, June 22, 1972, p. 3.

8. Karen Fernau, "Former Presidents' Food Preferences Revealed," *USA Today*, February 17, 2014, http://www.usatoday.com/story/news/nation/2014/02/17/presidents-favorite-foods/5547517/.

9. Author's interview with Marian Burros, August 11, 2014.

10. Quoted in Poppy Cannon and Patricia Brooks, *The Presidents' Cookbook*, New York: Funk and Wagnalls, 1968, pp. 8–9.

11. Ibid.

12. Ibid., pp. 57–64.

13. Ibid., pp. 353–354.

14. Ibid., pp. 370–382.

15. Ibid., pp. 383–393.

16. Henrietta Nesbitt, *The President's Cookbook: Feeding the Roosevelts and Their Guests*, Garden City, NY: Doubleday and Company, 1951, pp. 1–2, 8–9. See also Cannon and Brooks, *The Presidents' Cookbook*, pp. 430–440.

17. "King Tries Hot Dog and Asks for More," *New York Times*, June 12, 1939, p. 1.

18. Henry Haller, *The White House Family Cookbook*, New York: Random House, 1987, pp. 84–85.

19. Dana Prom Smith, "Ronald Reagan and Tomatoes," *Arizona Daily Sun*, August 8, 2009, http://azdailysun.com/lifestyles/home-and-garden/ronald-reagan-and-tomatoes/article_b3745d9a-9698-52f1-9556-38c439c8c064.html.

20. Jennifer Treuting, "Plate of the Union: The Picky Presidential Palate," http://delish.com/cooking-shows/food-tv/president-favorite-foods.

21. Author's interview with Marian Burros, August 11, 2014.

22. Quoted in Diane Maglio, "A Century of Style: Presidents," *Daily News Record*, May 14, 1999, p. 184.

23. Neil Steinberg, "Passing (on) the Hat: New Book Reveals America's Changing Love Affair with Men's Hats, and the President Who Bucked the Trend Altogether," *Chicago Sun-Times*, December 5, 2004, p. 14.

24. Kate Betts, "The Cool Factor," *Time*, June 21, 2007, http://content.time.com/time/specials/2007/article/0,28804,1635958_1635999_1634962,00.html.

25. Ibid.

26. Ibid.

27. Author's interview with Gregory Cummings, a specialist on Nixon at the National Archives and Records Administration, August 20, 2014.

28. "Men's Fashions Take a Cue from the President's Garb," *New York Times*, July 19, 1965, p. 20.

29. Myron Kandel, "Presidential Fashions Have Impact on Men's Clothing Style," *New York Times*, February 25, 1962, p. F1.

30. "Homburg Sales Give Lift to Danbury Hat Trade," *Hartford Courant*, April 26, 1953, p. E15.

31. Nina Hyde, "The Man in the White House Brought Back the Brown Suit," *Toronto Star*, February 4, 1988, p. J3.

32. Joe Battenfeld, "Clinton Sticks His Neck out for Hip Image," *Boston Herald*, December 21, 1993, p. 43.

33. Susan Watters, "The Politics of Fashion: Elections Can Be a Clothes Race," *Daily News Record*, October 30, 1996, p. 5.

34. Both critics quoted in Diane Maglio, "A Century of Style; Presidents," *Daily News Record*, May 14, 1999, http://www.highbeam.com/doc/1G1-54683868.html.

35. Claire McLean, quoted on website of the Presidential Pet Museum, http://presidentialpetmuseum.com/first_pet_book.

36. Ibid.

Chapter 17

1. Fred Inglis, *A Short History of Celebrity*, Princeton, NJ: Princeton University Press, 2010, p. 4.

2. Ibid., pp. 10–11.

3. "Peace Corps," John F. Kennedy Presidential Library and Museum, http://www.jfklibrary.org/JFK/JFK-in-History/Peace-Corps.aspx.

4. Jim Malone, "Peace Corps Among President Kennedy's Lasting Achievements," *Voice of America*, November 19, 2013, http://www.voanews.com/content/peace-corps-president-kennedy-lasting-achievement/1793504.html.

5. Cited in "The Roosevelts: An Intimate History: In the Arena (1901–1910)," PBS film by Ken Burns, September 2014.

6. Juliet Eilperin, "White House Call to End Sexual Assaults on Campuses Enlists Star Power," *Washington Post*, September 19, 2014, http://www.washingtonpost.com/politics/call-to-end-sexual-assault-on-campuses-enlists-star-power/2014/09/19/91ff1eb2-3e8d-11e4-b0ea-8141703bbf6f_story.html.

7. Ibid.

8. I was president of the White House Correspondents' Association (WHCA) and was in charge of the WHCA dinner in the mid-1990s. At that time, the event was attended by movie, TV, and music stars but it was not the celebrity-dominated spectacle it is today. I still go to the dinner but I now share the discomfort that other journalists have felt because of the glorification of celebrity there. The WHCA

board is considering ways to fix the problem, such as by limiting the tickets available to organizations that don't cover the White House and that pack their tables with movie and TV stars.

9. Margaret Sullivan, "When Coziness with Sources Is a Conflict," *New York Times*, Sunday Review, April 6, 2014, p. 12. Actually, Baquet had something wrong in his explanation. Aside from the national anthem, there is no tradition of singing songs at the WHCA dinner. Perhaps he was confusing it with the annual Gridiron dinner, where singing does take place.

10. Carroll Doherty, "7 Things to Know about Polarization in America," Pew Research Center, June 12, 2014, http://pewresearch.org/fact-tank/2014/06/12/7-things -to-know-about-polarization-in-america.

11. Dan Balz, "Pew Poll: In Polarized United States, We Live as We Vote," June 12, 2014, *Washington Post*, http://www.washingtonpost.com/politics/pew-poll-in -polarized-america-we-live-as-we-vote/2014/06/12/0b149fec-f196-11e3-914c -1fbd0614e2d4_story.html.

SELECTED READINGS

Beschloss, Michael. *Presidential Courage: Brave Leaders and How They Changed America 1789–1989.* New York: Simon and Schuster, 2007.

Blumenthal, Sidney, and Thomas Byrne Edsall, eds. *The Reagan Legacy.* New York: Pantheon Books, 1988.

Boller, Paul F., Jr. *Presidential Diversions: Presidents at Play from George Washington to George W. Bush.* Orlando, FL: Harcourt, 2007.

Branch, Taylor. *Pillar of Fire: America in the King Years 1963–65.* New York: Simon and Schuster, 1998.

Brinkley, Douglas, ed. *The Reagan Diaries.* New York: HarperCollins, 2007

Broder, David S. *Behind the Front Page.* New York: Simon and Schuster, 1987.

Brownstein, Ronald. *The Power and the Glitter: The Hollywood-Washington Connection.* New York: Pantheon, 1990.

Burns, James MacGregor, and Susan Dunn. *George Washington.* New York: Times Books, 2004.

Bush, George. *All the Best, George Bush: My Life in Letters and Other Writings.* New York: Scribner, 1999.

Cannon, Lou. *President Reagan: The Role of a Lifetime.* New York: Public Affairs, 1991.

Cannon, Poppy, and Patricia Brooks. *The Presidents' Cookbook.* New York: Funk and Wagnalls, 1968.

Carter, Jimmy. *Keeping Faith: Memoirs of a President.* Fayetteville: University of Arkansas Press, 1995.

———. *White House Diary.* New York: Farrar, Straus and Giroux, 2010.

Clinton, Bill. *My Life.* New York: Alfred A. Knopf, 2004.

Cook, Rhodes. *The Presidential Nominating Process*. Lanham, MD: Rowman and Littlefield Publishers, 2004.

Cooper, Andrew F. *Celebrity Diplomacy*. Boulder, CO: Paradigm Publishers, 2008.

Cronin, Thomas E. *On the Presidency: Teacher, Soldier, Shaman, Pol*. Boulder, CO: Paradigm Publishers, 2009.

Dallek, Robert. *Flawed Giant: Lyndon Johnson and His Times, 1961–1973*. New York: Oxford University Press, 1998.

———. *Harry S. Truman*. New York: Times Books, 2008.

———. *An Unfinished Life: John F. Kennedy, 1917–1963*. New York: Little, Brown, 2003.

Deakin, James. *Straight Stuff*. New York: Morrow, 1984.

Dickson, Paul. *Words from the White House: Words and Phrases Coined or Popularized by America's Presidents*. New York: Walker and Company, 2013.

Duffy, Michael, and Dan Goodgame. *Marching in Place: The Status Quo Presidency of George Bush*. New York: Simon and Schuster, 1992.

Feeney, Mark. *Nixon at the Movies*. Chicago: University of Chicago Press, 2004.

Fitzwater, Marlin. *Call the Briefing! Reagan and Bush, Sam and Helen: A Decade with Presidents and the Press*. New York: Times Books, 1995.

Fleischer, Ari. *Taking Heat: The President, the Press, and My Years in the White House*. New York: William Morrow, 2005.

Germond, Jack W., and Jules Witcover. *Whose Broad Stripes and Bright Stars? The Trivial Pursuit of the Presidency 1988*. New York: Warner, 1989.

Goldberg, Vicki, with the White House Historical Association. *The White House: The President's Home in Photographs and History*. New York: Little, Brown and Company, 2011.

Goldman, Peter, and Tom Mathews. *The Quest for the Presidency 1988*. New York: Simon and Schuster/Touchstone, 1989.

Goodwin, Doris Kearns. *No Ordinary Time: Franklin and Eleanor Roosevelt: The Home Front in World War II*. New York: Simon and Schuster, 1994.

Healy, Gene. *The Cult of the Presidency: America's Dangerous Devotion to Executive Power*. Washington, DC: Cato Institute, 2008.

Heilemann, John, and Mark Halperin. *Game Change: Obama and the Clintons, McCain and Palin, and the Race of a Lifetime*. New York: HarperCollins, 2010.

Holzer, Harold. *Lincoln at Cooper Union: The Speech That Made Abraham Lincoln President*. New York: Simon and Schuster Paperbacks, 2004.

———. *Lincoln and the Power of the Press*. New York: Simon and Schuster, 2014.

Hoyt, Linda Holden. *Presidents' Gardens*. Oxford, UK: Shire Publications, 2013.

Inglis, Fred. *A Short History of Celebrity*. Princeton, NJ: Princeton University Press, 2010.

Jamieson, Kathleen Hall. *Packaging the Presidency: A History and Criticism of Presidential Campaign Advertising*. New York: Oxford University Press, 1992.

Jeffries, Ona Griffin. *In and Out of the White House . . . From Washington to the Eisenhowers*. New York: Wilfred Funk, 1960.

Kantor, Jodi. *The Obamas*. New York: Little Brown, 2012.

Klein, Edward. *Blood Feud: The Clintons vs. the Obamas*. Washington, DC: Regnery Publishing, 2014.

Kuhn, Jim. *Ronald Reagan in Private; A Memoir of My Years in the White House*. New York: Sentinel, 2004.

Lederer, Richard. *Presidential Trivia*. Salt Lake City, UT: Gibbs Smith, Publisher, 2007.

Lindlop, Edmund, and Joseph Jares. *White House Sportsmen*. Boston: Houghton Mifflin Company, 1964.

Luntz, Frank. *Words that Work: It's Not What You Say, It's What People Hear*. New York: Hyperion, 2007.

Lynes, Russell. *The Tastemakers: The Shaping of American Popular Taste*. New York: Dover Publications, 1980.

Maraniss, David. *First in His Class*. New York: Simon and Schuster, 1995.

Matviko, John W., ed. *The American President in Popular Culture*. Westport, CT: Greenwood Press, 2005.

McCullough, David. *Truman*. New York: Simon and Schuster, 1992.

Miller, Merle. *Plain Speaking: An Oral Biography of Harry S. Truman*. New York: G. P. Putnam's Sons, 1974

Monkman, Betty C. *The White House: Its Historic Furnishings and First Families*. New York: Abbeville Press, 2014.

Morris, Dick. *Behind the Oval Office: Winning the Presidency in the Nineties*. New York: Random House, 1997.

Mundy, Liza. *Michelle, A Biography*. New York: Simon and Schuster, 2008.

Nixon, Richard. *In the Arena: A Memoir of Victory, Defeat, and Renewal*. New York: Simon and Schuster, 1990.

Obama, Barack. *Dreams from My Father: A Story of Race and Inheritance*. New York: Crown, 2007.

Patterson, Thomas E. *Out of Order*. New York: Knopf, 1993.

Perlstein, Rick. *Nixonland: The Rise of a President and the Fracturing of America*. New York: Scribner, 2008.

Pollard, James E. *The Presidents and the Press*. New York: Macmillan, 1947.

Popadiuk, Roman. *The Leadership of George Bush: An Insider's View of the Forty-First President*. College Station: Texas A&M University Press, 2009.

Reagan, Nancy, with William Novak. *My Turn: The Memoirs of Nancy Reagan*. New York: Random House, 1989.

Reagan, Ronald. *Ronald Reagan: An American Life*. New York: Simon and Schuster, 1990.

Reedy, George E. *The Twilight of the Presidency*. Cleveland and New York: New American Library/World Publishing Company, 1970.

Reeves, Richard. *President Kennedy: Profile of Power*. New York: Touchstone/Simon and Schuster, 1993.

Rollins, Peter C., and John E. O'Connor, eds. *Hollywood's White House: The American Presidency in Film and History*. Lexington: University Press of Kentucky, 2003.

Sabato, Larry. *Feeding Frenzy: How Attack Journalism Has Transformed American Politics*. New York: Free Press/Macmillan, 1991.

———. *The Kennedy Half-Century: The Presidency, Assassination, and Lasting Legacy of John F. Kennedy*. New York: Bloomsbury, 2013.

Salgo, Sandor. *Thomas Jefferson: Musician and Violinist*. Monticello, VA: Thomas Jefferson Foundation, 2000.

Saslow, Eli. *Ten Letters: The Stories Americans Tell Their President*. New York: Anchor Books, 2011.

Schickel, Richard. *Intimate Strangers: The Culture of Celebrity*. New York: Fromm International Publishing, 1986.

Schroeder, Alan. *Celebrity-in-Chief: How Show Business Took Over the White House*. Boulder, CO: Westview Press, 2004.

Schweizer, Peter, and Rochelle Schweizer. *The Bushes: Portrait of a Dynasty*. New York: Doubleday, 2004.

Skinner, Kiron K., Annelise Anderson, and Martin Anderson. *Reagan: In His Own Hand*. New York: Free Press, 2001.

Smith, Hedrick. *The Power Game*. New York: Ballantine, 1988.

Sorensen, Theodore C. *Kennedy*. New York: Harper and Row, 1965.

Stephanopoulos, George. *All Too Human: A Political Education*. Boston: Little, Brown, 1999.

Swarns, Rachel L. *American Tapestry: The Story of the Black, White, and Multiracial Ancestors of Michelle Obama*. New York: Amistad, 2012.

Taylor, Tim. *The Book of Presidents*. New York: Arno Press, 1972.

Tebbel, John, and Sarah Miles Watts. *The Press and the Presidency, from George Washington to Ronald Reagan*. New York: Oxford University Press, 1985.

Troy, Tevi. *What Jefferson Read, Ike Watched, and Obama Tweeted: 200 Years of Popular Culture in the White House*. Washington, DC: Regnery Publishing, 2013.

Truman, Margaret. *Harry S. Truman*. New York: William Morrow and Company, 1973.

Updegrove, Mark K. *Second Acts: Presidential Lives and Legacies After the White House*. Guilford, CT: Lyons Press, 2006.

Van Natta, Don, Jr. *First off the Tee: Presidential Hackers, Duffers, and Cheaters from Taft to Bush.* New York: Public Affairs, 2003.

Walsh, Kenneth T. *Feeding the Beast: The White House versus the Press.* New York: Random House, 1996.

———. *From Mount Vernon to Crawford: A History of the Presidents and Their Retreats.* New York: Hyperion, 2005.

———. *Prisoners of the White House: The Isolation of America's Presidents and the Crisis of Leadership.* Boulder, CO: Paradigm Publishers, 2013.

———. *Ronald Reagan: Biography.* New York: Park Lane Press, 1997.

Watterson, John Sayle. *The Games Presidents Play: Sports and the Presidency.* Baltimore: Johns Hopkins University Press, 2006.

Woodward, Bob. *The Agenda.* New York: Simon and Schuster, 1994.

———. *The Choice.* New York: Simon and Schuster, 1996.

Zelizer, Julian E. *Jimmy Carter.* New York: Times Books, 2010.

Index

About the Author

Kenneth T. Walsh is chief White House correspondent for *U.S. News & World Report*. He is the author of "The Presidency" column for the *U.S. News Weekly* and the daily blog "Ken Walsh's Washington" for usnews.com. He has won the most prestigious awards for White House coverage and is the former president of the White House Correspondents' Association. He has written six other books, including *Prisoners of the White House: The Isolation of America's Presidents and the Crisis of Leadership* (2013) and *Air Force One: A History of the Presidents and Their Planes* (2003). He is a frequent TV and radio commentator on national affairs and does commentary and analysis for WTOP, the all-news station in Washington, DC, every Sunday morning. He has taught in the School of Communication at American University in Washington, DC. Walsh also gives many speeches, both in the United States and abroad. He and his wife Barclay Walsh live in Bethesda, Maryland, and Shady Side, Maryland. They have two children, Jean and Chris.

14